THE RISE OF CONSUMER SOCIETY IN BRITAIN, 1880–1980

THEMES IN BRITISH SOCIAL HISTORY

edited by Dr J. Stevenson

This series covers the most important aspects of British social history from the Renaissance to the present day. Topics include education, poverty, health, religion, leisure, crime and popular protest, some of which are treated in more than one volume. The books are written for undergraduates, postgraduates and the general reader, and each volume combines a general approach to the subject with the primary research of the author.

THE RISE OF CONSUMER SOCIETY IN BRITAIN, 1880–1980

John Benson

LONGMAN
London and New York

Longman Group UK Limited,
Longman House, Burnt Mill,
Harlow, Essex CM20 2JE, England
and Associated Companies throughout the world.

*Published in the United States of America
by Longman Publishing, New York*

© Longman Group UK Limited 1994

First published 1994

ISBN 0 582 072891 CSD
ISBN 0 582 072883 PPR

British Library Cataloguing-in-Publication Data

A catalogue record for this book is
available from the British Library

Library of Congress Cataloging-in-Publication Data

Benson, John, 1945–
    The rise of consumer society in Britain, 1880–1980 / John Benson.
        p. cm. — (Theme in British social history)
    Includes bibliographical references and index.
    ISBN 0–582–07289–1 (case). — ISBN 0–582–07288–3 (paper)
    1. Great Britain—Social conditions—19th century. 2. Great
Britain—Social conditions—20th century. 3. Great Britain–
–Economic conditions—19th century. 4. Great Britain—Economic
conditions—20th century. I. Title. II. Series.
HN385.B46   1994
301'.0941—dc20   93–41571
                                                                      CIP

Set by 5C in 10 on 11pt Times Roman

Produced by Longman Singapore Publishers (Pte) Ltd.

Printed in Singapore

CONTENTS

ACKNOWLEDGEMENTS

I am pleased to take this opportunity to acknowledge the help that I have received in the preparation of this book. I am grateful to the British Academy for the award of a small personal research grant, and to the University of Wolverhampton for a period of study leave in which to complete the final draft of the manuscript.

I am grateful too for invitations to speak about the work as it was in progress. An earlier version of Chapter 6 formed the basis of a paper read to the School of Humanities and Social Sciences Research Seminar, University of Wolverhampton; and earlier, and very different, versions of the Introduction and Chapter 3 formed the basis of papers read to the History Research Seminar, University of Wolverhampton; the Social History Seminar, King's College, University of Cambridge; and the Seminar in Modern Social History, Institute of Historical Research, University of London.

I have also benefited from the advice and assistance of John Callaghan, Mark Clapson, Pat Green, Alan Hallsworth, Sharon Hasluck, Richard Hawkins, Paul Henderson, Peter Jackson, Roger Leese, Celia Lury, Laurence Pearl, Joan Prescott, Fiona Terry-Chandler, Margaret Walsh, Peter Watson, Janice Winship and Harvey Woolf. I have benefited too from the advice of those who have taken the trouble to read, and comment on, parts of the manuscript. Ina Zweiniger-Borgielowska read Chapter 3, Gareth Shaw Chapters 3 and 4, Jeff Hill Chapter 5, Mike Cunningham, Marci Green, Geoff Hurd and Andrew Thacker Chapter 6, David Fowler and Geoff Hurd Chapter 7, and Diane Collins, Elizabeth Roberts, Margaret Walsh and Ina Zweiniger-Borgielowska Chapter 8. I have benefited still more from the advice of George Bernard and Peter Thompson who took on the onerous task of reading, and commenting on, the whole of the manuscript, and I owe them a special debt of gratitude.

I also wish to draw particular attention to the support that I have received from John Stevenson, Paul Lewis and Malcolm Wanklyn.

John Stevenson proved once again to be an exemplary editor: enthusiastic, encouraging, critical and constructive. Paul Lewis and Malcolm Wanklyn proved to be the most generous of colleagues: they took over, unhesitatingly and uncomplainingly, a number of my duties and responsibilities, and so enabled me to take up, and benefit from, my period of study leave. However, once again my greatest debt is to my wife, Clare, without whose support neither this nor any other of my books would have been written.

JOHN BENSON
July 1993

LIST OF ABBREVIATIONS

Bristol	Avon County Reference Library, Bristol: Bristol People's Oral History Project, Transcript
Express and Star	Wolverhampton, *Express and Star*
Lancaster	University of Lancaster: The Quality of Life in Two Lancashire Towns, 1880–1930; Social and Family Life in Preston, 1890–1940; Social and Family Life in Preston, Lancaster and Barrow, 1940–70, Transcript
Mass-Observation	Mass-Observation Archive, File Report
RC	Royal Commission

*In memory of Charles Henry Thompson
(1910–93)*

INTRODUCTION

The study of consumption has become increasingly fashionable in recent years. Nor is this before time. For our understanding of modern Britain remains remarkably unbalanced: it is unbalanced in that whereas a good deal is now known about the ways in which the British people made their living, very little indeed is known about the ways in which they spent the money that they earned. So if it is true that demographers have managed to make sex and death boring, it could be said without too much exaggeration that historians have conspired to render consumption almost invisible.[1]

It is true, of course, that in seeking to understand the nature and causes of economic growth, economists, economic historians and market researchers have looked to the workings of the market and the nature of consumer demand.[2] However, it is only during the last ten years or so that social historians, sociologists, psychologists and scholars from other disciplines have begun to follow their lead. Spurred on by the pioneering work of early modern historians such as Neil McKendrick, John Brewer and J. H. Plumb, they have begun to examine a whole range of issues, some of them apparently trivial, most of them potentially fascinating: the Americanisation of Europe, the advertising of soap, the ownership of cars, the use of men's toiletries, consumer choice in mental health care, and popular attitudes towards austerity and rationing.[3]

Indeed, something of a new consensus seems to be emerging. It appears to be accepted – 'assumed' might be a better word – that Britain has undergone a consumer revolution, so that by the end of the period covered by this book Britain had become a 'consumer society' with a 'consumer culture'.[4] In fact, the term 'consumer society' has become a widely used description-cum-explanation of the state of contemporary Britain, finding a prominent place in both popular and scholarly analysis. For example, in their recent study of mass consumption and personal identity, psychologists Peter Lunt and Sonia Livingstone describe modern Britain in the following terms.

1

The material conditions of consumer society constitute the context within which people work out their identities. People's involvement with material culture is such that mass consumption infiltrates everyday life not only at the levels of economic processes, social activities and household structures, but also at the level of meaningful psychological experience – affecting the construction of identities, the formation of relationships, the framing of events.[5]

In his authoritative history of Britain between 1750 and 1985, Edward Royle refers time and time again to late twentieth-century Britain as a consumer society.

The lubricant to make the consumer society function smoothly was advertising, which was made all the easier with the advent of television . . . .
  Though society is no longer divided between the leisured and the non-leisured, in a consumer society those with most money are clearly differentiated from those with the least . . . .
  In the consumer society, religious activities have suffered irreparably from secular competition.[6]

However, this is not the end of the matter. For despite the growing consensus that Britain has become a consumer society, the history of consumption, consumers and consumer society could scarcely be more controversial. There are two major areas of debate. There is no agreement over when it was that Britain became a consumer society. In fact, as Paul Johnson has pointed out, 'Putting a date to the consumer revolution has become a highly competitive business'.[7] The consumer revolution occurred, and the consumer society emerged, so we are told, in the seventeenth century, in the eighteenth century, in the second half of the nineteenth century, between the two world wars, in the years following the Second World War, and during the 1980s.[8]

There is no agreement either over the consequences of the consumer revolution, and the advantages and disadvantages of living in a consumer society. Those on the right tend to see consumption as power: 'the consumer, empowered by a purified market, will be sovereign.'[9] Thus according to that guru of the new right, Arthur Seldon,

Ordinary people haven't done well out of democracy as it is operated. The market offers you one-man, one-vote every day. Politics offers you one-man, one-vote every thousand days. Purchasing power is to own a vote. A man doesn't have to know anyone with influence. He doesn't have to explain why he wants to do things. All he needs is coins. The ordinary man without cultural power could do better under a market system that offered choice between competing suppliers than in a system where access to goods is controlled by politics.[10]

According to Conservative MP, Teresa Gorman, consumption works to the particular benefit of women.

Women actually have enormous economic power in this country because they're the people who do the shopping, who spend most of the household budget . . . .

A duchess's £5 is worth exactly the same in Marks and Spencer as a pensioner's.[11]

Those on the left tend to disagree most profoundly: they see consumption as subordination, as a capitalist and/or patriarchal device which, whether deliberately or not, increases inequality, undermines class consciousness, and keeps women tied to the home and enslaved to fashion. Thus according to Ursula Huws, consumption entails commodification, 'the process by which goods replace services.'

Instead of simply paying for the use of a service, it is now necessary to pay the capital costs of providing it . . . . As a higher and higher proportion of the population become owners of these things, then the public provision of the service which they replace atrophies or becomes prohibitively expensive because the economies of scale have been lost . . . . The gap between the haves and have-nots is intensified.

Commodification, she goes on, results in 'the atomisation of community life and with it a loss of class identification and political consciousness . . . . Life based on the private ownership of commodities is individualised and isolated.'[12] Nor is this all. For, according to Ben Fine and Ellen Leopold, even to examine consumption is to endorse it:

the effect of directing attention to consumption through the market is to rewrite history favourably in terms of the rich and powerful, who act as the leading edge of change and as subjects to be emulated. The result is to construct a rationale in favour of contemporary consumerist society, however understood, and the role of those most privileged within it.[13]

In fact, these disagreements, deep-seated though they are, are not at all difficult to understand. For the study of consumer society remains beset by a combination of ideological, empirical and conceptual difficulties, difficulties that seem unfortunately to be mutually reinforcing.

The first difficulty is that the study of consumer society, like any subject of pressing contemporary concern, poses particular problems of subjectivity and objectivity: it is all too easy to let one's approval or disapproval of the society in which one lives direct, and dominate, one's approach to, and view of, the way in which it has developed. The second difficulty is related to, and tends to aggravate, the first. For while the study of consumer society has suffered from a surfeit of contemporary concern, it has suffered too from a shortage of empirical investigation: in such circumstances, it can be tempting, whether consciously or not, to compensate imaginatively – and ideologically – for the lacunae and limitations of the evidence that one has at one's disposal.

The third difficulty is the most intractable of the three. For while it seems to be accepted that Britain has become a consumer society, it is not at all clear upon what basis this conclusion has been reached. For the fact of the matter is that there is still no agreed way of defining, and identifying, a consumer society. Rather, there are two alternative definitions in use, the one economic, the other social-cum-cultural. The economic definition has the advantage, it seems, of precision. I. R. C. Hirst put it like this in 1977.

> Most people, I think, would use the phrase 'the consumer society'
> to refer to to the sort of life we live today and to certain features of
> it which seem likely to become even more prominent in the future
> such as car and colour-television ownership and holidays abroad.
> But the economist is likely to use the phrase rather differently. He
> distinguishes consumption from investment . . . . But the economist
> also distinguishes that part of the economy which is responsive to the
> preferences of the individual consumer from that which is controlled
> by collective decision. Very broadly the distinction is between the
> private and the public sectors of the economy and it [Britain] is
> the consumer society in the sense of an economy directed by the
> purchasing decisions of millions of individual consumers.[14]

The social-cum-cultural definition has the advantage, it seems, of coming closer to the complexity of reality. For although scholars such as Joan Thirsk, Neil McKendrick and Gary Cross seem to shy away from defining exactly what they mean by consumer society, they describe the consumer societies that they have studied in broadly similar terms: they are societies, it emerges, in which choice and credit are readily available, in which social value is defined in terms of purchasing power and material possessions, and in which there is a desire, above all, for that which is new, modern, exciting and fashionable.[15]

Unfortunately, whichever of the two definitions is adopted, serious difficulties remain. For neither definition resolves the dilemma of distinguishing clearly and incontrovertibly between consumption, saving and investment. It is not at all clear whether buying a house, owning a racehorse, joining a friendly society, taking out an insurance policy or placing a bet are understood most helpfully as consumption, as saving or as investment.[16]

There are other difficulties besides. The use of the economic definition produces a conclusion that seems to fly in the face of common sense. It transpires, for example, that the proportion of gross national product devoted to consumer expenditure – the most obvious indicator of individual spending – declined by more than twenty per cent between 1880 and 1959.[17] The use of the economic definition suggests therefore that Britain became less, rather than more, of a consumer society during the period covered by this book. This is a proposition that simply cannot be sustained.

The use of the social-cum-cultural definition raises difficulties of its own. For this definition does not make clear how widely or how deeply it is necessary for choice and credit, the material assessment of value and the desire for novelty to be embedded for them to produce a consumer society. Moreover, the definition is not easy to apply empirically, for it is extremely difficult to collect the evidence that is needed to assess popular attitudes towards issues as elusive as social value and the desire for novelty. Thus it is that the social-cum-cultural definition of consumer society suffers from the very complexity that seems initially to constitute its major attraction.

Accordingly, it is the aim of this book to confront some of the ideological, empirical and conceptual difficulties surrounding the study of consumer society. Its subject is the rise of 'consumer society', its focus the causes, course and consequences of the changes in consumption that took place in the hundred years or so between the late nineteenth century and the late twentieth century.

However, this is an enormous subject, and two qualifications need to be made at the outset. It must be stressed that both consumption and society are interpreted more narrowly than some would wish. For while it is accepted that consumption constitutes the individual and/or family selection, purchase, ownership and usage of goods and services, the focus here is primarily upon selection and purchase.[18] Moreover, while it is accepted that society should be interpreted as holistically as possible, the focus here is upon just three sectors of the economy: shopping, tourism and sport. However, they have not been selected at random: shopping has been chosen because in spite of its importance, it has aroused remarkably little scholarly or other interest; tourism and sport have been chosen, on the other hand, because they have received a good deal of attention, and have generated a number of provocative generalisations concerning the relationship between consumption and broader social and economic change. Thus it is believed that the decision to focus attention upon these three sectors of the economy will facilitate rather than impede, the attempt to elucidate the causes, course and consequences of changes in consumption, and thus to decide whether, and when, Britain underwent a consumer revolution, and became a consumer society.

The structure of the book is as follows. Part One examines the underlying changes that occurred in the demand for, and the supply of, consumer goods and services between 1880 and 1980. Part Two delineates the major changes that took place in consumers' experience of shopping, tourism and sport. Part Three considers the consequences that these changes had for certain key issues in modern British history:

the consolidation of national identity, the creation of youth culture, the emancipation of women, and the defusion of class tension.

NOTES AND REFERENCES

1. **J. de Vries**, 'Between Purchasing Power and the World of Goods: Understanding the Household Economy in Early Modern Europe', in **J. Brewer** and **R. Porter** (eds), *Consumption and the World of Goods*, Routledge, 1993, p. 85.

2. Among the economic historians who sought to make consumption visible were **E. W. Gilboy**, 'Demand as a Factor in the Industrial Revolution', in **R. M. Hartwell** (ed.), *The Causes of the Industrial Revolution in England*, Methuen, 1967; **W. Minchinton**, 'Patterns of Demand 1750–1914', in **C. M. Cipolla** (ed.), *The Fontana Economic History of Europe: The Industrial Revolution*, Fontana, 1973; **W. H. Fraser**, *The Coming of the Mass Market, 1850–1914*, Macmillan, 1981; **W. W. Rostow**, *The Stages of Economic Growth: A Non-Communist Manifesto*, Cambridge University Press, 1960. See also **R. Stone**, *The Measurement of Consumers' Expenditure and Behaviour in the United Kingdom 1920–1938*, I, Cambridge University Press, 1954; **R. Stone** and **D. A. Rowe**, *The Measurement of Consumers' Expenditure and Behaviour in the United Kingdom 1920–1938*, II, Cambridge University Press, 1966.

3. These were all the subjects of papers presented at the Social History Society Conference on 'Consumption, Standards of Living and Quality of Life', held at Roehampton Institute, January 1993. See also, **N. McKendrick**, **J. Brewer** and **J. H. Plumb**, *The Birth of a Consumer Society: The Commercialisation of Eighteenth-Century England*, Hutchinson, 1982. For anthropology, see **M. Douglas** and **B. Isherwood**, *The World of Goods: Towards an Anthropology of Consumption*, Allen Lane, 1979; for cultural studies, see **P. Willis**, *Common Culture: Symbolic Work at Play in the Everyday Cultures of the Young*, Open University Press, 1990; for semiology, see **R. Barthes**, *Elements of Culture*, Polity, 1989.

4. Britain was described in 1939 as a 'consumption economy' (**E. Hulton**, 'Spend at Christmas!', *Picture Post*, 9 December 1939), in 1968 as 'a modern, mass-consumption economy' (**D. E. Allen**, *British Tastes: An Enquiry into the Likes and Dislikes of the Regional Consumer*, Hutchinson, 1968), and in 1970 as a 'consumer capitalist society' (**E. P. Thompson**, 'The Business University', *New Society*, 19 February 1970).

5. **P. K. Lunt** and **S. M. Livingstone**, *Mass Consumption and Personal Identity*, Open University Press, 1992, p. 24.

6. **E. Royle**, *Modern Britain: A Social History 1750–1985*, Arnold, 1987, pp. 280, 283, 342.

7. **P. Johnson**, 'Conspicuous Consumption and Working-Class Culture in Late Victorian and Edwardian Britain', *Transactions of the Royal*

Historical Society, 38, 1988, p. 27. See also **J. Styles**, 'Manufacturing, Consumption and Design in Eighteenth-Century England' in Brewer and Porter *Consumption and the World of Goods*.

8. See, for example, **J. Thirsk**, *Economic Policy and Projects: The Development of a Consumer Society in Early Modern England*, Clarendon Press, 1978; McKendrick, et. al., *Consumer Society*; Fraser, *Mass Market*; **G. Cross**, *Time and Money: The Making of a Consumer Culture*, Routledge, 1993, p. ix; **J. H. Goldthorpe**, **D. Lockwood**, **F. Bechhofer** and **J. Platt**, *The Affluent Worker in the Class Structure*, Cambridge University Press, 1969; **M. J. Lee**, *Consumer Culture Reborn: The Cultural Politics of Production*, Routledge, 1993.

9. **I. Loveland**, 'The Consumer as an Impotent King', *Guardian*, 22 September 1990. Cf. *Social Audit*, Summer 1973, p. 17.

10. Cited in **P. Hennessey**, 'Market "the Measure of Democracy"', *The Times*, 24 December 1990. See also **R. Harris** and **A. Seldon**, *Shoppers' Choice: An Essay in the Political Economy of Obstruction by Sectional Interests to the Repeal of the Shop Acts*, Institute of Economic Affairs, 1984.

11. Cited in **G. Bedell**, 'The Woman Least Likely', *Guardian*, 16 December 1990.

12. **U. Huws**, 'Consuming Fashions', *New Statesman & Society*, 19 August 1988, p. 32. Also **E. Wilson**, *Only Halfway to Paradise: Women in Postwar Britain 1945–1968*, Tavistock, 1980, p. 12; **G. Reekie**, 'Knowing the Female Consumer: Market Research and the Post-War Housewife', unpublished paper, Griffith University, 1990; **J. Carey**, *The Intellectuals and the Masses: Pride and Prejudice among the Literary Intelligentsia, 1880–1939*, Faber and Faber, 1992; Cross, *Time and Money*, pp. 39, 55.

13. **B. Fine** and **E. Leopold**, 'Consumerism and the Industrial Revolution', *Social History*, **15**, 1990, p. 152.

14. **I. R. C. Hirst**, 'Consumer Choice and Collective Choice', in **I. R. C. Hirst** and **W. D. Reekie** (eds), *The Consumer Society*, Tavistock, 1977, p. 51.

15. Thirsk, *Economic Policy*; McKendrick, et al., *Consumer Society*; Cross, *Time and Money*.

16. *RC on Betting, Lotteries and Gaming, Report*, 1951, pp. 16–17; **W. Vamplew**, *The Turf: A Social and Economic History of Horse Racing*, Allen Lane, 1976, p. 12; **C. Campbell**, *The Romantic Ethic and the Spirit of Modern Consumerism*, Blackwell, 1987, pp. 37–41; Reekie, 'Female Consumer', p. 16.

17. **P. Deane** and **W. A. Cole**, *British Economic Growth 1688–1959: Trends and Structure*, Cambridge University Press, 1969, pp. 332–3. Also **N. F. R. Crafts**, *British Economic Growth during the Industrial Revolution*, Clarendon Press, 1985, pp. 62–3.

18. **R. Scott**, *The Female Consumer*, Associated Business Programmes, 1976, p. 55; *Final Report of the Committee on Consumer Protection*, 1962, pp. 1–2.

Part One

CONTEXT

Chapter 1

CHANGES IN DEMAND

It is axiomatic that the growth, and redirection, of consumption that have taken place over the past two hundred years could not have done so without corresponding changes in the scale, and distribution, of consumer demand. It is not surprising therefore that demand and consumption can sometimes prove difficult to disentangle. But disentangled they must be. For demand and consumption are not necessarily synonymous: one has only to think of the recurrent shortages of private-sector rented accommodation, or of the unsatisfied demand each year for cup-final and centre-court tickets. In fact, even when demand is disentangled from consumption, considerable difficulties remain. For in seeking to understand changes in demand, it is essential to distinguish between two distinct developments: changes in the ability to consume; and changes in the willingness to consume.

Accordingly, this chapter is divided into two: the first section considers the material changes that increased consumers' ability to consume; the second, and much briefer, section examines the ideological changes that increased consumers' willingness to do so.

It is relatively easy to document the material changes that increased consumers' capacity for consumption. For instance, it has long been recognised that demography and demand are intimately entwined, and that the growth of the population constituted a fundamental cause of the expansion of the domestic market.[1] Table 1.1 shows that the population of Britain grew more than five times between the early nineteenth and the late twentieth centuries. It doubled between 1801 and 1851, almost doubled again during the next fifty years, and increased by more than 50 per cent between 1901 and 1981. Of course, population growth does not always prove economically and socially beneficial. However, in nineteenth- and twentieth-century Britain, as opposed, say, to nineteenth-century Ireland or many developing countries today, population growth was accompanied by economic growth, with the result that wealth, income and free time all grew very significantly.

The rise of consumer society in Britain, 1880–1980

TABLE 1.1 The growth of demand, Great Britain, 1801–1981

Year	Population (millions)	Wealth accommodation owned/being purchased by occupier (%)	Income per person (a) at current prices (£)	Income per person (b) in real terms (1801=100)
1801	10.7	5	22	100
1851	20.9	5	25	113
1901	37.1	10	44	240
1951	48.9	31	231	363
1981	54.8	60	3,278	702

Sources: **T. Barker** and **M. Drake** (eds), *Population and Society in Britain 1850–1980*, Batsford, 1982, p. 205; **J. Benson**, *The Working Class in Britain, 1850–1939*, Longman, 1989, p. 54; **P. Deane** and **W. A. Cole**, *British Economic Growth 1688–1959: Trends and Structure*, Cambridge University Press, 1969, pp. 6, 8, 166, 175, 178; **M. Flinn**, 'Trends in Real Wages, 1750–1850', *Economic History Review*, **xxvii**, 1974, pp. 399–404; **A. H. Halsey**, *British Social Trends since 1900: A Guide to the Changing Social Structure of Britain*, Macmillan, 1988, pp. 182, 377; **Central Statistical Office**, *Key Data 1986 Edition*, HMSO, 1986, p. 8.

Certainly this growing population was becoming more wealthy. It is true of course that wealth and purchasing power must be distinguished from one another: we all know of elderly people who are asset-rich but income-poor; those, for example, who own large houses but exist on modest pensions. None the less, a person's wealth does provide some indication of the potential purchasing power at his (or her) disposal. For assets, in the form of property, savings, investments, pension rights and so on, provide one component, at least, of many people's incomes.[2] It has been suggested indeed that, 'other things being equal, an increase in wealth will lead to more spending and so to less saving'.[3]

Unfortunately it is impossible to plot in any precise way the growth of individual (or family) wealth over the past two hundred years. It is clear, however, that the ownership of physical and financial assets has become both more common and more valuable. There are a number of indicators: the growth of personal savings; the spread of home ownership; and the increase in the number of people leaving property when they die. It has been found, for example, that the number of people owning (or purchasing) the accommodation in which they live expanded enormously. Table 1.1 shows that owner-occupation grew from some 5 per cent of all accommodation during the first half of the nineteenth century, to about 10 per cent in 1914, (20 per cent in 1939), 30 per cent in 1951, and more than 60 per cent by the early 1980s. This expansion of home ownership was reflected in the increase in the housing and other forms of property that were left at death. It has been found that the number (and proportion) of adults who died leaving property increased dramatically between the mid-nineteenth and the mid-twentieth centuries: from just under 30,000 (15 per cent of those dying) in 1858 to more than 150,000 (33 per cent) in 1938–39. Moreover, it has been found that the average value of each estate nearly doubled: from £2,331 in 1858 to £3,640 in 1938–39.[4] Individually, it may be objected, none of these indicators is fully convincing; cumulatively, however, they do point to a sustained, and significant, increase in wealth-holding since about the middle of the nineteenth century.

The income (and credit) at the disposal of this growing, and increasingly wealthy, population also increased very greatly. Unfortunately, the assessment of individual (and family) income is no more straightforward than that of individual (and family) wealth. Once again, however, some progress can be made. For by combining the demographic data that were discussed above with the estimates that have been made of movements in incomes and prices, it is possible to provide a broad indication of the ways in which per capita incomes have grown over the past two hundred years. Such a calculation is most revealing. It suggests that while money incomes remained stubbornly low during the first half of the nineteenth century, they grew with increasing rapidity thereafter. Table 1.1 shows how average income per head grew by 75 per cent between 1851 and 1901, 500 per cent between 1901 and 1951, and by a massive 1,300 per cent between 1951 and 1981. Thus, whereas at the beginning of the nineteenth century the average person's income barely reached £20 per year, by the late twentieth century it had risen to well over £3,000.

Naturally such figures need to be adjusted for inflation if they are to reveal anything helpful about the release of potential purchasing power. This is not the place for a detailed examination of changes in the cost of living. All that needs to be made clear for the moment is that even when the growth of money incomes is adjusted to take account of changes in prices, there remains a major increase in real income per head. Table 1.1 confirms that the income, in real terms, of the average British consumer grew seven-fold between the early nineteenth and late twentieth centuries; it doubled between 1851 and 1901, grew by 50 per cent between 1901 and 1951, and almost doubled again during the final thirty years of the period. Increases on such a scale are of crucial significance in seeking to understand the changes in demand that have taken place in Britain during the past two hundred years. For, together with the growth of population and the expansion of wealth, they transformed the volume of potential purchasing power at the disposal of the British consumer. So it was that in 1957, for example, Harold Macmillan was moved to make his celebrated remark that 'Most of our people have never had it so good'.[5]

The amount of time at the disposal of the British consumer also increased very significantly. Once again, however, this is a difficult matter about which to generalise. Working people benefited less than those in middle-class occupations; farm workers, domestic servants and shop assistants worked longer hours than most other working-class groups; and the persistence of casual and seasonal work, overtime and un- (and under-) employment tends to undermine the validity of any generalisation based upon changes in 'normal' working hours.[6] None the less, two broad developments may be discerned: a decline in the length of the working week, and a decline in the length of the working year. It has been found, for example, that between 1880 and 1980 the 'normal' working week of manual workers – the most accessible guide to the time available for consumption – declined by practically a third: from nearly 60 hours (spread over six or seven days) to almost exactly 40 hours (spread over five days).[7] It has been found too that paid holidays became a great deal more common. So whereas in the mid 1930s only 1.5 million workers were entitled to paid holidays, the Holidays with Pay Act of 1938 extended the benefit to nearly eight times as many people. Indeed, it was estimated in the mid 1960s that 96 per cent of manual workers were entitled to a basic paid holiday of two weeks, with about 15 per cent receiving extra time in recognition of their long service.[8]

None the less, there are other material changes to consider. For scale is not the only aspect of purchasing power that needs to be understood. So too does its distribution. For it is clear that over the past two hundred years changes in the distribution of population, wealth and income have led inexorably to changes in the distribution of consumer purchasing power. It is a redistribution that tended to favour four broad, and often overlapping, groups: town dwellers and those living in the Midlands and South-west of England; adolescents and the elderly; women of all ages; most members of the middle class; and many members of the working class.

The geographical redistribution of purchasing power has been of considerable importance. The growth of population, wealth and income occurred so as to concentrate economic power increasingly in the urban and suburban areas of the Midlands and the South-east of England.[9] Thus it is a commonplace to assert that the proportion (and number) of the population living in urban and suburban areas has increased dramatically since the onset of industrialisation. Table 1.2 shows that in England and Wales, for instance, the proportion of urban dwellers rose from some 30 per cent of the population (2.8 million) in 1801, to 50 per cent (9.0 million) in 1851, and more than 75 per cent (25.1, 35.3, and 37.7 million) in 1901, 1951 and 1981.[10] The number of people living in large centres (with 50,000 or

TABLE 1.2 The redistribution of demand, Great Britain, 1801–1981: geography

| Year | The proportion (and number) of the population living in: | | | | | |
| | Urban areas | | Midlands and South-east England | | Greater London | |
	No. (mills)	%	No. (mills)	%	No. (mills)	%
1801	2.8	30	4.3	40	1.1	10
1851	9.0	50	8.2	39	2.7	13
1901	25.1	77	15.9	43	6.6	18
1951	35.3	81	22.4	46	8.4	17
1978/81	37.7	76	25.8	47	7.0	13

*Urban areas: refers to England and Wales only
Sources: **G. Alderman**, *Modern Britain 1700–1983: A Domestic History*, Croom Helm, 1986, p. 244; **T. Barker** and **M. Drake** (eds), *Population and Society in Britain 1850–1980*, Batsford, 1982, pp. 205–6; **Central Statistical Office**, *Key Data 1986 Edition*, HMSO, 1986, p. 8; **A. H. Halsey**, *British Social Trends since 1900: A Guide to the Changing Social Structure of Britain*, Macmillan, 1988, pp. 326, 329–30; **C. H. Lee**, *Regional Economic Growth in the United Kingdom since the 1880s*, McGraw-Hill, 1971, p. 213; **D. C. Marsh**, *The Changing Social Structure of England and Wales 1871–1961*, Routledge & Kegan Paul, 1977, pp. 96, 108, 285; **R. M. Reeve**, *The Industrial Revolution 1750–1850*, University of London Press, 1971, p. 205

more inhabitants) increased more rapidly still: from barely 4 per cent of the population in 1801, to 36 per cent in 1871, and more than 50 per cent by 1931.[11]

Nor is it difficult to point to the growing demographic domination of the Midlands and the South-east of England. Indeed, it is noticeable how towns and cities in different parts of the country are associated with different phases of economic growth: Bradford, Leeds, Manchester, Preston and Sheffield with the classic Industrial Revolution of the late eighteenth and early nineteenth centuries; Cardiff, Glasgow, Coventry, Leicester, Northampton, Nottingham and Oxford with the industrial developments of the late nineteenth and early twentieth centuries; and Dagenham, Hornchurch, Harrow, Hayes, Romford and Wembley with the economic restructuring of the inter-war years. The proportion (and number) of the British population living in the Midlands and South-east of England increased consistently between the early nineteenth century and the mid twentieth century: from some 40 per cent (4.3 and 8.2 million) in 1801 and 1851, to 46 per cent (22.4 million) in 1951, and 47 per cent (25.8 million) in 1978.[12] The demographic domination of London became more striking still. The proportion (and number) of the

British population living in the capital grew from 10 per cent (1.1 million) in 1801, to 13 per cent (2.7 million) in 1851, and 17–18 per cent (6.6 and 8.4 million) in 1901 and 1951. The significance of such figures can scarcely be overestimated. They mean that throughout the first half of the twentieth century more than one Briton in six lived in Greater London, and that despite some waning of metropolitan dominance after 1951, the capital remained home to one Briton in eight at the beginning of the 1980s.[13]

The geographical redistribution of population was almost bound to bolster the demand emanating from urban areas, and in particular from the towns and cities of the Midlands and South-east England. In fact, the impact of this demographic redistribution was reinforced by the geographical distribution – and redistribution – of wealth-holding and income-earning. It was seen above how difficult it is to measure changes nationally in levels of individual and family wealth-holding, and it is more difficult still to measure changes on a local or regional basis. None the less, certain generalisations can be offered. The innovatory investigations of David Rubinstein make clear that throughout the period covered by this book wealth was concentrated in commercial centres, especially in and around the City of London.[14] The study of home ownership confirms that this form of wealth-holding was always more common (and more valuable) in urban than in rural areas, and that it became more common (and more valuable) in the Midlands and South-east of England than in other parts of the country. Thus before the First World War the areas noted for their high levels of working-class owner-occupation included the South Wales coalfield, the Lancashire cotton towns, the Yorkshire woollen districts, and certain Northern shipbuilding centres. During the inter-war years these areas were joined by the growing towns of the Midlands: by 1939 over a third of the accommodation in Coventry, and more than 40 per cent of that in Oxford, was owner-occupied.[15] However, since the Second World War it is the South-east of England that has attained the highest levels (and values) of home ownership. By 1978/81 owner-occupation in South-east England (excluding Greater London) accounted for 63 per cent of all households in the region, compared to 35 per cent in Scotland, 56 per cent in the North of England – and 58 per cent throughout England and Wales as a whole.[16]

It is no easier to disaggregate income levels on a local or regional basis. However, two important points can be made. It seems clear that incomes were normally higher in urban than in rural areas: it has been found, for example, that in late nineteenth-century Britain real wages were highest in 'the northern counties, London, and parts of the midlands as far south as Birmingham'.[17] It is clear too that in recent years earnings have risen highest in the Midlands and South-east of England. It was found in 1978, for instance, that nearly a quarter of adult male workers in Greater London, and 14 per cent of those elsewhere in the South-east, were earning £6,000 or more a year – compared to less than 10 per cent in areas such as East Anglia, the West Midlands and the South-west of England.[18] It is generally acknowledged that in the early 1990s workers in London and the South-east of England earn some 30 per cent more than those living in the North of England.[19]

Thus the geographical distribution – and redistribution – of population, wealth and income have been mutually reinforcing. The result has been to concentrate consumer purchasing power increasingly – and disproportionately – in urban and suburban areas, and especially in those to be found south of that imaginary, but influential, line which is drawn between the Humber and the Bristol Channel.

The growth of population, wealth and income have also occurred in ways which, together, have increased the economic power of adolescent and elderly consumers. At first sight, the growth of adolescent purchasing power seems somewhat surprising.[20] For over the past hundred years British society has become less, rather than more, youthful: Table 1.3 shows that although the number of adolescents in England and Wales rose by 45 per cent between 1871 and 1961, the proportion of the population that this represented declined by very nearly 30 per cent.

However, this relative demographic decline was made up for by the economic improvement enjoyed by those in their mid-to-late teenage years. For despite the inability of the young to accumulate wealth and despite the increase in the number of pupils staying at school until their late teens,[21] adolescent purchasing power increased between the wars, and increased again in the years following the Second World War. Adolescents benefited indirectly from the improvements in adult incomes that were discussed above. They benefited directly

TABLE 1.3   The redistribution of demand, England and Wales, 1871–1981: age

Year	Adolescents (15–19 years)		Elderly (65+ years)	
	No.	%	No	%
1871	2.2	9.7	1.1	4.8
1901	3.3	10.0	1.5	4.7
1931	3.4	8.6	2.9	7.4
1951	3.2	6.9	4.8	11.0
1981	4.0	8.3	7.4	15.0

Sources: **D. C. Marsh**, *The Changing Social Structure of England and Wales 1871–1961*, Routledge & Kegan Paul, 1977, pp. 24–5; **A. H. Halsey**, *British Social Trends since 1900: A Guide to the Changing Social Structure of Britain*, Macmillan, 1988, pp. 104–6.

from the improvements in their own incomes; it has been found, for example, that whereas the real wages of adults rose by some 25 per cent between 1938 and 1958, those of adolescents increased twice as quickly over the same twenty-year period.[22] Indeed, it has long been recognised that the burgeoning youth culture of the 1960s had its material roots in the full employment and high wages of that and previous decades. 'Well, I started at three pound fifteen,' explains a Brighton man,

> but I know that one of the jobs I had that year was as a labourer in a factory and, well, I was absolutely quids in. I was getting taxis about. I mean a pound would buy you a bloody good night out. You could probably have eight or nine pints of beer and twenty fags and a couple of tanners for the juke box.[23]

Moreover, it seems likely that adolescents were able to retain a growing proportion of the (growing) incomes that they were receiving. Oral evidence reveals that before the Second World War working-class youths were normally allowed to keep only a very small part of their earnings – perhaps a penny in the shilling, or a shilling in the pound.[24] Social survey evidence suggests that even quite soon after the war they were able to retain a great deal more. It was found that in the East End of London, for example, a 'boy aged about 16 would get £6 or £7 of which he would give his mother £2, leaving £4 or £5 for himself, while a 20 year old earning £12 would give his mother £3 or £4, leaving himself £8 or £9'.[25] It seems that wage-earnings came to be regarded increasingly as belonging, not to the family, but to the wage-earner him (or her) self.[26]

The growth of adolescent economic power always occasioned considerable anxiety. Comparisons were made constantly with earlier, and supposedly less sophisticated, times. These concerns emerged well before the end of the nineteenth century: 'What would our grandmothers have thought of girls, sixteen or eighteen, parading the fair alone, dressed in jockey-caps . . . imitation open jackets and waistcoats, and smoking cigars or cigarettes?'[27] Such concerns resurfaced time and time again. In the 1960s, for instance, the Committee on Children and Young Persons observed that

> During the past fifty years there has been a tremendous material, social and moral revolution . . . . The material revolution is plain to see. At one and the same time it has provided more desirable objects, greater opportunities for acquiring them illegally, and considerable chances of immunity from the undesirable consequences of so doing.[28]

The growing economic power of the elderly aroused no such anxieties. Yet once again the growth itself seems somewhat surprising, for there remains a tendency to associate old age with frailty, incapacity and poverty. Although such an association certainly existed, it is important to appreciate that over the past hundred years a combination of demographic and material changes has wrought a fundamental, and beneficial, transformation in the economic circumstances of many elderly people.

The demographic changes of the twentieth century led to a substantial increase in the numbers of the elderly. As Table 1.3 shows, the proportion of the population aged 65 and above grew very substantially: from 5 per cent (a maximum of 1.5 million people) during the second half of the nineteenth century; to 7 per cent (practically 3 million) in 1931; 11 per cent (4.8 million) in 1951; and 15 per cent (well over 7 million) in 1981. These changes meant that by the end of the period the elderly outnumbered groups such as adolescents by very nearly two to one.

The elderly were also growing more wealthy. Indeed, it is generally recognised that wealth tends to increase with age, since most people accumulate property, personal possessions, pension rights and other assets during the course of their working lives. Thus house purchase is usually completed by the age of 60 or 65, and savings tend to peak at the time of retirement – and to diminish thereafter as they are drawn upon in order to finance expenditure.[29] Indeed, it has been shown that over the past hundred years the elderly have begun to accumulate more and more of these material assets. It will be clear from the discussion above that the growth of home ownership proved of considerable benefit to the elderly; and it will become apparent from the discussion below that the possession of pension rights proved enormously beneficial to them.

It is not surprising therefore that the incomes of the elderly were also rising. However, they did not do so to the extent that the increasing wealth of old age might lead one to suppose. One barrier was that old people did not necessarily find it easy (or desirable) to use their property and possessions to generate income on a day-to-day basis. Another was that it became less common for the elderly to continue in paid employment. Census data suggest that whereas during the late nineteenth century at least two-thirds of men and women in the workforce continued to be employed beyond the age of 65, by the 1920s this figure had fallen to less than 50 per cent, and by the 1980s to no more than 10 per cent.[30]

Nevertheless, the incomes of the elderly did rise very significantly. For it must be remembered that the purchasing power of old age did not necessarily depend solely – or even chiefly – upon wage-earnings. The incomes of the elderly, still more than those of other age groups, were often composed of several different elements: self-employment; charitable assistance; and, in particular, payments from statutory and private pension schemes.[31] In fact, the tendency of the elderly to retire from wage labour was offset, to a greater or lesser degree, by the likelihood that they would qualify for state and (increasingly) private pension provision.

Contemporary criticisms of the inadequacies of the state retirement pension make it easy to underestimate the benefits that it brought to the elderly. Certainly the level of state pensions was modest enough. The non-contributory scheme of 1908 paid a maximum of five shillings a week, compared to a 'normal' full-time working-class income of about twenty-five shillings.[32] Its value in real terms always hovered around this sort of level; thus, despite adjustments being made for inflation, the contributory scheme of 1911 paid allowances which, between 1950 and 1980, remained equivalent to no more than about 20 per cent of average male manual earnings.[33] Yet, whatever the parsimony of state provision, its coverage became well-nigh universal. Within four years of its inception, the non-contributory scheme of 1908 covered 60 per cent of those aged 70 or above; and by the early 1940s it, together with the contributory scheme of 1911, embraced some 84 per cent of the elderly population. By the end of the period practically all women over 60, and practically all men over 65, were drawing the state retirement pensions to which they were entitled.[34]

The endorsement in recent years of the virtues of private welfare provision makes it difficult to overlook any longer the contribution made by occupational pension schemes. The pioneering investigations of Leslie Hannah reveal the rapid growth in the proportion of the workforce protected in this fashion: from some 5 per cent in 1900, to 13 per cent in 1956, and nearly 50 per cent by the end of the period.[35] Hannah's work reveals too something of the financial implications that these schemes were to have for the elderly:

in 1979, when the state retirement pension for a single person was £19.50 per week, the average occupational pension then being paid was £18 per week . . . . This does, however, somewhat understate the benefits from occupational schemes of the newly retired, for it includes some pensions of long standing (some more than twenty years old) fixed in a period when benefits were less generous. In 1979, for example, the average male employee retiring from the public sector on pension could expect £28 from his occupational scheme, while for the private sector the figure was £20 a week. In addition, many employees could expect lump sums on retirement: in 1979 these averaged £4,000–£5,000.[36]

Even the discussion of changes in paid employment and in state and private pension provision does not exhaust the difficulties of determining the purchasing power of the elderly. For no matter how careful the calculation of these sources of income, one crucial problem remains: to assess the cumulative, rather than the individual, impact of the changes that took place. This is no easy matter. However, the few calculations that have been made confirm once again that the incomes of the elderly were rising very appreciably. Leslie Hannah suggests that

In 1951, the average disposable income of those over state pension age (including all income from occupational pensions, interest, etc., as well as the state pension and other social security benefits) was little more than two-fifths of the average non-pensioner's, but thirty years later the average pensioner enjoyed as much as two-thirds of the average non-pensioner's income.

This leads him to conclude, with, it must be said, a certain amount of exaggeration, that 'The generations retiring in the 1960s and 1970s enjoyed a lifetime of continually improving standards in which their retirement was truly a golden age.'[37]

The redistribution of economic power in favour of the elderly benefited women more than men. Women's greater longevity meant that they often inherited property and other assets on the death of their husbands; and it meant too that they derived particular advantage from the extension of statutory and private pension provision that was discussed above.[38] Moreover, women of all ages benefited from the more general redistribution of wealth and income that took place during the course of the twentieth century. It was a redistribution which, as is well known, aroused – and arouses – intense, and often acrimonious, differences of opinion.

These differences were – and are – exacerbated by the peculiar difficulties of documenting the growth of female purchasing power. Of course, it is simple enough to point to the paradox that, although women constituted a majority of the nation's population, they possessed only a minority of its wealth. (The precise combination of economic circumstances, legal constraints and social/cultural attitudes that caused the imbalance is difficult to disentangle, and need not detain us here.) However, the scale of the imbalance does need to be stressed. It has been found, for example, that in the mid nineteenth century women were only half as likely as men to leave property when they died;[39] and it has been calculated that even towards the end of the twentieth century women owned no more than about 40 per cent of the nation's wealth.[40] Nevertheless, it is also important to point out that this maldistribution became less acute as the period progressed. The best available estimates suggest that whereas in the late 1920s women held 33 per cent of the personal wealth in England and Wales, by the early 1970s this figure had risen by a fifth, to very nearly 40 per cent.[41]

It is well known that the combination of economic, legal, social and cultural constraints that prevented women from acquiring the same wealth as men also prevented them from earning the same pay. Not surprisingly, this inequality too has come in for the criticism – not to say contempt – of historians, politicians, feminists and working women alike.[42] Yet such dismay must not be allowed to obscure the fact that once again important changes were taking place: for a growth in the number of women in paid employment, and a rise in the level of their earnings, combined together to increase the strength, both individually and collectively, of female purchasing power.

The number of women identified as economically active rose significantly during the course of the twentieth century. Census data show that, although the proportion of women recorded in the workforce declined from just under 40 per cent in the third quarter of the nineteenth century to around 35 per cent during the first half of the twentieth century, it increased consistently thereafter, to 38 per cent in 1961 and 46 per cent in 1981. The number of women recorded as part of the workforce increased more than three-fold: from 2.8 million in 1851, to 5.2 million in 1901, 7.0 million in 1951 and 9.9 million in 1981.[43]

Women workers shared in the more general growth of wage-earnings that was discussed towards the beginning of the chapter. None the less, for the great majority of the period most women received only about half the pay of their male counterparts. There were several reasons for this other than overt discrimination: women remained concentrated disproportionately in low-wage occupations; they often worked shorter hours than men; and they did not normally remain in the workforce for as long.[44] Yet discrimination there was. Consequently it was only the equal-pay and associated legislation of the 1970s which, for all its limitations, began to address this longstanding and deep-seated inequality. Sidney Pollard makes the point.

> Women's earnings in manufacturing as a proportion of male remained remarkably stable from pre-war years until 1970, fluctuating gently around the 50% mark, with a light rise in wartime and a subsequent return to the pre-war level. The Equal Pay Act of 1970, phased to come into full force in 1975, brought a dramatic change, and its momentum was continued by the Sex Discrimination Act of 1975 which prohibited non-pecuniary discrimination such as access to jobs or promotion. By 1975, women's wages had risen to 57½% of men's and by 1978 to 61%, where they remained.[45]

As this discussion makes clear, it is possible to delineate, in broad terms at least, the changes that took place in women's wealth and earning capacity. However, it is a great deal more difficult to determine the ways in which these changes affected women's economic power, and thus their day-to-day influence over developments in consumer demand. This may seem somewhat surprising, for it has generally been agreed that most women exercised very little control over the finances of the households in which they lived. In an influential study of the welfare of women in English labouring families, Laura Oren describes in graphic detail the unequal distribution of resources which prevailed, she believes, throughout the period from 1860 to 1950. Many working-class wives did not know how much their husbands earned, many received inadequate housekeeping allowances, and many consumed far less food than their partners. Even 'Higher wages and greater prosperity in this century', she concludes, '. . . did not eliminate the uneven distribution of incomes between husbands and wives.'[46]

In fact, such views need to be modified in the light of recent oral investigations of working-class life in the late nineteenth and early-to-mid twentieth centuries. Elizabeth Roberts finds, for example, that

> in the majority of working-class marriages it would appear to be misleading and inaccurate to see the wife as downtrodden, bullied and dependent. She was much more likely to be respected and highly regarded, [the] financial and household manager, and the arbiter of familial and indeed neighbourhood standards.[47]

Carl Chinn goes further. He concludes that

> what distinguished all mothers of the poor, whether they worked or not, was their total command of the family finances in every respect, except for the money retained by a husband for his own pleasure . . . . She it was who paid the rent, who bought the clothes, who purchased the food and who applied for credit at the local corner shop. It was she who conducted all financial negotiations and it was upon her generalship that the family relied to supply it with a meal.[48]

It was the working-class mother, in other words, whose economic power exercised a decisive day-to-day influence over the scale, and nature, of consumer demand.

This new emphasis upon the role played by working-class women confirms the contention that in seeking to understand the growth and redistribution of consumer demand, attention needs to be directed not just to gender, generation and geography, but also to class. For, as was suggested earlier in the chapter, the redistribution of purchasing power occurred in such a way as to favour most members of the middle class and many members of the working class.

Both groups benefited, to some degree, at the expense of the upper class.[49] In all events, the last hundred years have seen a marked diminution in the economic, political and social authority of the landed aristocracy. They began the period rich, powerful and confident; indeed, during the first three-quarters of the nineteenth century their wealth and incomes probably grew as urban land values rose, as they involved themselves in industrial development, and as they sought to place their estates upon a more businesslike footing.[50] The result was that around the middle of the century the typical peer probably had an income of about £10,000 a year (400 times the national average), while magnates like the Dukes of Bedford, Bridgwater, Devonshire and Northumberland were each able to dispose of over £50,000 a year (2,000 times the national average).[51]

However, because the aristocracy owed its position primarily to its landed assets, it suffered when land began to lose its economic, political and social primacy. The so-called 'great depression' of the late nineteenth century reduced agricultural rents and profits.[52] The landed aristocracy suffered still more from the legislative changes of the twentieth century. Lloyd George's 'People's Budget' of 1909 began the process. It continued in 1919 when death duties on estates worth more than £2 million were raised to 40 per cent; and it was completed, some would say, in the 1960s and 1970s when capital gains tax was introduced, and estate duty was replaced by the more-difficult-to-avoid capital transfer tax.[53] The consequences were predictable. Many estates were broken up or reduced in size; many country houses were demolished or abandoned; and many aristocrats found themselves in straitened circumstances. 'The landed aristocracy in the inter-war years gradually settled down to a circumscribed style of living, which had previously been typical only of the impoverished arable land-owners.'[54] During the 1960s, to take one striking, albeit untypical example, the fifth Lord Redesdale, the descendant of a family that had once owned 30,000 acres in Northumberland, found himself running a laundry and dry-cleaning business in London.[55] It was a dramatic change: the economic and social ascendancy of the aristocracy was eroded, its power to dominate taste and demand considerably undermined.

The decline of the aristocracy coincided with – and was not unrelated to – the rise of the middle class.[56] Of course, to point to the rise of the middle class constitutes one of the most weary of all historical clichés. Yet it is a cliché that bears repetition, for the past two hundred years have seen a massive growth in the numbers, wealth and incomes of the middle class – and the resulting growth in middle-class purchasing power has had a profound impact upon the nature of consumer demand.

The middle class grew faster than any other. Table 1.4 shows that the number of people who can be identified as belonging to the middle class increased more than seventeen times: from some 1.3 million (an estimated 12.5 per cent of the population) in 1801, to 2.6 million (12.5 per cent) in 1851, 9.3 million (25 per cent) in 1901, 12.2 million (30 per cent) in 1951, and 22.6 million (40 per cent) in 1981.

The middle class was also growing more wealthy. It was not just that it came to contain some of the very richest in the land.[57] It was more that it came to contain many of those who might be termed the moderately rich. It is difficult to be precise. However, it has been found that there was a considerable increase in the value of property left by those who died. The number of estates worth between £1,000 and £10,000 grew from just over 6,000 (21 per cent of those dying) in 1858, to nearly 16,000 (24 per cent) at the turn of the century, and more than 46,000 (30 per cent) in 1938–39. These were substantial sums: for even in London during the late 1930s £1,200 would buy

TABLE 1.4. The redistribution of demand, Great Britain, 1801–1981: class

Year	All classes No. (mills)	Upper class No. (mills)	%	Middle class No. (mills)	%	Working class No. (mills)	%
1801	10.7	0.1	1.0	1.3	12.5	9.3	86.5
1851	20.9	0.2	1.0	2.6	12.5	18.1	86.5
1901	37.1	0.4	1.0	9.3	25.0	27.4	74.0
1951	48.9	0.5	1.0	12.2	30.0	36.2	69.0
1981	54.8	0.6	1.0	21.9	40.0	32.3	59.0

Sources: **T. Barker** and **M. Drake** (eds), *Population and Society in Britain 1850–1980*, Batsford, 1982, p. 205; **J. Burnett**, *A History of the Cost of Living*, Penguin, 1969, pp. 40, 292–3; **P. Deane** and **W. A. Cole**, *British Economic Growth 1688–1959: Trends and Structure*, Cambridge University Press, 1969, pp. 6, 8; **A. Marwick**, *British Society since 1945*, Penguin, 1982, pp. 40, 209; **R. C. O. Mathews**, **C. H. Feinstein** and **J. C. Odling-Smee**, *British Economic Growth 1856–1973*, Clarendon Press, 1982, p. 167; **H. Perkin**, *Origins of Modern English Society*, Ark, 1985, pp. 20–1; **E. Royle**, *Modern Britain: A Social History 1750–1985*, Arnold, 1987, p. 102.

an individual, architect-designed, detached house standing in up to half an acre of land.[58] It has been found too that there was a substantial redistribution of wealth-holding in favour of the middle class. Between 1923 and 1976 the proportion of marketable wealth possessed by the richest 20 per cent of the population (excluding the very richest 2 per cent) increased by more than a half, from 33 per cent, to 52 per cent, of the total.[59]

The middle class was also receiving higher, and more secure, incomes. It has been calculated, for example, that salary-earners' share of national income grew from less than 7 per cent in the mid nineteenth century, to almost 12 per cent in 1913, 20 per cent in 1951, and more than 26 per cent in 1973.[60] Certainly it is easy to point to the high, and rising, incomes of the upper middle class. It has been estimated that whereas in 1913–14 the typical doctor/general practitioner probably earned just under £400 a year, in 1935–37 he would probably receive £1,000, and in 1960 more than £2,500. This represented an improvement, in real terms, of just over 50 per cent in fifty years.[61] The lower middle class did better still. For as Geoffrey Crossick has pointed out, 'The basis for the broad commercial provision for a lower middle class market was initially simple growth of numbers, but equally significant were earnings – their size, regularity and security.'[62] Thus it has been estimated that in 1911–13 the average annual earnings of male bank clerks stood at £142, and that they increased to £368 in 1935, and to £1,040 in

1960. This represented an improvement in real terms of practically 75 per cent – and this over the same fifty-year period that the incomes of doctors rose by about 50 per cent.[63] Some further generalisation and comparison is possible. It has been calculated that between 1913–14 and 1978 the salaries of male clerks rose 60 per cent faster than those of higher professional such as doctors, lawyers, architects and accountants, and that the salaries of female clerks rose 70 per cent faster than those of lower professional such as teachers, librarians and social workers.[64]

The growth of middle-class purchasing power was matched – indeed, it was surpassed – by the growth in the purchasing power of the working class.[65] This, perhaps, is not surprising, for the working class was larger than any other. Table 1.4 shows that the number (although not the proportion) of people that may be identified as working-class increased some three and a half times: from 9.3 million (an estimated 86.5 per cent of the population) in 1801, to 18.1 million (86.5 per cent) in 1851, 27.4 million (74 per cent) in 1901, 36.2 million (69 per cent) in 1951, and 33.3 million (59 per cent) in 1981.

The growth of working-class purchasing power, unlike that of the middle class, owed very little to the redistribution of wealth. In fact, it has been calculated that in 1923 80 per cent of the population owned no more than 6 per cent of all marketable wealth, a figure which even in 1976 had risen to only 23 per cent.[66] This meant, for example, that even after the Second World War nearly two-thirds of the population possessed private capital worth less than £100 – too little obviously to generate any significant volume of day-to-day income.[67]

The working class benefited more – and more than the middle class – from the redistribution of incomes that was taking place. There is evidence that, although wage-earners comprised a steadily declining proportion of the population, their share of national income remained constant at around 40 per cent.[68] In fact, it has been calculated that between 1900 and 1981 the weekly wage-earnings of manual workers increased, in real terms, by well over 400 per cent.[69] There is evidence too that the semi-skilled and unskilled benefited more than the skilled. Guy Routh estimates that between 1913–14 and 1978 the rise in the average earnings of unskilled workers exceeded that of skilled workers by just under 33 per cent, while the rise in the earnings of semi-skilled workers exceeded that of skilled workers by just over 33 per cent.[70] The consequences were plain. When Peter Willmott and his team interviewed Bethnal Green boys born during the 1940s, they discovered that this was 'the first generation . . . to grow up without malnutrition and poverty'. A tailor's presser explained:

> You can have a lot more things than they would, the previous
> generation, television and things like that. And a working man can

own a motor-car and go out at week-ends . . . . What some people
call the good old days were really the bad old days.[71]

These, and the other, material changes considered so far in this
chapter were of truly fundamental importance. Indeed, it is no
exaggeration to claim that they revolutionised the British people's
capacity for consumption. For changes in the scale and distribution of
population, wealth and income transformed the scale and distribution
of purchasing power, and thus the size and nature of the domestic
market that suppliers of goods and services were seeking to satisfy.

However, material changes alone cannot account for changes in
the scale and nature of consumer demand. (It is perfectly possible,
after all, for improvements in prosperity to lead to increases in saving
rather than to increases in spending.[72]) Thus, in order to understand
the changes that have taken place in consumer demand, one further
step is required. It is necessary to take account of ideological as
well as material developments, to consider changes in consumers'
willingness – as well as in their ability – to consume the goods and
services that were made available to them.

Accordingly, it is the purpose of the remainder of this chapter to
consider briefly some of the major changes that have taken place in
attitudes towards consumption. This is not easily done. For although
the outstanding development, the increasing propensity to consume,
is easy enough to identify, it remains difficult to explain it in a way
that appears totally convincing. In fact, three major explanations
have been advanced: manipulation; emulation; and amelioration.
The first suggest that consumers were manipulated by advertisers
and other commercial interests; the second that consumers were
satisfying a deep-seated need to emulate their fellows; and the
third that they were satisfying a still more deep-seated need to
improve the material (and other) circumstances in which they found
themselves.[73]

The view that advertisers, producers and other commercial interests were able to manipulate – and increase – consumer spending
is one to which historians have given considerable credence.[74] For
according to Neil McKendrick and his colleagues, the consumer
revolution of the eighteenth century was made possible by 'the
efforts of those busy, inventive, profit-seeking men of business whose
eager advertising, active marketing and inspired salesmanship did so
much . . . to usher in a new economy and a new demand structure
in English society'.[75] According to Edward Royle, 'The lubricant to
make the consumer society' of the late twentieth century 'function
smoothly was advertising, which was made all the easier with the
advent of television.'

Now products could be recommended within the privacy and security
of 18.7 million homes, and the message repeated every quarter of an

hour with all the sincerity an actor or actress could summon until the image of the product was firmly planted in the viewers' minds. People were persuaded to want bigger, better and allegedly different goods.[76]

There is no doubt, of course, that once manufacturers, retailers and advertisers identified those groups whose economic power was growing, they made vigorous, and imaginative, efforts to persuade them to increase, and change, their spending. It will be seen in the chapter which follows that adolescents, the elderly, women and the working class were all targeted. Thus working-class women appeared to offer a particularly attractive market. They were bombarded with advertisements: first for basic household goods like soap and patent medicine; then for furniture, clothing and fashion accessories; and more recently for specialised/luxury products such as confectionery, consumer durables and convenience foods.[77]

Consequently it is easy to believe that if advertisers were urging increases, or changes, in spending, and if consumers were increasing, or changing, their spending, then the latter must have been manipulated by the former. However, such an argument must be treated with very great caution, for it can be both condescending and illogical. It is condescending in so far as it implies that consumers were the passive victims of forces beyond their control; it is illogical in so far as it suggests that consumers might not have their own reasons for wishing to increase, or change, their spending.[78]

Dissatisfaction with theories dependent upon the manipulation of the consumer has led scholars to look to explanations based upon the consumer's innate desire for social emulation. For, as Thorstein Veblen pointed out nearly a hundred years ago, the consumption of goods and services satisfies social as well as material needs. 'The motive that lies at the root of ownership', he asserted, 'is emulation.' 'No class of society, not even the most abjectly poor, forgoes all customary conspicuous consumption . . . . Very much of squalor and discomfort will be endured before the last trinket or the last pretense of pecuniary decency is put away.'[79] It is a view that Harold Perkin did much to popularise some twenty years or so ago:

> If consumer demand . . . was the key to the Industrial Revolution,
> social emulation was the key to consumer demand. By the eighteenth
> century nearly everyone in England and the Scottish Lowlands
> received a money income, and nearly everyone was prepared to spend
> a large part of it in 'keeping up with the Joneses'.[80]

More recently, Paul Johnson has taken up the concept of conspicuous consumption as 'a potentially powerful analytical device which can be used to throw light on consumption patterns of workers in late-Victorian Britain'.[81]

These are appealing arguments, and ones for which their supporters have been able to marshal a good deal of empirical support. Harold Perkin cites Daniel Defoe who, along with other eighteenth-century commentators, castigated the 'flourishing pride' which 'dictated new methods of living to the people; and while the poorest citizens live like the rich, the rich like the gentry, the gentry like the nobility, and the nobility striving to outshine one another, no wonder all the sumptuary trades increase'.[82] Paul Johnson cites the worker in the East End of London who observed that 'There was snobbery even among the working classes, and the boys from Morrison Buildings, who were a little better off than we were and a little better dressed, used to sneer at our rags.'[83]

None the less, it seems that the emulative model, like the manipulative, rests upon an unduly restricted view of consumer motivation and behaviour. But so too does the third explanation that has been advanced to explain the consumer's increasing propensity to consume. The ameliorative (or instinctivist) model suggests that the desire to increase consumption resulted from an innate, and therefore persistent, desire to enjoy a higher standard of living. According to this view, the only thing that prevents consumers from increasing their consumption is their inability to do so. It is a view to which I – and many others – have subscribed.

> When real incomes rose, the first priority was to obtain enough food to eat and adequate accommodation in which to live. But once these basic needs had been met, priorities began to alter. The better off wished to enjoy some of the trappings of their new-found, if often insecure prosperity. They wanted to eat a more varied diet and wear more fashionable clothes; they planned to live in a more comfortable and better furnished home; and they expected to enjoy some at least of the new forms of leisure that were becoming available to those with the money to pay for them.[84]

It is a view to which I – and many others – still do subscribe. This is not to deny of course that consumers could be manipulated, or that consumers often used consumption as a means of social emulation. Nor is it to overlook the dangers of the ameliorative model itself. For it is deceptively simple, and in attempting to explain consumer behaviour in terms of inherent needs, it can degenerate all too easily into circular and/or determinist forms of reasoning.[85] Nevertheless, it does appear that the ameliorative (or instinctivist) model accords very closely with what is known about consumer behaviour in Britain over the past two hundred years. It will be seen in subsequent chapters that – with certain obvious exceptions – people in Britain did tend to increase their spending in line with increases in their wealth and in line, more particularly, with increases in their day-to-day disposable income.[86]

It will be clear by now, if it was not at the outset, that the study of consumer demand raises considerable conceptual and empirical difficulties. For although it has proved relatively straightforward to identify, and explain, consumers' increasing capacity for consumption, it has been found much more difficult to account satisfactorily for their increasing willingness to do so. Indeed, the growth and redirection of demand can be understood properly only when set alongside the growth and diversification of supply. Demand and supply, it will then be seen, were entwined in an intimate and symbiotic relationship.

NOTES AND REFERENCES

1. **E. W. Gilboy**, 'Demand as a Factor in the Industrial Revolution', in **R. M. Hartwell** (ed.), *The Causes of the Industrial Revolution in England*, Methuen, 1967, p. 123.
2. **A. B. Atkinson**, *Unequal Shares: Wealth in Britain*, Allen Lane, 1972, p. 5.
3. **R. Stone**, 'Private Saving in Britain, Past, Present and Future', *Manchester School of Economic and Social Studies*, **32**, 1967, p. 80. Also **M. Douglas** and **B. Isherwood**, *The World of Goods: Towards an Anthropology of Consumption*, Allen Lane, 1979, p. 25.
4. **W. D. Rubinstein**, *Men of Property: The Very Wealthy in Britain since the Industrial Revolution*, Croom Helm, 1981, pp. 28–30, 32. The figures for 1858 refer to England and Wales, those for 1938–39 to Great Britain.
5. **A. Marwick**, *British Society since 1945*, Penguin, 1990, p. 111.
6. See, for example, **H. Cunningham**, 'Leisure', in **J. Benson** (ed.), *The Working Class in England 1875–1914*, Croom Helm, 1984, p. 135; **J. Benson**, *The Working Class in Britain, 1850–1939*, Longman, 1989, pp. 14–15. Also **G. Cross**, *A Quest for Time: The Reduction of Work in Britain and France, 1840–1940*, University of California Press, 1989.
7. Cunningham, 'Leisure', pp. 135–6; **G. C. Cameron**, 'The Growth of Holidays with Pay in Britain', in **G. L. Reid** and **D. J. Robertson** (eds), *Fringe Benefits, Labour Costs and Social Security*, Allen & Unwin, 1965, pp. 281, 297; **M. A. Bienefeld**, *Working Hours in British Industry: An Economic History*, Weidenfeld & Nicolson, 1972, pp. 1, 40, 80; *British Labour Statistics: Historical Abstract 1886–1968*, Department of Employment and Productivity, 1971, p. 160.
8. Cross, *Quest*, p. 97; Cameron, 'Holidays', p. 285; **J. Stevenson**, *British Society 1914–45*, Penguin, 1984, p. 193.
9. See, for example, **G. A. Mackay** and **G. Lain**, *Consumer Problems in Rural Areas*, Scottish Consumer Council, 1982?
10. **T. Barker** and **M. Drake** (eds), *Population and Society in Britain 1850–1980*, Batsford, 1982, p. 205; **A. H. Halsey**, *British Social Trends since 1900: A Guide to the Changing Social Structure of Britain*, Macmillan, 1988, p. 326; **D. C. Marsh**, *The Changing Social Structure*

of England and Wales 1871–1961, Routledge & Kegan Paul, 1977, pp. 96, 108, 285.

11. Marsh, *Social Structure*, pp. 21, 71; **R. M. Reeve**, *The Industrial Revolution 1750–1850*, University of London Press, 1971, pp. 203, 205; **E. Royle**, *Modern Britain: A Social History 1750–1985*, Arnold, 1987, p. 20.

12. Barker and Drake, *Population and Society*, p. 206; **P. Deane** and **W. A. Cole**, *British Economic Growth 1688–1959: Trends and Structure*, Cambridge University Press, 1969, p. 6; Marsh, *Social Structure*, p. 98.

13. Halsey (ed.), *Social Trends*, pp. 329–30; Reeve, *Industrial Revolution*, p. 205.

14. Rubinstein, *Men of Property*, pp. 102–10, 238–9. See also **W. D. Rubinstein**, 'The Victorian Middle Classes: Wealth, Occupation, and Geography', *Economic History Review*, **xxx**, 1977.

15. **M. Swenarton** and **S. Taylor**, 'The Scale and Nature of the Growth of Owner-Occupation in Britain Between the Wars', *Economic History Review*, **xxxviii**, 1985, pp. 378, 388.

16. Halsey, *Social Trends*, p. 378; Marsh, *Social Structure*, p. 237.

17. **E. H. Hunt**, *British Labour History, 1815–1914*, Weidenfeld & Nicolson. 1981, p. 101.

18. **Central Statistical Office**, *Facts in Focus*, Penguin, 1980, p. 128. Also *British Labour Statistics*, pp. 392–3.

19. *Independent*, 15 September 1990. In 1979/80 average household income was £134 per week in Great Britain, £117 in Yorkshire and Humberside and £153 in South-east England. **J. Le Grand** and **R. Robinson**, *The Economics of Social Problems: The Market versus the State*, Macmillan, 1987, p. 194.

20. For the difficulties of defining adolescence, see **J. Rider** and **H. Silver**, *Modern English Society 1850–1970*, Methuen, 1970, p. 260.

21. Halsey, *Social Trends*, p. 262.

22. Rider and Silver, *Modern English Society*, p. 260. Also **P. Willmott**, *Adolescent Boys of East London*, Penguin, 1975, p. 21.

23. **B. Osgerby**, '"Well, It's Saturday Night an' I Just Got Paid": Youth, Consumerism and Hegemony in Post-War Britain', *Contemporary Record*, **6**, 1992, p. 294. Also Willmott, *Adolescent Boys*, p. 7; **M. Abrams**, *Consumer Spending in 1959 (Part II): Middle Class and Working Class Boys and Girls*, London Press Exchange, 1961.

24. **E. Roberts**, *A Woman's Place: An Oral History of Working-Class Women 1890–1940*, Blackwell, 1984, p. 43; **E. Roberts**, 'The Family', in **Benson** (ed), *Working Class* p. 26; Bristol, R01, p. 18; R02, p. 13; Lancaster, Mrs C5P, p. 5; Mrs R3P, p. 22; Mrs A1P, p. 7. Cf. **D. Fowler**, 'Teenage Consumers? Young Wage-Earners and Leisure in Manchester, 1919–1939', in **A. Davies** and **S. Fielding** (eds), *Workers' Worlds: Cultures and Communities in Manchester and Salford, 1880–1939*, Manchester University Press, 1992.

25. Willmott, *Adolescent Boys*, pp. 21–2. Also Lancaster, Mrs L2L, p. 37; Mrs P5B, p. 6; Mr R1P, p. 55; Mr R3B, p. 24.

26. **E. Roberts**, unpublished paper, University of Birmingham, October 1991.

27. **P. Thompson**, *The Edwardians*, Paladin, 1977, p. 71.
28. Marwick, *British Society*, p. 143.
29. *RC on the Distribution of Income and Wealth, Report No. 1*, 1975, pp. 110, 115; **L. Hannah**, *Inventing Retirement: The Development of Occupational Pensions in Britain*, Cambridge University Press, 1986, p. 125. **A. Hallsworth**, *Food Shopping and the Elderly*, Manchester Business School, 1990, pp. 5–7.
30. Hannah, *Inventing Retirement*, pp. 122–3, 154, 188.
31. Hannah, *Inventing Retirement*, pp. 7–8. Also **M. Abrams**, 'Some Background Facts', *Journal of the Market Research Society*, 25, 1983, p. 219; **J. Benson**, *The Penny Capitalists: A Study of Nineteenth-Century Working-Class Entrepreneurs*, Gill & Macmillan, 1983.
32. Benson, *Working Class*, pp. 50–3.
33. Hannah, *Inventing Retirement*, pp. 16–17; Benson, *Working Class*, pp. 50–1.
34. Halsey, *Social Trends*, pp. 496–7; Hannah, *Inventing Retirement*, p. 105.
35. Hannah, *Inventing Retirement*, pp. 13, 40, 126. Also **R. Fitzgerald**, *British Labour Management and Industrial Welfare*, Croom Helm, 1988.
36. Hannah, *Inventing Retirement*, pp. 126–7.
37. Hannah, *Inventing Retirement*, p. 126.
38. Hannah, *Inventing Retirement*, pp. 61, 117–21, 128. **L. Oren**, 'The Welfare of Women in Laboring Families: England, 1860–1950', in **M. S. Hartman** and **L. Banner** (eds), *Clio's Consciousness Raised: New Perspectives on the History of Women*, Harper & Row, 1974, pp. 236–7. In 1981 elderly women outnumbered elderly men by three to two. Abrams, 'Facts', p. 217.
39. Rubinstein, *Men of Property*, pp. 28–30.
40. *RC Distribution, Report No. 1*, p. 106.
41. *RC Distribution, Report No. 1*, pp. 99, 106.
42. See, for example, **S. Lewenhak**, *Women and Work*, Fontana, 1980; **A. Coote** and **B. Campbell**, *Sweet Freedom: The Struggle for Women's Liberation*, Picador, 1982.
43. Halsey, *Social Trends*, pp. 169–72; Hunt, *Labour History*, pp. 17, 29; **E. Roberts**, *Women's Work 1840–1940*, Macmillan, 1988, pp. 21–2; **E. Richards**, 'Women in the British Economy since about 1700: An Interpretation', *History*, **59**, 1974.
44. Benson, *Working Class*, pp. 58–9; Roberts, *Women's Work*, pp. 23–6; **S. Pollard**, *The Development of the British Economy 1914–1980*, Arnold, 1983, p. 321.
45. Pollard, *British Economy*, pp. 321–2.
46. Oren, 'Welfare', p. 236.
47. Roberts, *Woman's Place*, p. 124.
48. **C. Chinn**, *They Worked all their Lives: Women of the Urban Poor in England, 1880–1939*, Manchester University Press, 1988, p. 51. Also Oren, 'Welfare', pp. 231, 235; **L. A. Tilly** and **J. W. Scott**, *Women, Work, and Family*, Routledge, 1987, pp. 207–210.
49. The upper class (or aristocracy) is defined here economically, as those who derived their wealth and income primarily from the ownership

of land. See **J. V. Beckett**, *The Aristocracy in England 1660–1914*, Blackwell, 1986; **D. Cannadine**, *The Decline and Fall of the British Aristocracy*, Yale University Press, 1989; **F. M. L. Thompson**, *English Landed Society in the Nineteenth Century*, Routledge & Kegan Paul, 1963.

50. **S. G. Checkland**, *The Rise of Industrial Society in England 1815–1885*, Longman, 1964, pp. 281–3.

51. **J. Burnett**, *A History of the Cost of Living*, Penguin, 1969, p. 221. Also Rubinstein, *Men of Property*, pp. 60–1.

52. Beckett, *Aristocracy*, p. 468; Checkland, *Industrial Society*, pp. 288–9. For the decline of the gentry, see **G. E. Mingay**, *The Gentry: The Rise and Fall of a Ruling Class*, Longman, 1976, pp. 165–87.

53. Beckett, *Aristocracy*, pp. 477–8.

54. Thompson, *Landed Society*, pp. 337–8. Also Beckett, *Aristocracy*, pp. 176, 478–9.

55. Beckett, *Aristocracy*, p. 470. But see **F. M. L. Thompson**, 'English Landed Society in the Twentieth Century: I, Property: Collapse and Survival', *Transactions of the Royal Historical Society*, **40**, 1990.

56. The middle class is defined economically, as those who derived their wealth and income primarily from the ownership of property other than land, and from their employment in non-manual labour. See **J. Raynor**, *The Middle Class*, Longman, 1969.

57. Rubinstein, *Men of Property*, pp. 61, 70, 240.

58. Rubinstein, *Men of Property*, pp. 29–30, 32; **J. Burnett**, *A Social History of Housing 1815–1985*, Methuen, 1986, p. 252.

59. **D. Metcalf** and **R. Richardson**, 'Labour', in **A. R. Prest** and **D. J. Coppock** (eds), *The UK Economy: A Manual of Applied Economics*, Weidenfeld & Nicolson, 1980, p. 259.

60. **R. C. O. Mathews, C. H. Feinstein** and **J. C. Odling-Smee**, *British Economic Growth 1856–1973*, Clarendon Press, 1982, p. 164.

61. Burnett, *Cost of Living*, p. 298.

62. **G. Crossick**, 'The Emergence of the Lower Middle Class in Britain: A Discussion', in **G. Crossick** (ed.), *The Lower Middle Class in Britain 1870–1914*, Croom Helm, 1977, p. 34.

63. Burnett, *Cost of Living*, p. 299.

64. **G. Routh**, *Occupation and Pay in Great Britain 1906–79*, Macmillan, 1980, p. 125.

65. The working class is defined economically as those who derived their wealth and income primarily from their employment in manual labour. See Benson, *Working Class*, pp. 3–4.

66. Metcalf and Richardson, 'Labour', p. 259.

67. Stevenson, *British Society*, p. 331.

68. Pollard, *British Economy*, p. 188.

69. Calculated from Halsey, *Social Trends*, pp. 180, 182.

70. Routh, *Occupation*, pp. 120–1.

71. Willmott, *Adolescent Boys*, p. 20.

72. **C. Campbell**, *The Romantic Ethic and the Spirit of Modern Consumerism*, Blackwell, 1987, pp. 18, 40–1.

73. Campbell, *Romantic Ethic*, pp. 42–3. For criticisms of advertising, see *RC on Consumer Protection*, 1962, pp. 238–43.

74. See **R. H. Williams**, *Dream Worlds: Mass Consumption in Late Nineteenth-century France*, University of California Press, 1982, p. 3.
75. **N. McKendrick, J. Brewer** and **J. H. Plumb**, *The Birth of a Consumer Society: The Commercialisation of Eighteenth-century England*, Hutchinson, 1982, p. 6.
76. Royle, *Modern Britain*, p. 280–1.
77. **W. H. Fraser**, *The Coming of the Mass Market, 1850–1914*, Macmillan, 1981, pp. 135–6, 139, 142, 145; **T. R. Nevett**, *Advertising in Britain: A History*, Heinemann, 1982, pp. 68–9, 179.
78. Cf. **F. M. L. Thompson**, 'Social Control in Victorian Britain', *Economic History Review*, **xxxiv**, 1981, p. 189. Moreover, as Jim Obelkevitch has pointed out, successful products were sometimes advertised very lightly, and unsuccessful ones very heavily. **J. Oblekevitch**, unpublished paper, University of Warwick, March 1991.
79. **T. Veblen**, *The Theory of the Leisure Class*, Unwin Books, 1970, pp. 35, 70.
80. **H. Perkin**, *Origins of Modern English Society*, Ark Paperbacks, 1985, pp. 96–7.
81. **P. Johnson**, 'Conspicuous Consumption and Working-Class Culture in Late Victorian and Edwardian Britain', *Transactions of the Royal Historical Society*, **38**, 1988, pp. 30–1.
82. Cited Perkin, *Origins*, p. 92.
83. Johnson, 'Conspicuous Consumption', p. 34.
84. Benson, *Working Class*, p. 146.
85. Campbell, *Romantic Ethic*, p. 44.
86. Stone, 'Private Saving'.

Chapter 2

CHANGES IN SUPPLY

The relationship between demand, supply and consumption remains notoriously difficult to disentangle. It was seen in the previous chapter that the growth and redirection of consumption could not have taken place without corresponding changes in the scale and distribution of demand. It will be shown in this chapter that the growth and redirection of consumption could not have taken place without corresponding changes in the scale and distribution of supply.[1] Of course, supply and consumption were no more synonymous than demand and consumption. For not all goods and service find buyers: one has only to think of the periodic slumps that occur in the housing market, or of the many second and third division football matches that fail to attract spectators. Supply does not necessarily create its own demand.

However, when supply is disentangled from consumption, two major developments become apparent. Accordingly, this chapter, like the last, is divided into two. The first section considers the expansion in the supply of goods and services available to the consumer; the second, and slightly shorter, section examines the ways in which suppliers sought to direct these goods and services towards those consumers whose purchasing power was increasing most rapidly.

It is easy to show that the supply of goods and services available to the British consumer increased at an unprecedented rate during the past two hundred years. It is well known that the restructuring of the economy, the introduction of mechanisation and the adoption of other, organisational innovations exercised a most profound effect: these changes increased the supply (and reduced the cost) of traditional products such as food and housing, and made possible the introduction of a wide range of new products – from motor cars and television sets to breakfast cereals and package holidays.[2]

This growth in the supply of goods and services is measured most conveniently in terms of gross national (or domestic) product. Thus

The rise of consumer society in Britain, 1880–1980

Table 2.1 shows that the value, in real terms, of the goods and services produced by the British economy increased more than eight times during the nineteenth century, and a further four and a half times between 1901 and 1981. It shows too that even when allowance is made for the growth of the population, the real value per head of these goods and services increased very significantly: two and a half times during the course of the nineteenth century, and a further three times during the first eighty years of the twentieth century.

The growth in the supply of goods and services is measured more tellingly in terms of individual products. Tables 2.2 and 2.3 provide some indication of the changes that took place. They suggest that from the middle of the nineteenth century the supply of traditional products (such as food, housing and clothing) more than kept pace with the growth of population; and that from the end of the century the supply of consumer durables (such as carpets, cars, pianos and televisions) and of consumer services (such as retailing, travel, sport and entertainment) comfortably outstripped the growth of the population.

The supply of food, housing and clothing all kept pace with demand. For example, it would be difficult to exaggerate the changes that have taken place in the supply of food available to the British consumer. The volume, variety and quality of the food on super-market shelves today would come as an even greater surprise to our early nineteenth-century predecessors than it does to our late twentieth-century contemporaries from less industrialised parts of the world. Changes in British farming, advances in food processing, and the growth of foreign imports all had their effect. British agriculture expanded, became more efficient and, when it contracted, specialised

TABLE 2.1 The growth of gross national (domestic) product, Great Britain, 1801–1981

Year	At current prices (£ million)	In real terms (1801=100)	In real terms per head (1801=100)
1801	232	100	100
1851	523	226	116
1901	1,643	849	245
1951	11,293	1,899	416
1981	184,887	3,797	741

Sources: **D. Butler** and **J. Freeman**, *British Political Facts 1900–1968*, Macmillan, 1969, pp. 222–3; **Central Statistical Office**, *Key Data 1986 Edition*, HMSO, 1986, p. 66; **P. Deane** and **W. A. Cole**, *British Economic Growth 1688–1959: Trends and Structure*, Cambridge University Press, 1959, pp. 166, 175, 178; **B. R. Mitchell** and **H. R. Jones**, *Second Abstract of British Historical Statistics*, Cambridge University Press, 1971, p. 151

TABLE 2.2 The supply of staple products (food and housing), Great Britain, 1801–1969

| Year | Food | | Housing | |
| | cattle | wheat (for sale, i.e., production plus imports) | houses | Persons per house |
	(millions)	(million tons)	(millions)	
1801/11		.088	1.9	9.8
1850/51	4.2		3.4	8.0
1884		3.6		
1900/1	6.8			
1911			7.6	6.0
1939	8.2			
1950/51		5.9	13.8	3.7
1969/78	11.1	4.5	21.1	2.7

Sources: **J. Burnett**, *A History of the Cost of Living*, Penguin, 1984, pp. 206–7; **J. Burnett**, *Plenty and Want: A Social History of Food in England from 1815 to the Present Day*, Routledge, 1989, pp. 8, 116; **Central Statistical Office**, *Key Data 1986 Edition*, HMSO, 1986, p. 66; **D. Butler** and **J. Freeman**, *British Political Facts 1900–1968*, Macmillan, 1969, pp. 17, 63, 222–3; **P. Deane** and **W. A. Cole**, *British Economic Growth 1688–1959: Trends and Structure*, Cambridge University Press, 1969, pp. 8, 62, 166, 175, 178; **B. R. Mitchell** and **H. R. Jones**, *Second Abstract of British Historical Statistics*, Cambridge University Press, 1971, pp. 57, 61, 116

TABLE 2.3 The supply of consumer durables (carpets and cars), Great Britain, 1850–1980

| Year | Carpets | | Cars |
	for sale in UK (million yards)	(yards per house)	British production
1850	11.9	3.5	
1912/13	30.4	4.0	25,000
1929			182,000
1947			287,000
1950/2	31.3	2.3	476,000
1969/78	123.4	6.2	1,700,000
1980			924,000

Sources: **J. N. Bartlett**, *Carpeting the Millions: The Growth of Britain's Carpet Industry*, Donald, nd, pp. 66, 198–9; **S. Pollard**, *The Development of the British Economy 1914–1980*, Arnold, 1989, p. 289; **D. G. Rhys**, *The Motor Industry: An Economic Survey*, Butterworths, 1972, pp. 9, 14, 18, 21, 38

increasingly in products such as milk, eggs, fruit and vegetables that were difficult to import economically from overseas.[3] Food processing and manufacturing became more sophisticated. Late-nineteenth-century suppliers began to mechanise the production of staple items such as bread and biscuits, while their twentieth-century successors introduced new lines in snacks, confectionery, breakfast cereals and other convenience foods.[4] Moreover, an increasing amount of British food was imported from abroad: first, items like tea and coffee that could only be grown overseas; then, from about 1850, staple goods such as meat and cereals that could be produced more cheaply overseas; and finally, from the turn of the century, fruits, cheeses, wines and other items that had been regarded previously as exotic and/or unobtainable luxuries.[5]

The supply of housing also kept pace with the growth of the population. For although the building industry remained – and remains – technologically and organisationally conservative, it employed a workforce that was large enough, and grew fast enough (from 0.9 million in 1881, to 1.4 million in 1951, and 1.6 million in 1973), to enable it to increase many times over the number of houses that it was able to build: 80,000 a year in the 1880s, almost 230,000 in the early 1950s, and more than 260,000 during the late 1970s.[6] The impact of this expansion is revealed in Table 2.2. It shows that between 1801/11 and 1969/78 the number of houses available in Britain multiplied more than eleven times, an increase which (because it far outstripped the growth of population) meant that the average number of people living in each house declined from almost ten to fewer than three.

TABLE 2.4   The supply of consumer services (retailing and advertising), Great Britain, 1850/51–1978/80

| Year | Retailing Branches of multiples (with 10+ branches) | | Advertising Expenditure | |
	No.	Per 10,000 population	£ mill.	£ per head at current prices
1850/51			1	0.1
1880	1,564	0.5		
1905/7	15,242	3.8	10	0.3
1950/51	44,800	9.2	102	2.1
1978/80	66,343	12.1	2,562	46.8

Sources: **J. B. Jefferys**, *Retail Trading in Britain, 1850–1950*, Cambridge University Press, 1954, pp. 22, 61; **T. R. Nevett**, *Advertising in Britain: A History*, Heinemann, 1982, pp. 29, 70–1; **L. O'Brian** and **F. Harris**, *Retailing: Shopping, Society, Space*, David Fulton, 1991, p. 61; **S. Pollard**, *The Development of the British Economy 1914–1980*, Arnold, 1989, p. 327

The supply of consumer durables increased just as rapidly, but not until the second half of the nineteenth century. Indeed, the manufacturers of these products constituted the core of the so-called 'new' industries that came to prominence between the two world wars. These industries, together later with their overseas competitors, relied heavily upon the advantages to be derived from economies of scale and the adoption of new forms of mechanisation. They poured out a growing – and, it sometimes seemed, an endlessly changing – range of products to tempt the consumer: carpets, furniture and pianos; cycles, motor cycles and cars; and a huge variety of electrical goods from vacuum cleaners, cookers, refrigerators and freezers to radios, television sets and video recorders.

Not all consumer industries are equally well known. The carpet industry, for instance, has never attracted the attention that it deserves. However, it has been shown that a major transformation occurred during the second half of the nineteenth century: the scale of investment grew, the number of large firms increased, and the production of Axminster and woollen tapestry was mechanised. The result was that the value of goods produced by the average firm grew from less than £20,000 in 1850 to more than £115,000 in 1913. It has been shown too that a second transformation occurred in the years following the Second World War. The number of large firms increased once more, the control of stock was improved, and the production of tufted rugs and carpets was simplified and made cheaper by the introduction of man-made fibres.[7] The consequences of these two periods of change can be seen clearly in Table 2.3: the amount of British carpet available for sale increased two-and-a-half times during the second half of the nineteenth century, and practically four times during the final thirty years of the period.

The motor industry, of course, is far better known. Indeed, with its large firms, new technologies and advanced techniques of mass production, it came to stand as a symbol of twentieth-century manufacturing industry. Its concentration of ownership was remarkable, with firms like Austin, Ford, Morris Motors and Vauxhall coming to dominate.[8] Its expansion of output was extraordinary: for despite the criticisms levelled at the industry in recent years, Table 2.3 shows that its production of private cars increased from just 25,000 in 1913, to almost half a million in 1951, and practically twice that number in 1980. In fact, even these figures do not reflect fully the post-war growth in the supply of motor cars. They are misleading in that they overestimate the number of vehicles available in Britain in the early 1950s (when two-thirds of British output was exported), and that they underestimate the number available in the early 1980s (when 40 per cent of domestic sales were imported from abroad).[9]

The supply of consumer services has received far less attention than the supply of consumer durables. In fact, the service sector as a whole was so seldom the source of organisational innovation, technological breakthrough or class confrontation that it always tends to be overlooked.[10] Yet there can be no justification for such neglect. Industries such as retailing, marketing, advertising, entertainment, tourism and sport began to assume a new, and major, importance in late Victorian and Edwardian Britain – an importance that they maintained, and increased, during the following hundred years.

The growth of retailing was central to the growth of supply. It was not just that the number of people employed in trade doubled between 1851 and 1901, and increased by a further 40 per cent between 1901 and 1951.[11] It was also that the development of co-operative, department and multiple stores enabled retailing to begin to enjoy some of the economies of scale that had been pioneered by manufacturing industry.

The process of change began with the establishment of retail co-operation in the 1840s. Forty years later there were nearly a thousand co-operative societies with over half a million members, and by 1914 the movement's 1,385 societies had more than 3 million members and a turnover of £88 million a year. The stores began to diversify: for although they continued to concentrate upon groceries and provisions, they also started to sell meat, milk, bread, greengrocery, clothing and household goods. 'Where this was carried out under one roof', explains Michael Winstanley, 'co-op establishments began to resemble department stores for the working classes, even aping them in their architectural embellishments, the Lancaster society expending £22,000 in 1905 on imposing central premises with a Renaissance facade.'[12] Their customers recognised the significance of these, and subsequent, changes: 'really the Co-ops they were the first sort of supermarket weren't they in a way, but they just didn't keep up with the times'.[13]

Department stores proper also expanded rapidly during the second half of the nineteenth century. By 1900 there were more than two hundred such stores, with every major town and city home to at least one: Liverpool had its Lewis's, Manchester its Kendal Milne, Glasgow its John Anderson, Wolverhampton its Beatties, and Sheffield its Cockaynes. London had a whole number: Debenhams, Harrods, Selfridges, Whiteleys, the Army and Navy, Dickens and Jones, and Marshall and Snelgrove. By the turn of the century Whiteleys alone employed 4,000 people, and Harrods 6,000 – and there were said to be a further ten firms with a workforce of a thousand or more. By this time, points out W. H. Fraser, 'most department stores were concentrating on the upper end of the market. Services like lifts, escalators, restaurants and rest-rooms were regarded as more important than low prices.'[14]

The process of change accelerated after the First World War. For, although multiple (or chain) store retailing was already well established in 1914, almost a thousand new branches were opened between the wars. By 1927–28 Woolworths had 280 stores, and Liptons 615; by 1939 Marks and Spencer had 250 branches, a staff of over 18,000, and a turnover of more than £23 million. 'By the outbreak of the Second World War', remarks John Stevenson, 'Marks and Spencer, Lipton's, Sainsbury's and Woolworths had become household names in almost every medium-sized town, bringing with them a wider range of food-stuffs, clothing and household goods than had been available at the traditional corner shop and retailer.'[15] The process of change culminated in the years following the Second World War. The 1950s and 1960s saw the opening of some 25,000 self-service stores and supermarkets, with chains of large stores controlled by firms such as Tescos, Fine Fare and Sainsburys; the 1970s saw the opening of the country's first hypermarkets, huge stores covering 50,000 square feet or more of floor space, and carrying as many as 30,000 different product lines.[16]

Retailing, it is clear, underwent a fundamental transformation. For despite the resilience of small firms (and the resurgence recently of corner shops), retailing, like food processing and consumer goods manufacturing, experienced an important, if easily overlooked, form of industrial revolution. 'There is no doubt', it was explained in 1977, 'that the revolution in food retailing which began over a century ago is still in motion today. And this revolution has brought immeasurable benefits to consumers in the form of a wider variety of goods and lower prices.'[17]

The growth and bureaucratisation of credit also brought consumers considerable benefits. For, although the poor continued to rely for many years upon traditional sources of credit for the purchase of food and basic necessities, the better-off working class were encouraged to use hire purchase (as well as mail order and credit cards) for the purchase of furniture, electrical goods, motor cars and other consumer durables.[18] For example, the use of hire purchase multiplied twenty times between 1918 and 1938, bringing 'a wide range of household goods such as furniture within the reach of sections of the community who could not previously have afforded them'.[19] By 1966 credit sales accounted for almost 10 per cent of all consumer expenditure – 45 per cent of spending on cars, 41 per cent of spending on furniture and floor coverings, and 42 per cent of spending on radios, electrical goods and other household appliances.[20] The Molony Committee of 1962 explained succinctly the benefits of the credit relationship between supplier and consumer. 'By arranging credit for his customer, the shopkeeper sells goods for which he could not find a cash market; by receiving credit, the consumer obtains the use of goods for which he could not afford to pay immediately.'[21]

The growth of retailing was matched in certain respects by the growth of tourism. For here too the last hundred years have seen the growth, concentration and diversification of supply. Here too three major developments stand out: the growth during the late nineteenth century of the seaside holiday resort; the foundation between the wars of the holiday camp movement; and the expansion since the Second World War of the package holiday industry.

The growth of the seaside resort is only just receiving the attention that it deserves. Thanks to the efforts of scholars like John Walton and James Walvin, it is now possible to discern certain key elements in the development of towns such as Blackpool, Brighton, Rhyl, Scarborough and Southend. There was a considerable, and growing, investment in accommodation, entertainment and public amenities. For example, the 1850s and 1860s saw a spate of pier building: it cost £40,000 to erect Southport pier, and nearly £70,000 to complete Weston-super-Mare's Birnbeck pier.[22] The 1880s and 1890s saw a rash of investment in large entertainment complexes: it took £60,000 to build Rhyl's Winter Gardens and half a million pounds to construct Blackpool's Tower and Gigantic Wheel. The results were sometimes spectacular. By the turn of the century, the Palace at Rhyl boasted a large ballroom, extensive roof gardens, forty shops and offices, table-tennis rooms and an imitation Venice featuring 'real Gondolas propelled by real Italians'. The basement of Blackpool Tower contained a restaurant, a billiard room, an aquarium, a menagerie and a Grand Pavilion – 'perhaps the finest ballroom in England, where, without any extra charge, you are permitted to enjoy one of the finest variety entertainments imaginable'.[23]

The holiday camp movement has still not received the attention that it deserves. Yet it too has become a British institution, its achievements and absurdities celebrated in the television series *Hi di Hi*. Billy Butlin built his first camp at Skegness in 1936 – supposedly after meeting a group of disconsolate holidaymakers huddling in a bus shelter to avoid the rain of a British summer. Two years later he, together with Fred Pontin, Harry Warner and other less well-known entrepreneurs, had founded more than two hundred camps with accommodation for 30,000 visitors a week – half a million people a year. As the cost of building and running the camps increased, so their ownership became more and more concentrated. By the early 1980s there were a hundred or so camps, eighty of them operated by a handful of companies: Butlin's, Ladbroke's, Warner's and Haven Holidays.[24]

No doubt, the post-war expansion of the package holiday industry will find its historian in due course. It is well known, however, that war-time advances in aircraft technology, a post-war surplus of military planes, and political support for private sector airlines enabled entrepreneurs like Freddie Laker, Harold Bamberg (of Eagle Airways) and Vladimir Raitz (of Horizon Holidays) to begin to provide Continental package tours on a scale, and at a price, that had not been seen before. By 1981 Britain's ten largest air tour operators were authorised by the Civil Aviation Authority to carry more than 4 million passengers annually: the market leader, Thomson Holidays, was alone permitted to carry almost a million holidaymakers a year.[25]

The growth of retailing and tourism was matched, in turn, by the growth of spectator sport (and gambling).[26] Once again, the past hundred years have seen the growth, concentration and diversification of supply. In this case, two major developments may be discerned: the commercialisation, from the late nineteenth century, of sports like boxing, cricket, soccer and horse-racing; and the expansion, since the Second World War, of television coverage of these, and other sports, such as darts, snooker, Rugby league and American football.

The late nineteenth-century commercialisation of sport is beginning to find its place in the general histories of the period. For example, F. M. L. Thompson explains in his recent study of Victorian Britain that 'The rise of mass spectator sports, played by professionals, financed by gate-money, and calling for large investments in specially equipped grounds in prime urban sites, came suddenly and dramatically in the 1880s and 1890s.'[27] Horse-racing was one of the first sports to be affected, with companies across the country enclosing courses, charging for admission, and seeking dividends for their shareholders: Sandown Park led the way in 1875, and was followed by Derby in 1880, Leicester in 1884, Hamilton in 1887, Nottingham in 1892, Haydock in 1898 and Newbury in 1906. 'Clearly, by the end of the nineteenth century, racing was as much a part of the economic as the social scene: it was an industry as well as a sport.'[28]

Football, too, was becoming a business, though not in the same way as racing – and certainly not in the same way as retailing or tourism. Professional football aimed for sporting success rather than for profit maximisation. In fact, as Wray Vamplew has pointed out, 'each club was supplying two different markets with the same product: the demand of the partisan supporter was for a winning team; the demand of the less committed was for a close, high-quality encounter'.[29] The result was that clubs attempted both to exploit and to control competition within the industry. On the one hand, they invested in new grounds, sought to acquire the best players, and 'changed their organizations into business enterprises and adopted company status with the intention of winning matches and championships'.[30] On the other hand, they declined to compete with one another by raising players' wages or lowering admission charges. Indeed, the professional clubs' own organisation, the Football League, was formed in 1885 as 'a kind of non-profit-making cartel in which the power of the largest clubs was limited by the smallest'.[31] For as

Tony Mason explains, 'It was not that football and business . . . were expected to inhabit separate spheres. But each was expected to know its place and in sport business was the lesser partner.'[32]

The expansion of televised sport has occurred too recently for it to find its way into the textbooks. It is clear, however, that television's need for inexpensive live programmes coincided both with sport's need to generate income and with advertising's desire to be associated with an attractive and popular product. The independent television companies concentrated upon horse-racing, soccer, wrestling and darts; the BBC ranged more broadly, covering not only soccer, Rugby, cricket and tennis but also minority sports such as swimming, snooker and skiing. 'In newspaper terms', explained ITV's head of sport, 'the BBC is much more *Telegraph* and we are the *Mirror* or even the *Sun*'.[33] Whatever the differences between the two networks, the growth of televised sport proceeded apace. It has been calculated that by the late 1980s, for example, sport accounted for 17 per cent of the BBC's entire output of programmes.[34]

The transformation of spectator sport was not unique. For, as has been seen already in this chapter, entrepreneurs in all parts of the economy sought to increase the supply, reduce the cost and widen the range of goods and services available to the consumer. Moreover, entrepreneurs in all parts of the economy sought to direct this growing supply of goods and services towards those sections of the community whose purchasing power was increasing most markedly: town dwellers; the young; women; most members of the middle class; and many members of the working class.

Entrepreneurs concentrated their attention increasingly upon the growing number of consumers to be found in the urban and suburban areas of the country. Indeed, these areas assumed a major role in the production and distribution, as well as the consumption, of food, goods and services. It would be easy to overlook this connection between urbanisation and the supply of food. In fact, the new food-processing industries of the late nineteenth century were all established in urban areas: fish curing and canning in East Coast ports like Hull and Grimsby; biscuit making (by Peek Frean, and Huntley and Palmer) in southern cities like London and Reading; and chocolate making (by Cadbury, Fry and Rowntree) in regional centres such as Birmingham, Bristol and York.[35]

It would be much more difficult to overlook the connection between urbanisation and manufacturing. After all, it was seen in the previous chapter that individual towns and cities became identified with particular phases of economic growth, and thus with the production of particular types of product. Bradford, Leeds, Preston and Manchester became associated with woollen and cotton clothing; Sheffield with cutlery and metal goods; Leicester with hosiery and footwear; and Oxford, Coventry and Dagenham with motor cars. For more than two hundred years urban growth and industrial growth have been inextricably entwined.

It would be almost impossible to overlook the fact that retailing, sport and most other consumer services became concentrated overwhelmingly in urban areas. Retailers, of course, always tended to follow their customers. It has been found recently, for example, that the late-nineteenth-century decline of rural hawking and peddling was more than counterbalanced by its expansion in urban areas.[36] It has been recognised for many years that the late-nineteenth- and twentieth-century expansion of co-operative, departmental and multiple retailing depended upon the rapid expansion of the urban population. Newsagent W. H. Smith established his empire by building up a chain of station bookstores.

> Broadly speaking, railway stations interested Smith's in proportion to their size. The great termini of the great cities provided, obviously, the best markets and therefore cost Smith's the highest rents. Conversely, there were village stations – like Elsham, Appleby and Frodingham on the Trent, Ancholme and Grimsby Railway in the bare windswept plains of north Lincolnshire – where the rail proprietors were anxious to see Smith's involved but where the volume of passenger traffic of a sparsely populated countryside could not possibly support the relatively high costs of maintaining a bookstall and the necessary staff.[37]

Spectator sports like professional football took place exclusively in urban areas. It has been found that in 1911 all but eight of the ninety-seven English urban districts with populations of 50,000 or more had a professional football team of their own; indeed, these ninety-seven towns included every club in the Football League with the exception of Glossop and Gainsborough Trinity.[38] In fact, an 'ex-director' of one major club believed that no town with a population of fewer than 50,000 could possibly sustain a first-class professional team. Certainly there seemed to be a correlation between population size and sporting success: it has been estimated that in 1937–38 the average population of districts containing a first division club was well over 330,000, while the average of those containing a club from the third division north was well under 100,000.[39]

Suppliers of leisure, like suppliers of other services and goods, also made increasing efforts to identify, and satisfy, the needs of particular age groups. Invariably, however, they paid much greater attention to the young than they did to the old. Indeed, throughout most of the period manufacturers and retailers did little more for the elderly than package their products in the small quantities which were all that the poor (of any age) were able to afford. It was only from the 1960s that suppliers made serious efforts to exploit the new-found purchasing power at the disposal of the elderly. Builders and developers began to provide sheltered housing, nursing home accommodation and retirement homes ('Retire to Devon where the daffs bloom early and the air is mild'[40]), while tour operators such as Saga, Golden Circle and Golden Days began to specialise in holidays for the over-fifties.[41] Even record companies began to show some interest. 'They do not confine their advertising to the latest numbers featuring in "top of the tops",' it was explained in 1980. 'They capitalise on the nostalgia of older people for reminders of their youth.'[42]

Other manufacturers and retailers made much greater efforts to tap the adolescent market. The suppliers of fashion goods were among the first to do so. Late-nineteenth-century manufacturers of clothing and footwear attempted to attract the attention of the fashion-conscious teenage consumer, with the result that soon there was 'enough choice for the working-class girl to be able to concern herself with fashion and style and not solely with price'.[43] The suppliers of consumer services were not slow to follow suit. The number of dance halls proliferated during the inter-war years; by 1930 a provincial town like Rochdale, with a population of 100,000, was able to offer its young people five or six commercially organised dances every Saturday night during the summer months of the year.[44]

It was during the 1960s, of course, that suppliers of both services and goods came to recognise most clearly the great, and growing, potential of the teenage market. Edward Royle, like many others, takes a jaundiced view of the ensuing relationship between supply and demand:

> Perceiving the shift in the age structure of the population in the 1960s towards the 10–19 age-group (of whom there were 22 per cent more in 1961 than in 1951), the advertisers created 'teenagers', and persuaded them to need clothes, 'pop' music records and teenage magazines in which their 'problems' were magnified and then discussed.[45]

Whether or not teenage demand could be manipulated quite so easily, the music industry was quick to see the possibilities. A handful of large companies, led by Decca and EMI, proved enormously successful. Indeed it seems that in the mid-1970s the record companies were more profitable than most other British firms, a profitability which was based upon their output of 160 million records a year – more than 100 million of which were apparently bought by consumers between the ages of 12 and 20.[46] 'The Beatles did not get their MBEs for charitable works. They got them for their considerable contribution to British exports.'[47]

Publishing, catering and tourism also began to look to the teenage consumer. Publishers saw that they too could exploit the surge of interest in pop music. The first magazines for teenage girls appeared in the mid-1950s, and a decade later firms like D. C. Thompson and Fleetway Publications were producing nearly a dozen titles a week, with a combined circulation of some 3 million copies.[48] Caterers saw that they might be able to exploit the desire of older teenagers to spend time with their friends. Milk bars tempted them with chromium-plated interiors, bar stools and exotically named milk shakes; coffee bars with live music, juke boxes and an air of metropolitan bohemia; and public houses with refurbishment, entertainment and a veneer of sophistication.[49] Nor was this all, for tour companies saw that they would be able to benefit from the desire of those in their late teens and twenties to escape for longer periods of time. Companies catering for the young based their entire marketing strategy upon a heady cocktail of cheap drink, unlimited sun – and potential sexual adventure.[50]

Producers, retailers and advertisers all recognised the growing importance of the female consumer. They knew that women played a central role in the family's consumption of food, clothing and household goods; and they saw them assuming an increasingly independent role as consumers of products such as cigarettes, beauty aids, fashion goods and eventually motor cars.

Food manufacturers and processors sought to appeal to housewives by emphasising the cost, quality, and later the convenience of their products. A glance through the advertising columns of any late-nineteenth- or early twentieth-century newspaper will reveal the efforts made by food and drink manufacturers to reassure the housewife about the health-giving qualities of their new, mass-produced, branded products. Even apparently unpromising items like cocoa were marketed in this way. Cadbury's cocoa was described as 'a most valuable beverage for ATHLETES', while van Houten's cocoa was claimed to be 'A Perfect Beverage', and brought with it testimonials from the *Lancet* and the *British Medical Journal*.[51] Between the wars it was the convenience of branded foods that manufacturers sought to emphasise. Middle-class housewives learning to manage their homes without domestic help were bombarded with advertisements for drinks, relishes, confectionery and breakfast cereals. Quaker Oats was advertised as the 'no-trouble' breakfast, while the advantage of Camp coffee, it was claimed, was that 'There's absolutely NO WAITING'.[52]

The manufacturers of household goods also stressed the benefits that their products would bring to the overburdened housewife. Indeed, the advertising campaigns of detergent manufacturers have long been met with public scepticism – and of course with feminist derision. 'Why Does a Woman Look Older Sooner than a Man?' demanded one early Lever soap advertisement. The reason, naturally, was the burden of the weekly wash. Yet even in the 1890s the solution lay near to hand; for with Sunlight soap 'the work is so cut down that a young girl or delicate woman can do a family wash and not get tired'.[53] In the years following the First World War the manufacturers of consumer durables also began to target the middle-class housewife. 'It's So *Silly* To Go On Wearing Myself Out', declared the exhausted homemaker in one 1938 Hoover advertisement: for with a vacuum cleaner, 'I Can Have a Maid at 4d a Day'.[54]

Gradually manufacturers and advertisers began to realise that housewives did not wish to be regarded exclusively as homemakers. Thus although food manufacturers continued to stress the cost, quality and convenience of their products, other businesses began to appeal to women eager to reduce, or at least control, their calorific intake. Some campaigns were ingenious indeed. According to one 1930 advertisement, it was easy for lovely young women to retain their figures because 'When tempted to over-indulge – to eat between meals, they say: "*No thanks, I'll smoke a Kensitas instead.*"'[55]

The publishing, beauty, fashion, medical and motor industries were among those to recognise – though sometimes with considerable reluctance – that the growth in female purchasing power meant that women were able to purchase goods and services for themselves as well as for their husbands and children. Thus publishing, beauty and fashion assumed major prominence between the wars.

> Women's magazines boomed as never before. At one end of the spectrum were the expensive high-quality magazines, such as *Vogue*, founded in 1916, and *Harper's Bazaar* (1929). There were also lavish and relatively expensive magazines concerned with the home, such as *Homes and Gardens* (1919), followed by *Woman and Home* (1926) and the *Woman's Journal* (1927). Less expensive and more widely read were *Woman's Weekly* (1911), followed by the more colourful *Woman's Own* (1932). By 1939 the most successful was *Woman*, launched in 1937 and priced at 2d., carrying romantic stories, hints on fashion and cosmetics, features on home management and recipes.[56]

Soap manufacturers began to advertise their products in new ways: Cuticura soap was a beauty aid; Lifebuoy toilet soap prevented body odour; while Lux toilet soap kept skin soft and smooth – indeed, it was used by film stars as beautiful as Barbara Stanwyck.[57] The medical and pharmaceutical industries also changed the thrust of their advertising. In the late nineteenth century drug manufacturers claimed to be able to relieve women of basic gynaecological disorders; in the 1930s medical firms advertised products reputed to offer them 'Radiant Health in Middle Age'; while in the 1980s private health companies like BUPA competed by offering to screen women for breast cancer.[58] Even the motor industry recognised eventually that many women had a say in the purchase of the family car, and that many too were buying cars for their own use. Gradually the advertising images began to change, the scantily clad model draped over the bonnet of the car giving way to the busy housewife or career woman using the car as part of her day-to-day life.[59]

The increasing attention paid by suppliers to women, the young and the inhabitants of urban areas, did much to redirect goods and services towards those groups whose purchasing power was increasing most rapidly. However, the outstanding development, and that which did most to align supply with demand, was the increasing attention that entrepreneurs from all sectors of the economy began to pay to the growing working-class market.

Food producers and processors were among the first to see the possibilities. Even the manufacturers of health and convenience foods (that are associated usually with middle-class consumption) began to reorganise their marketing in an attempt to woo the working-class consumer. For example, the Hovis Bread Company acquired a national reputation in the late nineteenth century by tasteful advertising in high-status periodicals like the *Strand, Black & White* and the *Illustrated London News*. However, early in the new century it tried to widen its appeal by publishing full-page spreads in popular daily papers such as the *Graphic* and the *Daily Mail*.[60] The manufacturers of breakfast cereals proved more schizophrenic still in their pursuit of the working-class consumer. For while they too placed genteel advertisements in high-class magazines, they were also prepared to organise campaigns that included stunts such as draping advertising banners across the white cliffs of Dover.[61]

The suppliers of basic foodstuffs were much more determined – and much more successful – in targeting the working-class consumer. They had little choice. For whether they imported items like meat and tea, or manufactured products like margarine and biscuits, they depended for their success upon the growing working-class market. Thus within twenty years of frozen meat beginning to arrive in large quantities from Australasia and Argentina, five firms (Eastman's, W. & R. Fletcher, James Nelson & Sons, the London Central Meat Company and the River Plate Fresh Meat Company) had acquired well over 4,000 shops and stalls. These firms competed chiefly for working-class custom: their premises were so spartan that they 'were often little more than rudimentary stalls in side streets, dealing strictly in cash, their main purpose being to clear as much meat as possible at the lowest acceptable price before it deteriorated'.[62]

The suppliers of consumer goods needed to be equally – if not more – resourceful if they were to persuade the working-class consumer to invest in the less essential, and much more expensive, products that they had for sale. Thus even before the turn of the century piano shops were offering easy terms from as little as 1s 6d week (for a £10 instrument), while furniture shops were stressing that with their low prices and easy terms, they were able to provide 'Furniture For All

Classes'.[63] Such initiatives continued, and accelerated, during the course of the twentieth century. Between the two world wars both manufacturers and electricity supply companies introduced deferred payment schemes in their attempts to promote domestic demand for electrical appliances such as radios, cookers, boilers and vacuum cleaners.[64] In the years following the Second World War, the motor industry too turned its attention towards the working-class consumer. In the mid-1950s, for instance, Ford introduced its 'Popular' at a basic price of £275, while Austin advertised its two-door A30 as 'a fully equipped small car of low cost'.[65]

The suppliers of consumer services seemed to recognise more readily than entrepreneurs in other sectors of the economy the opportunities offered by the growth of working-class purchasing power. Retailers, of course, were particularly well placed to see the changes that were taking place. Those active in retail co-operation – working men themselves – aimed specifically to satisfy the increased purchasing power at the disposal of the skilled working class.[66] Department store proprietors also aimed to capture some, at least, of the growing working-class market. For although they usually began by seeking to satisfy middle-class needs, they were not averse to accepting the custom of those lower down the social scale. Indeed, it has been suggested that during the inter-war years one of the primary functions of stores like Stones of Upminster was to teach upwardly mobile East Enders how to use their new-found wealth and income.[67] However, it was the proprietors of multiple (or chain) stores who concentrated most single-mindedly upon capturing the working-class market. Thomas Lipton led the way. Opening his first shop in Glasgow in 1871, he had built up an empire of five hundred shops by the outbreak of the First World War. His principles and practices were simple: he looked for 'small profits, quick returns'; he opened long hours and charged low prices on a limited range of basic products.[68]

Entrepreneurs in other tertiary-sector industries also recognised the growth of working-class purchasing power. They were active in everything from tourism to television, from football to fast food. In tourism, for instance, the growth of seaside resorts, holiday camps and package tours depended very much upon their appeal to this growing, and relatively untapped market. Coastal towns like Rhyl, Morecambe, Bridlington, Blackpool and Southend all developed strategies designed to attract the working-class visitor.[69] So too did Billy Butlin, who advertised his first holiday camp with the slogan, 'Holidays with pay – holidays with play. A week's holiday for a week's wage'.[70] It seems that in catering too the success of the fast-food industry depended very heavily upon its appeal to the working-class consumer. John Walton has shown that during the final quarter of the nineteenth century fish-and-chip shops spread rapidly across the West Riding of Yorkshire, the cotton towns of Lancashire and many working-class districts of London. He concludes that by the turn of the century, 'In some working-class districts there must have been, quite literally, a fish and chip shop on every street.'[71] In death, as in life, there was little escape from entrepreneurs determined to target the new working-class market. For undertakers knew only too well how to exploit the widespread fear of a pauper's funeral. It cost just six shillings to hire a black horse and glass hearse, explained a Barnsley funeral director in 1902: they were, he added, 'very suitable for working people'.[72]

The study of these, and other, sources of supply is not without certain complications. It is difficult, for instance, to determine the extent to which producers stimulated, rather than simply satisfied, the changes that were taking place in consumer demand; and it is not always easy to avoid slipping into a classical (or neo-classical) view of the economy in which every demand is satisfied, and every supplier finds a purchaser. None the less, it has been seen that the study of supply raises rather fewer conceptual or empirical difficulties than the study of demand. Accordingly, it has been possible to identify two major developments. It is clear that the supply of goods and services available to the British consumer expanded at an unprecedented rate over the past two hundred years; and it is clear too that this expanding supply was directed increasingly at those groups whose purchasing power was growing most visibly. This confirms the suggestion, which was made at the end of the previous chapter, that the growth and redirection of consumer demand can be understood only when set alongside the growth and redistribution of supply.

NOTES AND REFERENCES

1. **W. Minchinton**, 'Patterns of Demand 1750–1914', in **C. M. Cipolla** (ed.), *The Fontana Economic History of Europe: The Industrial Revolution*, Fontana, 1973, pp. 82–3; **R. H. Williams**, *Dream Worlds: Mass Consumption in Late Nineteenth-century France*, University of California Press, 1982, pp. 3, 84–5.

2. For general surveys, see **E. J. Hobsbawm**, *Industry and Empire*, Penguin, 1969; **E. Royle**, *Modern Britain: A Social History 1750–1985*, Arnold, 1987. Cf. Williams, *Dream Worlds*, pp. 3, 9–10, 84–5.

3. **J. Burnett**, *Plenty and Want: A Social History of Food in England from 1815 to the Present Day*, Routledge, 1989, pp. 8–9, 119–25.

4. **T. A. B. Corley**, 'Nutrition, Technology and the Growth of the British Biscuit Industry, 1820–1900', in **D. J. Oddy** and **D. S. Miller** (eds), *The Making of the Modern British Diet*, Croom Helm, 1976, pp. 24, 39.

5. Burnett, *Plenty and Want*, pp. 15–16, 114–17, 225–9.
6. **A. H. Halsey**, *British Social Trends since 1900: A Guide to the Changing Social Structure of Britain*, Macmillan, 1988, p. 384; **H. W. Richardson** and **D. H. Aldcroft**, *Building in the British Economy between the Wars*, Allen & Unwin, 1968, p. 26.
7. **J. N. Bartlett**, *Carpeting the Millions: The Growth of Britain's Carpet Industry*, Donald, nd, pp. 19, 35, 102–4, 191–201.
8. **J. Benson**, *The Working Class in Britain, 1850–1939*, Longman, 1989, p. 13.
9. Hobsbawm, *Industry and Empire*, p. 252; **A. Marwick**, *British Society since 1945*, Penguin, 1990, p. 324.
10. Benson, *Working Class*, p. 21.
11. **P. Deane** and **W. A. Cole**, *British Economic Growth 1688–1959: Trends and Structure*, Cambridge University Press, 1969, p. 143.
12. **M. J. Winstanley**, *The Shopkeeper's World 1830–1914*, Manchester University Press 1983, p. 38; also p. 37. Membership reached 5 million in 1926 and 9 million in 1943. See **G. D. H. Cole**, *A Short History of the British Working-Class Movement 1789–1947*, Allen & Unwin, 1948, p. 484.
13. Lancaster, Mr S9P, p. 52.
14. **W. H. Fraser**, *The Coming of the Mass Market, 1850–1914*, Macmillan, 1981, p. 132. Also Winstanley, *Shopkeeper's World*, pp. 34–5; Benson, *Working Class*, p. 25; **G. Shaw**, 'The Evolution and Impact of Large-scale Retailing in Britain', **J. Benson** and **G. Shaw** (eds), *The Evolution of Retail Systems*, Leicester University Press, 1992.
15. **J. Stevenson**, *British Society 1914–15*, Penguin, 1984, p. 113. Also Benson, *Working Class*, p. 25; Winstanley, *Shopkeeper's World*, pp. 38–9; Fraser, *Mass Market*, p. 120.
16. Royle, *Modern Britain*, pp. 279–80; **J. P. Johnson**, *A Hundred Years Eating: Food, Drink and the Daily Diet in Britain since the Late Nineteenth Century*, Gill & Macmillan, 1977, pp. 85–6. **C. Gardner** and **J. Sheppard**, *Consuming Passion: The Rise of Retail Culture*, Unwin Hyman, 1989, ch. 7. For the resilience of small firms, see Benson, *Working Class*, p. 26.
17. Johnson, *Eating*, p. 87. For changes in market research and advertising, see **T. A. B. Corley**, 'Consumer Marketing in Britain 1914–60', *Business History*, **29**, 1987; **D. West**, 'From T Square to T Plan: The London Office of the J. Walter Thompson Advertising Agency, 1919–70', *Business History*, **29**, 1987.
18. *RC on Consumer Credit, Report*, 1971, pp. 35; 42; **P. Johnson**, 'Credit and Thrift and the British Working Class, 1870–1939', in **J. Winter** (ed.), *The Working Class in Modern British History: Essays in Honour of Henry Pelling*, Cambridge University Press, 1983.
19. Cited **M. Tebbutt**, *Making Ends Meet: Pawnbroking and Working-Class Credit*, Leicester University Press, 1983, p. 194.
20. *RC on Consumer Credit, Report*, 1971, p. 111.
21. *RC on Consumer Protection, Report*, 1962, p. 164.
22. **J. K. Walton**, *The English Seaside Resort: A Social History 1750–1914*, Leicester University Press, 1983, p. 164. Also **J. Walvin**, *Beside the Seaside*, Allen Lane, 1978.

23. Walton, *Seaside Resort*, p. 176; also p. 175; **E. W. Gilbert**, 'The Growth of Inland and Seaside Health Resorts in England', *Scottish Geographical Magazine*, January 1939. Cf. Fraser, *Mass Market*, pp. 223–4.

24. Royle, *Modern Britain*, p. 265; Stevenson, *British Society*, p. 394; **J. C. Holloway**, *The Business of Tourism*, Macdonald & Evans, 1985, pp. 35, 139–40.

25. Holloway, *Tourism*, pp. 36–7, 171. See also **P. Brendon**, *Thomas Cook: 150 Years of Popular Tourism*, Secker & Warburg, 1991.

26. For gambling, see **M. Clapson**, *A Bit of a Flutter: Popular Gambling and English Society, c. 1823–1961*, Manchester University Press, 1992.

27. **F. M. L. Thompson**, *The Rise of Respectable Society: A Social History of Victorian Britain*, Fontana, 1988, p. 295.

28. **W. Vamplew**, 'The Sport of Kings and Commoners: The Commercialization of British Horse-racing in the Nineteenth Century', in **R. Cashman** and **M. McKernan** (eds), *Sport in History: The Making of Modern Sporting History*, University of Queensland Press, 1979, p. 321. Also Fraser, *Mass Market*, p. 216.

29. **W. Vamplew**, 'The Economics of a Sports Industry: Scottish Gate-money Football, 1890–1914', *Economic History Review*, **xxxv**, 1982, p. 566.

30. Vamplew, 'Sports Industry', p. 567. See also **T. Mason**, *Association Football and English Society 1863–1915*, Harvester, 1981; **C. P. Korr**, 'West Ham United Football Club and the Beginnings of Professional Football in East London, 1895–1914', *Journal of Contemporary History*, **13**, 1978.

31. **R. Holt**, *Sport and the British: A Modern History*, Oxford University Press, 1990, p. 285; also pp. 283–4.

32. **T. Mason**, *Sport in Britain*, Faber & Faber, p. 89; also p. 3.

33. Holt, *Sport*, p. 321.

34. Holt, *Sport*, p. 317.

35. **J. Tunstall**, *The Fishermen*, MacGibbon & Kee, 1962, ch. 1; Corley, 'Nutrition', p. 18; Johnson, *Eating*, p. 44.

36. **J. Benson**, 'Hawking and Peddling in England and Wales, 1850–1939', unpublished paper, pp. 4–5.

37. **C. Wilson**, *First with the News: The History of W. H. Smith 1792–1972*, Cape, 1985, pp. 98–9. Also **J. Benson**, *British Coalminers in the Nineteenth Century: A Social History*, Longman, 1989, p. 91; **P. Mathias**, *Retailing Revolution: A History of Multiple Retailing in the Food Trades Based upon the Allied Suppliers Group of Companies*, Longmans, Green & Co., 1967, p. 98.

38. Mason, *Association Football*, pp. 215, 221. Also Holt, *Sport*, pp. 166–8.

39. Mason, *Association Football*, p. 221.

40. *Express and Star*, 13 June 1964.

41. Holloway, *Tourism*, p. 127; **G. F. Thompson**, '"If You Can't Stand the Heat Get Off the Beach": The United Kingdom Holiday Business', in **A. Tomlinson** (ed.), *Consumption, Identity, and Style: Marketing, Meanings, and the Packaging of Pleasure*, Routledge, 1990, p. 208; *Express and Star*, 2 June 1965.

42. **E. Ornstein** and **A. Nunn**, *The Marketing of Leisure*, Associated Business Press, 1980, p. 206.

43. Fraser, *Mass Market*, p. 61. **B. Osgerby**, '"Well, It's Saturday Night an' I Just Got Paid": Youth, Consumerism and Hegemony in Post-war Britain', *Contemporary Record*, **6**, 1992, p. 295.

44. Stevenson, *British Society*, pp. 397–8.

45. Royle, *Modern Britain*, p. 281. Also **C. Alderson**, *Magazines Teenagers Read: With Special Reference to Trend, Jackie and Valentine*, Pergamon, 1968, p. 115. See too the speech of the President of the National Association of Head Teachers, reported in *Express and Star*, 16 May 1964.

46. **D. Harker**, *One for the Money: Politics and Popular Song*, Hutchinson, 1980, pp. 87–8, 109; **M. Brake**, *The Sociology of Youth Culture and Youth Subcultures: Sex and Drugs and Rock 'n' Roll*, Routledge & Kegan Paul, 1980, p. 155.

47. Harker, *Popular Song*, p. 87. 'Luxembourg Specials' were transistor radios that promised real 'thrillsville'. *Express and Star*, 28 May 1964.

48. Alderson, *Magazines*, p. 5.

49. Burnett, *Plenty and Want*, p. 264. Also **R. Hoggart**, *The Uses of Literacy: Aspects of Working-class Life with Special Reference to Publications and Entertainments*, Penguin, 1958, p. 248.

50. Holloway, *Tourism*, p. 127; Thompson, 'Holiday Business', pp. 208–9.

51. E.g., *Wolverhampton Chronicle*, 5 July 1899; *Barnsley Chronicle*, 1 November 1902. As late as 1950 Walls ice cream was advertised as 'More Than a Treat – *a food*', *Express and Star*, 2 January 1950.

52. E.g., *Express and Star*, 1, 14, 15 January 1930; Burnett, *Plenty and Want*, pp. 261, 265, 310. Working-class wives were also targeted as consumers of products such as shredded wheat: see, for example, *Daily Mail*, 17 January 1930.

53. *Wigan Observer*, 30 July 1892. Also *Wolverhampton Chronicle*, 5 July 1899; *Sunday Pictorial*, 6 September 1942; Fraser, *Mass Market*, p. 142.

54. **C. Davidson**, *A Woman's Work Is Never Done: A History of Housework in the British Isles 1650–1950*, Chatto & Windus, 1986, p. 129.

55. *Express and Star*, 15 January 1930. Also *John Bull*, 23 March 1940.

56. Stevenson, *British Society*, pp. 406–7.

57. *Express and Star*, 2 January 1930; 15, 17 May 1935; *Home Notes*, 20 January 1945.

58. *Express and Star*, 7 January 1930; 13 May 1935; 3 January 1980; **T. Richards**, *The Commodity Culture of Victorian England: Advertising and Spectacle, 1851–1914*, Verso, 1990, pp. 205–6.

59. *Express and Star*, 2 January 1990. Cf. **V. Scharff**, *Taking the Wheel: Women and the Coming of the Motor Age*, Free Press, 1991, ch. 7.

60. **E. J. T. Collins**, 'The "Consumer Revolution" and the Growth of Factory Foods: Changing Patterns of Bread and Cereal Eating in Britain in the Twentieth Century', in Oddy and Miller (eds), *Modern British Diet*, p. 30; Fraser, *Mass Market*, p. 167.

61. Collins, 'Consumer Revolution', p. 37.

62. Winstanley, *Shopkeeper's World*, p. 142. Also Burnett, *Plenty and Want*, pp. 117–23.

63. E.g., *Wigan Observer*, 30 July 1892; *Wolverhampton Chronicle*, 30 August 1899; Merthyr, *Pioneer*, 11 January 1913; *Daily Mail*, 9 January 1900, 20 January 1930; *Daily Herald*, 5, 7 April 1919; *Bristol Evening Post*, 5 March 1952.

64. **S. Bowden**, 'Credit Facilities and the Growth of Consumer Demand for Electrical Appliances in England in the 1930s', *Business History*, **32**, 1990.

65. *Express and Star*, 8 June 1955, *Bristol Evening Post*, 5 March 1952. Also **G. Maxcy** and **A. Silberston**, *The Motor Industry*, Allen & Unwin, 1959, pp. 112, 116.

66. Burnett, *Plenty and Want*, p. 126; Fraser, *Mass Market*, pp. 121–8; Winstanley, *Shopkeeper's World*, pp. 36–9.

67. **B. Lancaster**, 'British Department Stores and Society since 1850', unpublished paper, University of Warwick, November 1989.

68. Winstanley, *Shopkeeper's World*, p. 38. Also Burnett, *Plenty and Want*, p. 127.

69. Walton, *Seaside Resort*, pp. 59, 67–8, 213–14.

70. **A. Tomlinson** and **H. Walker**, 'Holidays for All: Popular Movements, Collective Leisure, and the Pleasure Industry', in Tomlinson (ed.), *Consumption, Identity and Style*, p. 226.

71. **J. K. Walton**, 'Fish and Chips and the British Working Class, 1870–1930', *Journal of Social History*, **23**, 1989, pp. 243, 248.

72. *Barnsley Chronicle*, 1 November 1902.

Part Two

CHANGES

Chapter 3

SHOPPING

The study of consumption remains bedevilled by the lack of interest shown in the mechanisms by which demand and supply were brought into contact with each other. Thus it seems extraordinary that shopping, by far the most important of these mechanisms, is still almost completely overlooked. For even those scholars who have shown some interest in consumption have tended to concentrate their attention more upon ownership and usage than upon selection and purchase – while even those scholars who have shown some interest in selection and purchase have tended to concentrate their attention more upon marketing and retailing than upon spending and shopping.[1]

Accordingly, it is the purpose of this chapter to consider the British experience of shopping. It will examine, in particular, the ways in which the changes in demand and supply that were discussed in the previous chapters interacted with one another to influence the ways in which shoppers selected and purchased the products that they consumed. This chapter, like those before it, is divided into two. The first, rather brief, section considers the changing experience of shoppers generally; the second, and considerably longer, section examines the changing experiences of elderly, adolescent, female and working-class shoppers, the groups whose growing purchasing power suppliers and retailers made such determined efforts to capture.

It will be argued that the past hundred years have seen what amounts to a total transformation in the British experience of shopping. It will be shown that there have been three major developments: a large increase in the amount of money spent; a major shift in the type of retailer patronised; and a substantial change in the type of product purchased.

It is clear, of course, that there has been an enormous increase in the amount of money spent on shopping. None the less, it is surprisingly difficult to quantify the scale of the increase, for the statistics of retailing/shopping are neither as easy to obtain nor as easy to interpret as might be imagined. It is important to recognise, above all else, that consumer expenditure cannot be regarded as synonymous with retail expenditure. After all, consumers do not go shopping, in any generally accepted sense of the term, for housing, for public transport or (since the introduction of public utilities) for fuel, light and power. Thus in recording the amount of money spent on shopping, Table 3.1 shows expenditure only on products such as food and drink, clothing, household goods and consumer durables that were normally purchased at retail outlets.

Provided that these reservations are borne in mind, Table 3.1 provides a serviceable enough indication of changes in retail expenditure. It shows that as incomes rose, so too too did the amount of money spent on shopping. It suggests, not very helpfully, that between 1860/61 and 1980/81 expenditure (at constant prices) increased nearly two hundred times, and expenditure per head (again at constant prices) increased nearly one hundred times. It suggests, much more helpfully, that real expenditure per head increased nearly five-and-a-half times. It doubled between 1860/61 and 1900/1, increased by 60 per cent during the first half of the twentieth century, and by very nearly a further 60 per cent in the thirty years between 1950/51 and 1980/81.

Table 3.1 shows too that the amount of money spent on shopping did not increase quite as rapidly as the amount of money that

TABLE 3.1   Expenditure on shopping, United Kingdom, 1860/61–1980/81

Year	Expenditure At constant prices (£ million)	Expenditure per person		
		At current prices (£)	In real terms (1860/61=100)	As % of income
1860/61	371	12.8	100	49
1900/1	862	20.8	214	47
1950/51	4,967	101.6*	341	44
1980/81	71,762	1,309.5*	536	40

* Population: Great Britain
It is assumed (a) that expenditure on shopping = expenditure on food, furniture and household goods, clothing, alcoholic drink and tobacco, and motor vehicle purchase; and (b) that this expenditure remained constant at 53% of total consumer expenditure. See **C. More**, *The Industrial Age: Economy and Society in Britain 1750–1985*, Longman, 1989, p. 373.

Sources: **J. Benson**, *The Working Class in Britain, 1850–1939*, Longman, 1989, p. 54; **P. Deane** and **W. A. Cole**, *British Economic Growth 1688–1959: Trends and Structure*, Cambridge University Press, 1969, pp. 332–3; **S. Pollard**, *The Development of the British Economy 1914–1980*, Arnold, 1983, pp. 315, 326.

shoppers had at their disposal. It suggests that, whereas real spending on shopping increased just under five-and-a-half times in the 120 years between 1860/61 and 1980/81, real incomes increased more than six times in the 130 years between 1850/51 and 1980/81. Thus expenditure on shopping constituted a declining proportion of average consumer income: it accounted for practically 50 per cent of incomes in 1860/61, less than 45 per cent in 1950/51, but only 40 per cent in 1980/81. Changes such as these suggest that Keynes was probably correct to claim, more broadly, that 'men are disposed, as a rule and on the average, to increase their consumption as their income increases, but not by as much as the increase in their income.'[2] Whether or not he was correct about consumption, he certainly was about shopping. For it is clear that as consumers' incomes rose so, to a lesser extent, did the amount of money that they spent on shopping.

It is clear, too, that as incomes rose, and spending on shopping increased, so shoppers changed the type of retailer with whom they did business. However, once again, some caution is necessary. For even when retail expenditure is disentangled from consumer expenditure, considerable complications remain to be resolved. It is obviously impossible to estimate accurately the proportion of retail trade done by street-sellers, market-stall holders or black marketeers, and it is surprisingly difficult to calculate with any precision the proportion done by independent shops, department stores, chain stores and mail-order houses.[3]

Although precision may be impossible, generalisation is not. It is perfectly possible to indicate, in broad terms, the extent to which shoppers patronised the new types of retail outlet whose development was discussed in the previous chapter. The quantitative evidence suggests, and the qualitative evidence confirms, that the century between 1880 and 1980 saw a fundamental transformation both in retail provision and in shopping behaviour. For it was during these years that British shoppers transferred the bulk of their custom from small, local retailers (like hawkers and pedlars, market-stall holders and corner shopkeepers) to larger, more centralised, and more impersonal outlets (such as co-operative stores, department stores, chain stores, supermarkets, hypermarkets and mail-order houses). Table 3.2 provides some indication of the periods during which, and the pace at which, shoppers turned to these more modern types of outlet. It shows, for example, that between 1915 and 1980/81 the contraction of small, independent shops was counterbalanced – and no doubt caused – by the expansion of large, heavily capitalised undertakings: the former's share of retail trade declined from over 80 per cent to barely 30 per cent, while the latter's share increased from 10 per cent to more than 60 per cent.

It would be difficult to exaggerate the scale and significance of such changes. For they helped to transform people's day-to-day experience

TABLE 3.2   The proportion of retail trade done by different types of fixed shops, 1800–1980/1 (percentages)

Year	Independents	Co-operatives	Department stores	Chain stores
	(1–9 outlets)			*(10+ outlets)*
1800	100	0	0	0
1915	82	8	2	8
1939	65	11	5	8
1980/81	31	6		63

Source: **S. Pollard**, *The Development of the British Economy 1914–1980*, E. Arnold, 1983, pp. 111, 303.

of the most important of the mechanisms by which demand and supply were brought into contact with one another. During the early and middle years of the nineteenth century most people did their shopping at their own front door, at a small local shop or at a nearby market; by the middle and later years of the twentieth century most people did their shopping at a city-centre department store, at a nationally-owned chain store, or at an out-of-town supermarket or hypermarket.

It is clear, too, that as incomes rose, as spending on shopping increased, and as the trade done by different outlets altered, so too there were changes in the types of product that were purchased. However, once again some caution is necessary. For even if retail expenditure can be disentangled from consumer expenditure, and estimates made of the trade done by different types of outlet, it remains difficult to discover precisely which products shoppers were purchasing. Yet the attempt must be made. For in seeking to understand shopping behaviour, it is obviously essential to try to identify as clearly as possible any changes in the kinds of item on which shoppers were spending their money.

Table 3.3 attempts to do this by providing an indication of the proportion (though not the volume) of consumer spending devoted to certain broad categories of product. It suggests that during the twentieth century there were two major periods of change. The years between the two world wars saw a substantial increase in the proportion of consumer expenditure spent on household goods, and a very large increase (from a very low base) in the proportion spent on the purchase of motor vehicles. The years following the Second World War saw a substantial decline in the proportion of consumer expenditure that went on food, and a modest decline in the proportion that was devoted to the purchase of clothing. These developments suggest an inverse relationship between income level and food consumption. They confirm, as Ernest Engel suggested

TABLE 3.3 The proportion of consumer expenditure spent on different categories of product, 1913–85 (percentages)

Year	Food	Furniture, floor coverings, hardware, electricals and textiles	Clothing	Alcoholic drink	Tobacco	Car and motor-cycle purchase
1913	28	4	10	8	2	0.6
1937	26	6	10	6	4	1
1965	22	7	9	6	6	3
1985	14	7	7	8	3	5

Source: **C. More**, *The Industrial Age: Economy and Society in Britain 1750–1985*, Longman, 1989, p. 373.

long ago, that as income rises, so the proportion of it spent on food tends to decline. They confirm, as economists put it, that food has a backward-sloping demand curve.[4]

Nor is this all. For there were changes within, as well as between, the proportions of consumer spending devoted to these broad categories of product. There were changes in the design, as well as the amount, of clothing bought; changes in the nature, as well as the number, of consumer durables obtained; and changes in the quality, as well as the quantity, of motor vehicles purchased. Thus Table 3.4 provides some indication of the ways in which food consumption developed. It shows that the decline in the proportion of consumer spending devoted to food was accompanied by a change in the types of food that were consumed. It reveals that as incomes rose, shoppers tended to reduce their consumption of staple products like bread

TABLE 3.4 Food consumption per person per annum, United Kingdom (pounds weight)

Year	Bread, wheat and flour	Potatoes	Other vegetables	Meat	Fruit
c. 1890	200	176		96	
1909–13	211	208	60	135	61
1924–28	198	194	78	134	91
1934	197	210	98	143	115
1950	188	202	112	99	59
1983	100	130	143	124	93

Source: **J. Burnett**, *Plenty and Want: A Social History of Food in England from 1815 to the Present Day*, Routledge, 1989, pp. 113–14, 267, 305–6.

and potatoes, and to increase their consumption of more expensive products such as meat, fruit and vegetables. These developments suggest, then, an inverse relationship between income level and staple food consumption. They confirm that staple foods, like foods generally, have a backward-sloping demand curve, that 'as incomes rise people tend to reduce their consumption of bread and to eat other foods' such as meat, fruit and vegetables.[5]

The difficulties of obtaining and interpreting national retailing/ shopping statistics make it unwise, perhaps, to comment with any confidence about changes in the British experience of shopping. None the less, it seems possible to identify three important, and seemingly unambiguous, developments. It has been shown that as consumers enjoyed higher incomes, so, to a lesser extent, they increased their spending on shopping; that as they increased their spending on shopping, so they patronised new types of retailer; and that as they patronised new types of retailer, so they changed the type of product that they purchased.

Nor does the shortage of reliable national statistics preclude the possibility of discussing the experiences of particular groups of shoppers. Indeed, such a shortage may even be beneficial in so far as it compels those seeking to understand the complex history of shopping to turn from impersonal, aggregate indicators of behaviour to more personal, disaggregated indicators of behaviour, attitudes and aspirations. Accordingly, the remainder of this chapter is devoted to a consideration of the changing experiences of elderly, adolescent, female and working-class shoppers. It will be argued that for most people in these groups, shopping became easier and more enjoyable, and that for many, it assumed a new, albeit rather less straightforward, importance.

The elderly were affected far less than other groups. Poverty and lack of mobility made it difficult for them to benefit to the same extent as other shoppers from the changes that were taking place in the retail sector of the economy. Thus it was not until the final decade or so of the period that elderly people in large numbers began to find their shopping either easier or more enjoyable – or more important to them. In fact, the concerns of the elderly remained remarkably unchanged, with food shopping, in particular, continuing to loom threateningly large.

Poverty meant that old people – like poor people generally – continued to devote a relatively high proportion of their expenditure to the purchase of food. Indeed, it was recognised almost 150 years ago that the poor of all ages were doubly disadvantaged: 'The poorer a family, the greater the proportion of its total expenditure that must be devoted to the provision of food.'[6] It was a trap from which the elderly, like the poor, found it difficult to escape. Thus it was discovered that even in the early 1980s, at the end of a century and more of economic advance, those living in 'elderly' households remained 'over-spenders' on food and fuel, their expenditure on such basic items accounting for 33 per cent of the average elderly budget, compared to 27 per cent of the average non-elderly budget.[7]

Poverty and lack of mobility meant that old people – like poor people generally – continued to shop for food more frequently, and in a narrower range of outlets, than those living around them. Sometimes, no doubt, elderly people saw their regular trips to the local shops as a vital means of keeping in touch with friends and neighbours. Often, however, they had little choice but to shop frequently. For there was a fundamental paradox at the heart of nineteenth- and twentieth-century developments in food retailing: price savings could be obtained best by those shoppers who needed them least. It required a certain level and/or regularity of income to be able to shop with cash at the new co-operative, departmental and chain stores that began to open during the second half of the nineteenth century.[8] It required a certain level and/or regularity of income – not to mention the use of a motor car – to be able to shop in bulk at the supermarkets and hypermarkets that sprang up on the outskirts of built-up areas during the second half of the twentieth century. These were barriers that many elderly people were quite unable to surmount. Thus when researchers from the University of Bristol and the University of Wales Institute of Science and Technology carried out a large-scale survey of shopping habits in Cardiff during 1982, they discovered, not very surprisingly, that those living in 'retired' households were less likely than other groups to travel to superstores and supermarkets, and more likely to shop in nearby co-operative and independent stores. 'Price competition', they concluded, 'has allowed savings to be made by consumers who can use the larger stores, but has increased the relative disadvantage for those who depend upon smaller grocery outlets.'[9]

It is true that the 1960s and 1970s saw the emergence of a growing minority of old people who, as homeowners and members of private pension schemes, were better able to enjoy their retirements unfettered by poverty and poor mobility. However this 'comparatively affluent minority of the elderly' did not really use their prosperity to change the ways in which they shopped. It was reported in 1983 that they 'spent much of their additional money on better housing (which they usually own), on transport and vehicles (primarily running a car) and on services (mainly hotel and holiday expenses).'[10] It transpired indeed that the expenditure per head of old people holidaying abroad was 60 per cent greater than that of the non-elderly who took holidays abroad.[11] So it seems clear that the elderly were affected relatively little by changes in retailing – and it will be seen from the discussion which follows that they were affected less than almost any other major group in the population.

Young people were affected far more profoundly, with shopping assuming a growing, and often a central, importance in teenage life. For whereas during the early years of the period most young people's experience of shopping was confined to helping – more or less reluctantly – with the purchase of food for the family, by the end of the period many adolescents were involved – with very great enthusiasm – in the purchase, for themselves, of an extensive, and apparently ever-changing, cornucopia of consumer goods.

Naturally, not all young people were affected to the same extent. For even at the beginning of the period those from upper-class and middle-class homes did not have to concern themselves with such mundane matters as family food shopping. However, young people from working-class homes had little choice but to become involved. Indeed, for many years the physical and financial constraints of working-class life meant that young people of all ages participated on a regular basis in shopping for food. They were sent to the local shops to ask for credit.[12] They were sent long distances to shops and markets that charged low prices or were prepared to sell in small quantities – splitting, for example, a twopenny, half-pound packet of margarine into two quarter-pound packages.[13] They were sent back and forth to the local shops at which the family was known: 'this easy access often meant that food was bought in dribs and drabs daily, even meal by meal.'[14]

However, both food retailing and food buying were changing. Between the wars these perpetual trips to the local shops were supplemented, and sometimes replaced, by less frequent visits to chain stores like Liptons and Home and Colonial.[15] During the 1960s and 1970s these visits, in their turn, began to be superseded by weekly or fortnightly excursions to supermarkets like Fine Fare, Tescos and Sainsburys.[16] Young people became less involved. For even the most appealing child was unable to persuade a chain store manager to offer credit or break his stock up into smaller units. Even the most responsible teenager was unlikely to be entrusted with the family car, given the housekeeping money, and sent to the supermarket with instructions to buy enough food to last the family for a week or two.

Teenagers' declining involvement in food buying was more than made up for by their growing participation in other forms of shopping. Indeed, by the end of the period shopping had assumed a major importance in the lives of many teenagers: they scanned magazine and television advertisements, they went window shopping with their friends, and they spent part of their weekends buying such clothes, records and other products as they were able to afford.

Clothes, of course, had long been a symbol of youthful independence. However, it was an independence in which not all teenagers were able to share. For although young people from upper-class and middle-class homes no doubt took as much, if not more, interest in what they wore as those from working-class homes, they had less opportunity to choose clothes for themselves. For example, Gwen Raverat recalls how little autonomy she was allowed by her middle-class family in turn-of-the-century Cambridge: 'I thought all my clothes horrible. I can't remember liking a single coat or hat or frock in all my youth, except for one pinafore with pink edges.'[17] Henry Vigne remembers how constrained his choices were when he was a pupil at Harrow school a few years later: 'I used to have five pounds in the summer term and three pounds in the two winter terms. I spent it on all sorts of oddments; books occasionally, a certain amount of food.'[18]

Young people from working-class homes had greater opportunities to indulge their tastes in fashion.[19] For although they had less money to spend, they had more freedom in deciding how to spend it. Not even the poorest were excluded. Mary Purslowe lived in what was reputed to be 'the worst street in North London': yet on Saturday afternoons during the First World War – just after Henry Vigne went to Harrow – she and a group of her friends used to visit nearby Chapel Street, 'a street-market mecca for the poorest of Islington's fashion-conscious youngsters'.[20] Other teenagers followed where Mary Purslowe and those like her had led. Indeed, commentators like George Orwell recognised very clearly the importance of clothes to the young people who grew up during the years of the Depression.

> The youth who leaves school at fourteen and gets a blind-alley job is out of work at twenty, probably for life; but for two pounds ten on the hire-purchase he can buy himself a suit which, for a little while and at a little distance, looks as though it has been tailored in Savile Row. The girl can look like a fashionplate at an even lower price. You may have three halfpence in your pocket and not a prospect in the world, and only the corner of a leaky bedroom to go home to; but in your new clothes you can stand on the street corner, indulging in a private daydream of yourself as Clark Gable or Greta Garbo, which compensates you for a great deal.[21]

Shopping for clothes assumed a greater importance still in the years following the Second World War. In 1960 the *Sunday Graphic* reported with horror on the number of clothes that teenagers were buying. It found a boy, earning five pounds a week, who owned five suits, two pairs of slacks, a pair of jeans, a jacket, an overcoat, eight shirts, twenty-five ties and five pairs of shoes; it discovered a 16-year-old typist who owned six dresses, nine skirts, an Italian suit, a mackintosh, an overcoat, a pair of boots and four pairs of shoes.[22]

These were the years during which records joined clothes as symbols of youthful independence. For as the marketing industry was quick to appreciate, 'The explosion of the record business in the 1960s coincided with the arrival at pocket-money age of the children born during the post-war baby boom'.[23] It coincided too with the arrival of the full employment and high wages which, as was seen in Chapter 1, provided the material basis for the burgeoning youth culture of this and subsequent decades.[24] Buying records helped to determine the pattern of the teenage weekend, with those intending – or pretending – to spend their money jammed into record-shop booths listening to the latest releases. Buying records helped to sustain the vitality of a growing music industry: it has been estimated, for example, that during the late 1950s those aged between 15 and 24 spent £15 million a year on records and record players – and accounted for 40 per cent of the entire market in recorded music.[25] Indeed, some commentators have gone so far as to claim that 'The era of the youth-driven retail economy started with the birth of the "teenager" in the late 1950s and early 1960s'.[26]

This, of course, is to exaggerate both the amount, and the economic impact, of the money that teenagers devoted to shopping. In fact, the importance of teenage shopping cannot be assessed solely in economic terms: it is essential to appreciate, for instance, that the £15 million a year that 15 to 24 year-olds spent on records and record players during the late 1950s represented considerably less than 2 per cent of the money that they had at their disposal.[27] The importance of teenage shopping can be assessed only when measured in less narrowly economic terms. For by the end of the period, shopping had come to assume a leading role in several, quite disparate aspects of teenage life. It was shopping, of course, that linked teenagers to the suppliers of the consumer goods that they wished to purchase. However shopping performed other functions besides. It offered teenagers a common, and, it should be noted, a commercial culture against which to compare themselves; and it helped to provide them with a means of shaping, and filling, large parts of their leisure time: 'Looking at commodities, gaining some kind of enjoyment from the socialness of the town centre and sharing in its movement and perhaps glamour are apparently attractions equally for the employed and the unemployed.'[28]

Women's experience of shopping changed even more profoundly than that of teenagers. For although women retained their traditional responsibility for the purchase of food, family clothing and small household goods, they acquired some say in the purchase of consumer durables, and attained an important – and increasingly independent – role in the purchase of the consumer goods that were produced by, for example, the beauty, fashion, medical and motor industries.

Women did not relinquish their responsibility for buying the family's food, clothing and household goods. However it was a responsibility that became considerably easier for them to sustain. The growth of family purchasing power, the improvement of public and private transport, and the expansion of co-operative, chain-store and supermarket retailing meant that food shopping came to occupy a less worrying, and a less prominent, place in the lives of the majority of women. With more money to spend, a greater choice of places at which to spend it – and more likelihood of owning a refrigerator and having access to a car – women began to shop less frequently, but in larger quantities. This was a most important development. The oral, autobiographical and social survey evidence confirms that throughout the nineteenth and early twentieth centuries most working-class women – and therefore most women – went shopping for food daily, or even several times a day. For instance, A. J. Hobson reported early this century that

> A single family has been known to make seventy-two distinct purchases of tea within seven weeks, and the average purchases of a number of poor families for the same period amount to twenty-seven. Their groceries are bought largely by the ounce, their meat or fish by the halfpennyworth.[29]

Such practices gave way in the face of rising prosperity. Both personal observation and marketing investigation confirm that by the end of the period it had become rare for women to shop for food several times a day, and unusual for them to do so every day of the week. A survey carried out in 1971 suggested that 'During an average week, the housewife will make at least three grocery trips. Four out of ten housewives shop daily for necessities and five out of ten shop more than four times a week.' However, the change was greater than these figures might lead one to suppose. For 'Of these trips at least one will be a major trip, usually to a supermarket and two-thirds of housewives will use a supermarket regularly for food purchases.'[30] Shopping at a supermarket was very different, and could be much more pleasant, than shopping at a corner shop. As one middle-class housewife explained to Ann Oakley in the early 1970s, 'I quite enjoy going round a supermarket if I've got the time, and lots of money, and I know I can choose all these lovely foods.'[31]

It goes without saying that not all housewives had the time and money to enable them to choose all the 'lovely foods' that supermarkets had on display. It goes without saying, therefore, that not all housewives found the transition from corner shop to chain store and supermarket entirely to their liking. Many working-class women regretted the lack of credit and the demise of bargaining, that traditional 'competition between two protagonists who bluff, haggle and insult their way to the act of purchase'.[32] Many middle-class women regretted the lack of subservience and the loss of that comforting 'feeling of being waited on and one's every whim catered for by a willing assistant'.[33] Many women, of all classes, disliked the anonymity of chain store and supermarket shopping.[34] Indeed, it has been suggested that most women found chain store and supermarket shopping less satisfying emotionally than other forms of food purchasing. They seemed to feel that buying large quantities of food for use at some time in the future was less rewarding than buying small quantities of food for use almost immediately.[35]

Whatever the deep-seated emotional costs of chain-store and supermarket shopping, women had to adapt to the growing interest that their families began to take in choosing, and later in buying, the food that was needed. Children certainly knew what they liked. It was estimated in 1970, for instance, that school-age children exercised an influence over some 15 per cent of family food purchases, especially, as might be expected, those involving bread, cakes, biscuits, confectionery, ice cream and breakfast cereals.[36] Husbands too knew what they liked, and what they wanted their wives to buy. It was found during the late 1960s and early 1970s, for example, that husbands were able to influence their wives' choice of products both indirectly (by making known their general preferences) and directly (by suggesting the purchase of the particular 'cheese, pickles and sauces, breakfast cereals, meat pies and sausages, toothpaste and biscuits' that they liked).[37]

Moreover, husbands began to do more to help their wives to buy, as well as to choose, the food that the family required. It was claimed in the late 1960s that 'husbands helped with shopping in 8 per cent of cases every day or most days and helped "regularly" with shopping 35 per cent of the time.'[38] Fifteen years later it was calculated that a quarter of husbands were occasionally sent out with instructions to do the grocery shopping: 'They are given a shopping list and told what to buy where'. Nor was this all. For it was reported that just over a third of young husbands regularly accompanied their wives on their major grocery-buying trips.[39] This growing involvement on the part of husbands had a considerable effect. It enabled women shoppers – especially those with young children – to carry, and therefore to buy, larger amounts of food; and it encouraged them, it seems, to purchase new and/or additional products. A survey carried out for J. Walter Thompson in 1968 concluded that

> the presence of the husband stimulates the housewife to buy more than she would otherwise have done. This may not account for *all* the difference between the spending patterns of the housewives who do and those who do not shop with husbands but it is likely to account for a considerable part of it.[40]

Normally, no doubt, such interest and assistance proved of considerable advantage to hard-pressed wives and mothers, no matter what their social status or economic circumstances. Yet it did nothing to alter the fundamental balance of power within marriage. For food shopping remained overwhelmingly, and unambiguously, a female responsibility. It has been seen that even towards the end of the period many husbands still showed little interest in what food was bought, and most husbands certainly did not accompany their wives on their major grocery-buying trips. The typical supermarket shopper was (and still is) a woman – and often, of course, a woman with young, and fractious, children in tow.[41] Indeed, even when husbands did show an interest in what food was bought, and did agree to accompany their wives on grocery-buying trips, they – along with their wives, their children and almost everybody else – continued to believe that food shopping was, at root, a job for women. The men's involvement was purely voluntary; the men, after all, were only helping.[42]

Moreover, women's involvement in shopping was never confined to the purchase of food. For it was women who shopped for virtually every one of the small 'domestic' items that they and their families required. Thus it was that throughout the whole of the period under discussion women were responsible for buying much of the family's clothing and footwear, and almost all of its soap, detergents, polishes, insecticides, bed linen, soft furnishings, medicines, toothpaste, toothbrushes and shaving products – in fact, it was estimated during the early 1970s that women bought 40 per cent of men's razor blades, and 50 per cent of the electric razors that were purchased as presents.[43]

Women became involved too in shopping for consumer durables. They joined with their husbands in saving for, selecting and purchasing the carpets, pianos, radios, radiograms, vacuum cleaners, washing machines, motor cars, television sets, dishwashers and video recorders that became available as the period progressed. Yet it is not at all easy to interpret correctly the nature of the influence that women were able to bring to bear when families were buying such items. However, it seems that, as might be expected, women's influence was at its strongest when families were buying 'domestic' durables such as carpets, vacuum cleaners and washing machines, and at its weakest when they were buying more 'masculine', more expensive and less overtly 'domestic' products such as video recorders and motor cars.[44] Rosemary Scott summarised the situation as she believed it to be in the mid-1970s:

> there will be more family involvement, particularly by the husband, in those purchase decisions where the product is perceived of as important to the family as a whole, or is more expensive and less frequently purchased. There will be more housewife influence operating on those products which are small, inexpensive and more frequently purchased which the family tends to take for granted, for example, food and household goods.[45]

Whatever the nature of the influence that women managed to bring to bear upon their husbands, it seems to have had its effect. For by the end of the period the sales of what marketing strategists called 'housewife-dominated durables' appeared almost to be approaching saturation point: in 1979 practically three-quarters of households in the country possessed a washing machine, 90 per cent had a refrigerator, and 94 per cent a vacuum cleaner. Suppliers of such products would just have to accept, explained the magazine *Retail Business*, that with such high levels of ownership, manufacturers and retailers were now operating primarily in a 'replacement market'.[46]

Of course, buying food and small household goods, and helping to buy larger consumer durables, did not exhaust women's involvement in shopping. For as the period progressed, women assumed an increasingly important – and an increasingly independent – role as purchasers of small consumer goods. They bought both traditionally 'feminine' products (like beauty aids, fashion goods and sanitary protection) and 'masculine' and/or gender-free products (like cigarettes, alcohol and motor cars). In fact, the markets for the two types of product were converging. 'The housewife will be a car buyer and cigar smoker,' it was argued in 1976: 'the career woman will be a detergent and nappy purchaser, the mother will want to buy investment, sparking plugs and cosmetics.'[47] Such claims should not be taken too literally – few housewives smoked cigars, and few mothers bought sparking plugs as often as they did cosmetics. Yet such a claim remains of some value in so far as it helps to draw attention once again to the complexity of women's changing experience of shopping.

It would be difficult to ignore women's increasing importance as purchasers of those goods that had been regarded traditionally as 'feminine' products. Indeed, it will be recalled from the previous chapter that the manufacturers, retailers and advertisers of beauty, fashion and medical products were among the first to recognise the growing purchasing power at the disposal of the female population. Many of their marketing initiatives, it can be seen, were successful in finding a ready, not to say an enthusiastic, welcome among large numbers of women shoppers.

Sales of beauty and fashion products grew rapidly from the late nineteenth century onwards. For although it is impossible to estimate with any accuracy the amount of money that was spent on such goods, it seems clear that women of all ages turned with alacrity, and apparent pleasure, to the growing volume and variety of clothing, footwear, slimming aids and cosmetics that were displayed so invitingly in the new department stores, in the rapidly expanding chain stores and, by the end of the period, in the fashionable boutiques and specialist shops that seemed sometimes to spring up almost overnight.[48] The results of almost any mid twentieth-century marketing study will serve to illustrate the point. For example, a cosmetics and toiletries survey carried out in 1971 revealed that

11 per cent of women owned six or more different types of eye shadow, and that two-thirds of those who used lipstick and nail varnish carried more than one type in their handbag and/or kept more than one type at home on their dressing table.[49]

Sales of sanitary protection also grew rapidly, but not until towards the end of the period. For although the sanitary towel had been patented in 1892, and output had received a boost after the First World War (when factories making bandages turned to the production of disposable towels), sales remained stubbornly low. Elizabeth Roberts reports, for example, that none of the respondents that she interviewed in Barrow, Lancaster and Preston can remember using a disposable towel until after the end of the Second World War.[50] Yet a quarter of a century later this was a highly successful industry. Sanitary protection was advertised expensively and aggressively; firms like Lillets, Lilia White and Tampax were making determined efforts to woo young shoppers; and it was estimated that retail sales had reached a level of almost £60 million a year.[51]

It would also be difficult to ignore women's increasing importance as purchasers of those consumer goods that had been regarded traditionally as 'masculine' and/or gender-free. Once again the 1960s seemed to constitute something of a turning point, with women becoming involved more than ever before: they began to buy everything, it seems, from Coca-Cola to cigarettes, from marijuana to motor cars.

It is surely no coincidence that there was a rash of reports on women consumers published during the early 1970s. It was found, for example, that a large minority of women participated in the decision whether or not to buy a car – and that a small, though growing, minority were beginning to buy cars in their own right.[52] It was found too that there was an increase in the number of women buying alcoholic drinks for consumption at home. A survey carried out for IPC Magazines in 1970 suggested that more than 40 per cent of such purchases were made by housewives who, in three-quarters of the cases, also took the decision which brand to buy – indeed it was noted that 'In 38 per cent of the purchases the money for drink came out of the housekeeping.'[53] It was found as well that women's consumption of cigarettes was beginning to increase – and this at the same time as men's purchases were beginning to decline. For example, during the 1960s female smokers increased their consumption of cigarettes by almost 40 per cent (from thirty-one to forty-three a week) while male smokers managed to lower theirs by about 4 per cent (from seventy-eight to seventy-five a week). Such changes made it possible for a representative of cigarette manufacturer W. D. and H. O. Wills to point out at the end of the decade that with 43 per cent of women over the age of sixteen smoking, 35 per cent of the British market for cigarettes and tobacco products could now be accounted for by female consumers.[54]

High though they are, such figures seem less surprising when set alongside more broadly based estimates of female consumption. For it has been calculated that by the mid 1970s women's spending accounted for the clear majority – some 54 per cent (by value) and 75 per cent (by sales) – of all the consumer expenditure that took place in the country.[55] Thus women shoppers ended the period more visible, and no doubt more powerful, than they had ever been before.

Such developments were of critical importance. For these changes in women's shopping, together with the changes in elderly and adolescent shopping discussed earlier in the chapter, had an impact upon all classes of society. The landed aristocracy, it has been seen, 'gradually settled down to a circumscribed style of living, which had previously been typical only of the impoverished arable land-owners.'[56]

The middle class lost their servants, but found other ways to enjoy the good food, fashionable clothes and consumer goods with which the department and specialist stores attempted to woo them. Indeed, in certain respects, the middle-class experience of shopping changed remarkably little. For although middle-class consumers had to learn to do their own shopping and to put up with declining standards of service, they, more than most, had the time, the money and the confidence to ensure that shopping remained a satisfying and enjoyable experience. Little, it seems, was allowed to stand in the way of the determined middle-class shopper. For example, when Mass-Observation carried out an investigation into shopping in 1948, it found that for middle-class housewives who were not working, 'the family shopping is by no means the drudgery and torment that is often suggested. In fact most of these housewives openly confess to enjoying it.'[57] Rationing was a challenge, explained one woman: 'I think shopping will lose much of its thrill when all controls go. I enjoy the scheming and contriving to make coupons go as far as possible.'[58] Others were more enthusiastic still: 'I love shopping', concluded a young housewife who worked part-time as an assistant in a nursery school. 'I like the simple act of buying but enjoy buying special treats and expensive things more than every-day necessities.'[59]

The working-class experience of shopping changed much more profoundly. Indeed it could scarcely be otherwise. For not only did working people comprise a clear, albeit declining, majority of the population, but their growing economic power proved a major, and apparently irresistible, attraction to an increasing number of manufacturers, retailers and advertisers.

It would be difficult to exaggerate the changes that took place in working people's experience of food shopping. It has been seen, for example, that as people became more prosperous, they began to spend a smaller proportion of their incomes upon food – and a smaller proportion still upon staple products such as bread and potatoes.[60] Indeed, this inverse relationship between income level and food – and staple food – consumption meant of course that well-off workers tended to change their spending habits more than the poor. According to Derek Oddy, the foremost historian of late nineteenth-century working-class diet, 'Not until income exceeded 30s. per week was there a marked improvement in standards'. However, the improvement could then be dramatic, with families earning thirty shillings or more a week eating twice as much meat and drinking twice as much milk as those earning less than eighteen shillings.[61] This relationship between income level and food consumption proved remarkably resilient. Thus according to a survey carried out by the Food Policy Unit of Manchester Polytechnic in 1984, low income families in the North of England continued to respond to adverse circumstances in time-honoured fashion: they reduced their spending on fish, fruit, fresh meat and vegetables, and increased it on bread, chips, beans and fried foods.[62]

It has been seen, too, that working-class women began to patronise the new types of retailer that sought so hard to secure their custom: they turned first perhaps to the local co-operative store, then to branches of the national chains, and finally to the large supermarkets and hypermarkets that opened after the Second World War.[63] It was not only women who changed their habits. In his classic study of York in the mid 1930s, Seebohm Rowntree laid great emphasis upon the impact of these new forms of retailing. There is one passage that is worth citing at considerable length.

> There are three large chain stores in York: Woolworth's, Marks and Spencer, and British Home Stores. They affect the lives of the workers in two different ways.
>
> First they place within the reach of people of limited means a range of goods far wider than was available to them before, and sold in many cases at prices noticeably lower than those charged elsewhere. This does not affect the minimum cost of maintaining a family in a state of physical efficiency, for the advantage in price is not to be found in the bare necessities of life, such as flour, sugar, tea, milk, cheap cuts of meat, potatoes etc., but rather in such goods as tinned foods, confectionery, biscuits, clothing, crockery, glass-ware, toilet articles, tools, stationery and hundreds of other miscellaneous goods which people of limited means buy.
>
> A second way in which these stores affect the lives of the workers is that they provide a form of entertainment! There is no doubt that thousands of people enter the stores just for the fun of having a look round. They see a vast assortment of goods displayed which they may examine at their leisure without being asked to buy.[64]

The number of people visiting these shops almost defies belief. Rowntree and his team 'took a census of the people entering one or other of the three stores on a Friday and Saturday in June 1936, and found the numbers to be 22,292 on Friday and 46,703 on Saturday.' Although they admitted that the latter figure was somewhat inflated because 'Saturday in York is market day and a certain number of people come into the city from the neighbouring villages', their findings remain striking in the extreme. They concluded that the 'great majority' of 'those patronizing these chain stores' were 'working people', and that the Saturday figure of 46,000 visitors was 'equal to almost one-half of the total population of the city'.[65]

This does not mean that working people abandoned older-established forms of food retailing. For it has been seen already that the elderly, like poor people generally, continued to use a more restricted range of outlets than the better-off. Many nineteenth- and even twentieth-century families liked to patronise the familiar and convenient street hawker: 'They can't be persuaded that they can buy as cheap at the shops; and besides they are apt to think shopkeepers are rich and street-sellers poor, and that they may as well encourage the poor.'[66] Many twentieth-century families continued to buy – and almost beg – from corner shops and market stalls: "Cus I can remember the days when they give the meat away on a Saturday night. They was open to 10, 11 o'clock at night in them days. No refrigerators in the shops. Whatever meat was left'd be bad before Monday.'[67] The association between poverty and such old-established forms of shopping was never completely eliminated. It was found that even in the early 1980s, for instance, 'retired' households in Cardiff made less use than younger ones of the 'multiple and co-operative stores in which price savings were greatest.'[68] The paradox persisted: savings were made most easily by those who needed them least.

The changes in working people's experience of buying food were matched, and in some ways exceeded, by the changes in their experience of buying consumer durables. For whereas at the beginning of the period working-class families simply did not buy consumer durables in the sense that they are understood today, by the end of it most working-class families had been able to purchase a whole number: a television, a record player, a radio or two, a three-piece suite, a refrigerator, a washing machine, a vacuum cleaner and so on.[69]

This transformation in the ownership of consumer durables was made possible by a combination of new methods of production, new types of retailing, and new forms of credit. It was seen in the previous chapter that between 1918 and 1938 the use of hire purchase multiplied twenty times, bringing 'a wide range of household goods such as furniture within the reach of sections of the community who could not previously have afforded them'.[70] Both agricultural and industrial areas were affected. In a farming village on the Oxfordshire-Northamptonshire border,

> a man who kept a small furniture shop came round selling his wares on the instalment plan. On his first visit . . . he got no order at all; but on his second one of the women, more daring than the rest, ordered a small wooden washstand and a zinc bath for washing day. Immediately washstands and zinc baths became the rage. None of the women could think how they had managed to exist so long without a washstand in their bedroom.[71]

In a mining village in South Wales, B. L. Coombes and his wife moved into two rented rooms during the First World War: 'I remember how proud I felt when I saw them furnished for the first time, and realised that all that shining new furniture was ours – even if most of it still had to be paid for.'[72] In the Leicestershire coalfield, 'You could earn up to five quid a week' during the Second World War:

> we were able to get a radiogram, some new coco matting . . . we had a three piece suite, one of those Rexine suites, it must have cost fifty quid, a lot of money, and you could go out and get your pints![73]

The changes in working people's experience of buying food and consumer durables were matched in turn by changes in their experience of buying other, often less expensive, consumer goods. It has been seen already that young people showed a growing interest in buying clothes and records, and women a growing interest in shopping for products such as beauty aids and fashion goods. Men too became involved: although often reluctant to shop for food or clothing, they became interested, many of them, in buying such reassuringly 'masculine' products as cigarettes, gardening and do-it-yourself equipment, not to mention motor cars and motoring accessories.[74]

One result of these changes was that the interests of working-class and other shoppers tended to converge somewhat in the years following the Second World War.

> The motor car, once a middle-class status symbol, now became a leveller, as ownership extended yearly to lower income groups, and it was closely paralleled by radio and television sets, by other domestic electric and gas appliances, by furniture and furnishings in the home and even by clothes and fashion goods, particularly among the young.[75]

Thus in their celebrated study of the 'affluent worker' in Luton during the early 1960s, John Goldthorpe and his collaborators discovered that,

> In the sphere of domestic consumption, at least, there was little evidence at all of any restricting influence being exerted by traditional

working-class norms. Considering, for example, refrigerators and cars – two high-cost and characteristically 'middle-class' possessions – the extent of ownership proved to be roughly comparable between our manual and nonmanual samples: 58% of the former as against 56% of the latter had refrigerators and 45% as against 52% owned cars.[76]

The value of such insights makes it difficult to understand the continuing neglect of shopping. For as W. G. McClelland pointed out thirty years ago, 'It can fairly be claimed that retailing, to a greater extent than most other types of economic activity and in particular than manufacturing, affects and is affected by the society in which it takes place. Few people, apart from those who work there, see inside a factory or a mine; everyone goes into shops.'[77] It is hoped, therefore, that the present chapter goes some way towards remedying this scholarly imbalance. Certainly it shows that there was a fundamental transformation in people's day-to-day experience of shopping, the most important of the mechanisms by which demand and supply were brought into contact with one another. It was a transformation which, as will be seen in subsequent chapters, was to exercise a profound influence upon many aspects of social and economic life. It was a transformation which must find a place in any serious discussion of the development of British society over the past hundred years.

NOTES AND REFERENCES

1. For studies of ownership and usage, see **M. Douglas** and **B. Isherwood**, *The World of Goods: Towards an Anthropology of Consumption*, Allen Lane, 1979 and **A. Tomlinson** (ed.), *Consumption, Identity and Style: Marketing, Meanings, and the Packaging of Pleasure*, Routledge, 1990. For studies of marketing and retailing, see **R. Scott**, *The Female Consumer*, Associated Business Programmes, 1976; and **R. East**, *Changing Consumer Behaviour*, Cassell, 1990. Cf. **R. Samuel**, 'Introduction: Exciting to be English', in **R. Samuel** (ed.), *Patriotism: The Making and Unmaking of British National Identity, Volume 1 History and Politics*, Routledge, 1989, pp. xlvii-iii.

2. **M. J. Artis** (ed.), *The UK Economy: A Manual of Applied Economics*, Weidenfeld & Nicolson, 1986, p. 12.

3. See, for example, **E. Smithies**, *The Black Economy in England since 1914*, Gill & Macmillan, 1984.

4. **W. Minchinton**, 'Patterns of Demand 1750–1914', in *The Fontana Economic History of Europe: The Industrial Revolution*, **C. M. Cipolla** (ed.), Fontana, 1973, p. 115. Also **G. J. Stigler**, 'The Early History of Empirical Studies of Consumer Behaviour', *Journal of Political Economy*, lxii, 1954.

5. Minchinton, 'Patterns of Demand', p. 82.

6. Stigler, 'Consumer Behaviour', p. 98.

7. **M. Abrams**, 'Some Background Facts', *Journal of the Market Research Society*, **251**, 1983, pp. 219–20. The elderly were also more reluctant than those from other age groups to use hire purchase. *RC on Consumer Credit, Report*, 1971, p. 116.

8. For example, **M. J. Winstanley**, *The Shopkeeper's World 1830–1914*, Manchester University Press, 1983, pp. 36–9.

9. **C. Guy**, 'The Food and Grocery Shopping Behaviour of Disadvantaged Consumers: Some Results from the Cardiff Consumer Panel', *Transactions of the Institute of British Geographers*, **10**, 1985, p. 181; also pp. 182–9.

10. Abrams, 'Facts', p. 222. See also **A. Hallsworth**, *Food Shopping and the Elderly*, Manchester Business School, 1990.

11. Abrams, 'Facts', p. 215.

12. **E. Roberts**, *A Woman's Place: An Oral History of Working-Class Women 1890–1914*, Blackwell, 1984, p. 148. Lancaster, Mr C1P, p. 2; Mrs P1P, p. 52; Bristol, R05, p. 5.

13. **C. Chinn**, *They Worked All Their Lives: Women of the Urban Poor in England, 1880–1939*, Manchester University Press, 1988, p. 64. Also **C. Steedman**, *Landscape for a Good Woman: A Story of Two Lives*, Virago, 1986, p. 42.

14. **J. Burnett**, *Plenty and Want: A Social History of Food in England from 1815 to the Present Day*, Routledge, 1989, p. 167. Also Roberts, *Woman's Place*, p. 23; Chinn, *Worked All Their Lives*, p. 64; Lancaster, Mrs P3L, p. 10.

15. **J. Stevenson**, *British Society 1914–45*, Penguin, 1984, p. 113; Lancaster, Mrs R3P, p. 7.

16. Scott, *Female Consumer*, p. 5.

17. **G. Raverat**, *Period Piece: A Cambridge Childhood*, Faber & Faber, c. 1952, p. 255.

18. **T. Thompson**, *Edwardian Childhoods*, Routledge & Kegan Paul, 1981, p. 161.

19. **B. Williamson**, *The Temper of the Times: British Society since World War II*, Blackwell, 1990, p. 150.

20. **J. White**, *The Worst Street in North London: Campbell Bunk, Islington, Between the Wars*, Routledge & Kegan Paul, 1986, p. 201.

21. **G. Orwell**, *The Road to Wigan Pier*, Penguin, 1937, p. 79.

22. **P. Laurie**, *The Teenage Revolution*, Anthony Blond, 1965, pp. 20–1. Also Scott, *Female Consumer*, p. 189. See also 'Men's Wear', *Retail Business*, July 1980, p. 60.

23. 'Tapes and Records', *Retail Business*, April 1978, p. 39.

24. **P. Willmott**, *Adolescent Boys of East London*, Penguin, 1975, p. 7.

25. **D. Harker**, *One for the Money: Politics and Popular Song*, Hutchinson, 1980, p. 74. Also 'Records and Tapes', *Mintel*, April 1980, p. 55; 'Records and Tapes', *Retail Business*, September 1981, p. 29.

26. **C. Gardiner** and **J. Sheppard**, *Consuming Passion: The Rise of Retail Culture*, Hyman, 1989, p. 213. Cf. **D. Fowler**, 'Teenage Consumers? Young Wage-Earners and Leisure in Manchester, 1919–1939', in **A. Davies** and **S. Fielding** (eds), *Workers' Worlds: Cultures and*

Communities in Manchester and Salford, 1880–1939, Manchester University Press, 1992.

27. Harker, *Money*, p. 74. Also Laurie, *Teenage Revolution*, p. 72.
28. **P. Willis**, *The Social Condition of Young People in Wolverhampton in 1984*, Wolverhampton Borough Council, 1985, p. 46.
29. Burnett, *Plenty and Want*, p. 167.
30. Scott, *Female Consumer*, p. 5. Also **W. G. McClelland**, 'The Supermarket and Society', *Sociological Review*, **10**, 1962, pp. 133–4; **P. Coldstream**, 'The Great Supermarket Revolution', *New Society*, 1 November 1962.
31. **A. Oakley**, *Housewife*, Penguin, 1974, p. 131. Cf. Mass-Observation, 1531, 'Shopping Survey', 1942. This book makes a good deal of use of Mass-Observation material: see **P. Summerfield**, 'Mass-Observation: Social Research or Social Movement?', *Journal of Contemporary History*, **20**, 1985.
32. Scott, *Female Consumer*, p. 61.
33. Scott, *Female Consumer*, p. 61. Also **L. M. Harris**, *Buyer's Market: How to Prepare for the New Era in Retailing*, Business Publications, 1963, p. 60.
34. McClelland, 'Supermarket', pp. 139–41; Coldstream, 'Supermarket'.
35. Scott, *Female Consumer*, p. 57.
36. Scott, *Female Consumer*, pp. 43–4. Also Lancaster, Mrs A1P, p. 41.
37. Scott, *Female Consumer*, p. 129. Also p. 81.
38. Scott, *Female Consumer*, p. 78. Also Lancaster, Mrs A1P, p. 53.
39. **P. Davis**, 'The Shape of Retail Trading Policies', *Retail & Distribution Management*, September–October, 1982, p. 8.
40. Scott, *Female Consumer*, p. 81.
41. Davis, 'Policies', p. 8; Scott, *Female Consumer*, pp. 8, 68, 78–9; Oakley, *Housewife*, p. 93.
42. Lancaster, Mrs R3B, p. 10; Mrs R4B, p. 14; Mrs L2L, p. 12; Mass-Observation, 3055, 'A Report on Shopping', 1948, p. 9; Scott, *Female Consumer*, p. 8.
43. Scott, *Female Consumer*, pp. 23, 33–7, 42–3.
44. Scott, *Female Consumer*, pp. 124, 134.
45. Scott, *Female Consumer*, p. 124.
46. 'Domestic Washing Machines', *Retail Business*, December 1979, p. 21. Also 'Vacuum Cleaners', *Retail Business*, June 1980, pp. 20–6; Scott, *Female Consumer*, pp. 45–53.
47. Scott, *Female Consumer*, p. 204.
48. **J. Benson**, *The Working Class in Britain, 1850–1939*, Longman, 1989, p. 146; **J. B. Jefferys**, *The Distribution of Consumer Goods: A Factual Study of Methods and Costs in the United Kingdom in 1938*, Cambridge University Press, 1950, pp. 318–37.
49. Scott, *Female Consumer*, p. 174.
50. Roberts, *Woman's Place*, p. 18; Jefferys, *Distribution*, p. 383.
51. 'The Sanitary Protection Market', *Retail Business*, August 1978, p. 37; Scott, *Female Consumer*, pp. 169–70.
52. Scott, *Female Consumer*, p. 164.
53. Scott, *Female Consumer*, p. 163.
54. Scott, *Female Consumer*, p. 162.

55. Scott, *Female Consumer*, p. ix.
56. **F. M. L. Thompson**, *English Landed Society in the Nineteenth Century*, Routledge & Kegan Paul, 1963, pp. 337–8.
57. Mass-Observation, 3055, p. 1.
58. Mass-Observation, 3055, p. 2. Also 3160, 'A Report on the London Middle-Class House-Wife and her Food Problems', 1949, p. 3.
59. Mass-Observation, 3055, p. 1. Also p. 8.
60. Minchinton, 'Patterns of Demand', p. 82.
61. **D. J. Oddy**, 'Working-Class Diets in Late Nineteenth-century Britain', *Economic History Review*, **xxiii**, 1970, pp. 318, 320. Also *British Labour Statistics: Historical Abstract 1886–1968*, Department of Employment and Productivity, 1971, pp. 380–83.
62. Burnett, *Plenty and Want*, p. 325.
63. Winstanley, *Shopkeeper's World*, pp. 36–9; **J. P. Johnson**, *A Hundred Years Eating: Food, Drink and the Daily Diet in Britain since the late Nineteenth Century*, Gill & Macmillan, 1977, pp. 68–87.
64. **B. S. Rowntree**, *Poverty and Progress: A Second Social Survey of York*, Longman, Green and Co., 1941, pp. 218–9.
65. Rowntree, *Poverty and Progress*, p. 219.
66. **H. Mayhew**, *London Labour and the London Poor*, Constable, 1968, I, p. 60. Also National Museum of Labour History, Manchester, *Report of the Co-operative Congress*, 1955, p. 62.
67. Chinn, *Worked All Their Lives*, p. 66. Also **C. C. Hosgood**, 'The Pigmies of Commerce and the Working-Class Community – Small Shopkeepers in England 1870–1914', *Journal of Social History*, **22**, 1989.
68. Guy, 'Shopping Behaviour', p. 189. Also Mass-Observation, A12, 'Anti Semitism Survey', 1938, p. 12; Lancaster, Mrs G5P, p. 9.
69. **J. Rule**, *The Labouring Classes in Early Industrial England 1750–1850*, Longman, 1986, pp. 46–71; 'Domestic Washing Machines', p. 21; *British Labour Statistics*, p. 394.
70. Cited **M. Tebbutt**, *Making Ends Meet: Pawnbroking and Working-Class Credit*, Leicester University Press, 1983, p. 194. Indeed, some shoppers paid by instalments, not because they were unable to pay cash, but so that they would have some redress if anything went wrong. Lancaster, Mrs M11B, p. 2.
71. **F. Thompson**, *Lark Rise to Candleford*, Penguin, 1973, p. 125.
72. **B. L. Coombes**, *These Poor Hands: The Autobiography of a Miner Working in South Wales*, Gollancz, 1939, p. 91.
73. **C. P. Griffin**, *The Leicestershire Miners: Vol. II, 1914–1945*, NUM Leicester Area, 1988, p. 52.
74. **C. More**, *The Industrial Age: Economy and Society in Britain 1750–1985*, Longman, 1989, p. 373.
75. **S. Pollard**, *The Development of the British Economy 1914–1980*, Arnold, 1983, p. 324.
76. **J. Goldthorpe**, **D. Lockwood**, **F. Bechhofer** and **J. Platt**, *The Affluent Worker in the Class Structure*, Cambridge University Press, 1969, p. 39.
77. McClelland, 'Supermarket and Society', p. 133.

Chapter 4

TOURISM

The study of tourism has aroused greater interest than that of shopping. Yet even those scholars who have shown an interest in this form of consumption have often approached it in a somewhat partial fashion: they find it difficult to define precisely what it is that they are studying; they seem to pay greater attention to certain forms of tourism than to others; and they tend to display relatively little interest in the impact that tourism had upon those who participated in it.[1]

It is the purpose of this chapter, by recognising – and seeking to remedy – such limitations, to provide a properly balanced consideration of the British experience of tourism. Accordingly, this chapter, like the last, is divided into two. The first, and shorter, section examines the major statistical indicators of changes in tourist activity; the second, and considerably longer, section examines the more personal, albeit less precise, evidence of changes in the experiences of elderly, adolescent, female, and aristocratic, middle-class and working-class tourists.

It will be argued that the past 150 years have seen a major transformation in the British experience of tourism. It will be shown that, as with shopping, there have been three major developments: a large increase in the volume (and value) of consumption; a major change in the types of people participating; and a substantial reorientation in the range of activities undertaken.

However, as so often, such claims are easier to make than they are to substantiate satisfactorily. For the discussion of tourism is bedevilled, still more than that of shopping, by an unwieldy combination of conceptual and empirical difficulties.

It is easy enough to agree upon a basic definition of tourism. 'Tourism', it has been said, 'denotes the temporary, short-term movement of people to destinations outside the places where they normally live and work and their activities during the stay at these destinations'.[2] Unfortunately such a straightforward definition is not always easy to apply in practice. For it is often difficult to decide whether the term 'tourism' should be used to describe travel over very short distances and/or very short periods of time; travel that involves no, or negligible, expenditure; and travel that is undertaken for business and vocational, rather than for recreational, reasons. For the purposes of this book, a study of the rise of consumer society, it has been decided to adopt a definition that directs attention towards those forms of tourism which – whatever their scale – involved consumers in some financial outlay and were undertaken primarily for recreational reasons.

Even when such a definition has been decided upon, it remains difficult to use it to compile even the most basic information concerning the growth of British tourism. For the statistical data are both chronologically and methodologically incomplete. It was not until 1951 that the British Travel Association began to organise sample household surveys of the volume, value and nature of British tourism. And even then, the evidence collected remains disappointingly opaque. It does not distinguish clearly between the number of people taking holidays and the number of holidays that were taken; while, as might be expected, it proves far less informative about small-scale forms of tourism (like day trips) than about larger-scale, more expensive activities (such as annual holidays).[3]

Although these conceptual complications and empirical deficiencies cannot be fully overcome, there is no doubt that the importance of virtually all forms of tourism has increased with the growth of prosperity during the past 150 years. For tourist expenditure has always been highly income-elastic: it has been claimed, for example, that when a person's income rises by 1 per cent, his or her expenditure on tourism is likely to increase by $1\frac{1}{2}$ per cent.[4]

Of course, small-scale tourism remains impervious to any attempt at statistical precision. It is difficult, after all, to decide at what point a visit to friends, a walk to the shops, a trip to the cinema, or a day out at a football match should be described as forms of tourism. Even when such distinctions can be made, it is impossible to compile convincing estimates – let alone accurate statistics – of the number of visits being made. None the less, it seems clear that the day (and part-day) trip/excursion has always been the most common, as well as the most easily overlooked, form of tourist activity. Visits were – and still are – made to every conceivable type of destination, attraction and event: fairs and markets, theatres and shops, beauty spots and historic sites, seaside resorts and rural retreats, religious services and political meetings, sporting events and family celebrations.

It seems clear too that the number of people taking such trips

– and the number of trips being taken – began to increase dramatically with the improvements in transport and the growth in working-class purchasing power that took place during the second half of the nineteenth century. It was a development that was recorded with some distaste by many commentators of both left and right. Ex-Chartist leader Thomas Cooper was aghast at the sight of Lincoln workmen pawning their beds so that they could afford to go on railway excursions.[5] Journalist Ewing Ritchie reported that after four weeks in Southend-on-Sea, he 'began to tremble at the very sight of an excursion'.[6] It was a development that was recorded more dispassionately by other late-nineteenth- and early-twentieth-century observers. Thus it is known that, whereas in 1844 Brighton received some 15,000 railway passengers from London over the Easter weekend, in 1862 it attracted nearly nine times that number of visitors on Easter Monday alone;[7] it has been pointed out that, whereas in 1892 the FA cup final attracted a crowd of some 33,000, in 1923 an estimated 150,000 supporters turned up to see the match at the newly opened Wembley Stadium.[8]

However, it was not until half a century later – at the very end of the period covered by this book – that estimates were first made of the full extent of such small-scale tourism. It was claimed, for example, that during the 1980s as many as 500 million day trips were taken annually, a figure which, if accurate, means that every man, woman and child in the country was making an average of nine trips a year – one every five or six weeks.[9] Of these trips, some 20 per cent were to the seaside, 25 per cent to attractions recognised by the travel industry, with the remaining 55 per cent being made to the homes of friends, relatives and so on.[10] There was – and is – an interesting correlation between destination and distance. It has been found that there is a minimum distance 'below which people do not think they are getting away from home and are therefore not very likely to travel. So there tends to be an 'average' travel time . . . . [Day] Excursionists spend on average about 1½–2 hours travelling to a destination.'[11]

It is apparent, then, that there has been a major transformation in the incidence and importance of small-scale tourism. For over the past 150 years the day (and part-day) trip has become a regular, if largely unremarked, feature in the lives of the majority of the British population.

It is not surprising that larger-scale forms of tourism have attracted both more attention and, in recent years, more serious and sustained attempts at statistical analysis. For it is easier to recognise – and thus to quantify – those forms of tourism that involve spending a night or more away from home. It is not difficult to accept that visits which are undertaken for pleasure, and which involve the purchase of accommodation as well as travel can be described unambiguously as forms of tourism. Nor is it difficult to recognise that during the second half of the twentieth century such tourism can be measured reasonably easily – and reasonably accurately – by the use of household, destination and similar surveys.[12]

Nevertheless, for the greater part of the period covered by this book it is necessary to rely, once again, upon the observations of informed contemporaries. They all agreed that the holiday habit was spreading both more widely and more deeply. Factory inspector Robert Baker remarked in 1875 that 'The working class are moving about on the surface of their own country . . . spending the wealth they have acquired 'in seeing the world' as the upper classes did in 1800, as the middle class did in 1850, and as they themselves are doing in 1875.'[13] Sixty years later, in 1935, the compilers of *The Survey of London Life and Labour* observed that 'An annual summer holiday is today taken for granted by a very large and increasing number of Londoners.'[14]

Such contemporary views have been corroborated by the work of historians such as John Walton and James Walvin who have done so much to further the serious study of British tourism. The former confirms that the 1870s

> saw the beginning of the rapid development of the seaside holiday
> habit among the industrial working classes of Lancashire, and to a
> lesser extent the West Riding. In these areas the seaside holiday,
> as opposed to the day-trip, became popular at least a generation
> before it became commonplace among working people elsewhere.[15]

The latter confirms that 'Whereas before 1914 the working-class seaside visitors had tended to be trippers, by the late 1930s they tended to stay for a week or more.'[16]

Fortunately by the late 1930s (and still more by the early 1950s) it is possible to supplement such claims with the statistical data assembled by the British Tourist Authority, the National Tourist Boards and other organisations interested in the operations of the country's tourist industry. Certain key elements of these data have been brought together in Table 4.1, and will be of considerable interest to anyone interested in the history of British holiday-making. Indeed, Table 4.1 is even more compelling than it may appear at first sight. For the information which it contains refers, not to all holidays, but only to those involving stays of four or more nights away from home. Yet it shows that even when the definition of holiday-making is restricted in this way, the forty years between 1939 and 1979 saw a major expansion in this, the most important form of British tourism. The number of holiday-makers increased very rapidly: from some 15 million in 1939, to 25 million in 1951, 30 million in 1966, and 35 million in 1979. The proportion of the population taking holidays

TABLE 4.1 Holidays away from home of four nights or more, United Kingdom, 1939–79

Year	Holiday-makers No. (mills)	% of Pop'n*	Holidays No. (mills)	£ (mills)	Direct expenditure Per head (a) of total pop'n (£)	(b) of pop'n taking holidays (£)
1939	15	33				
1951	25	50	26.5	380	7.8	15.5
1966	30	56	36.5	870	16.6	29.6
1971	33	59	41	1,448	25.9	43.9
1979	35	63	49	4,950	88	140

* Population: Great Britain

Sources: **A. J. Burkart** and **S. Medlik**, *Tourism: Past, Present and Future*, Heinemann, 1981, pp. 86–7, 274; **J. C. Holloway**, *The Business of Tourism*, Pitman, 1989, p. 33; **C. More**, *The Industrial Age: Economy and Society in Britain 1750–1985*, Longman, 1989, p. 280; **S. Pollard**, *The Development of the British Economy 1914–1980*, Arnold, 1983, p. 340; **H. Robinson**, *A Geography of Tourism*, Macdonald & Evans, 1979, pp. 221, 223–4.

increased almost as rapidly: from some 33 per cent in 1939, to 50 per cent in 1951, 56 per cent in 1966, and 63 per cent in 1979. The amount of money that these holiday-makers spent on their holidays increased more rapidly still: from £380 million (£15.5 per holiday-maker) in 1951, to £870 million (£29.6) in 1966, and £4,950 (£140) in 1979.

This was a transformation of truly massive proportions. For as J. A. R. Pimlott maintained nearly half a century ago in his pioneering study of *The Englishman's Holiday*, the annual summer holiday 'ranks high amongst our cultural exports': it represents, he believed, 'a revolutionary advance in the art of living' and it 'has had far-reaching consequences'.[17] In fact, as can be seen today, the annual summer holiday is a form of consumption in which most people manage to participate – and in which most other people would certainly like to.

These changes in the number, cost and importance of holidays were accompanied by changes in the popularity of different types of travel. There have been two seemingly contradictory, but largely complementary, developments: the growth of group tourism; and the expansion, in recent years, of independent travel.

It has become increasingly common for tourists to travel and/or stay together in groups. Nor is this by any means a new phenomenon.

For it is not always appreciated that during the second half of the nineteenth century neighbours, workmates, and members of sports and special interest groups quite often spent their holidays together. It seemed odd, remarked the *Saturday Review* in 1860, that 'The quietest sort of people are uncomfortable unless they, at least once a year, tie themselves together in batches and go prowling over the tops of unexplored Alps.'[18] It is striking, observes John Walton, that in late-nineteenth-century Lancashire 'whole towns go on holiday, and find resorts to look after their needs'. He believes that

> The communal nature of the cotton holidays was conducive to good behaviour among visitors who were often self-regulating. For its Wakes visitors Blackpool had none of the anonymity of a cosmopolitan or metropolitan resort. Dissolute or reprehensible behaviour was likely to come to the notice of relatives, friends and workmates.[19]

Of course, it is much more widely recognised that the years between the two world wars saw the successful establishment of one of the most communal of all forms of mass tourism, the seaside holiday camp. It has been estimated, for example, that the number of holiday-camp visitors increased from about 750,000 (3 per cent of all holiday-makers) in 1951 to 2.1 million (6 per cent) in 1963.[20] The camps' mass catering, organised activities and 'obligatory conviviality' were regarded with some distaste by the few scholars who took the trouble to study them. Thus, according to one post-war researcher, the camps exploited 'the indolence of people who want a holiday but who are too lazy to organise it for themselves'.[21] According to another,

> The camps were often just dormitories receiving busloads of young men and women from the mills, mines and factories during wakes weeks or similar breaks in the work routines. The emphasis was on exhausting physical sports: soccer and wrestling mostly, and boisterous drinking and dancing in the evening.[22]

None the less, it was the late 1960s and early 1970s that saw the most rapid increase in group tourism. The crucial development was the expansion of the package (or inclusive) holiday, the system whereby the tour operator, rather than the tourist, combined transport and accommodation into a single, convenient product. Of course, the package holiday already had a long history, with the most famous of all British travel agents, Thomas Cook, beginning his career as a tour operator as early as the 1840s.[23] However, it was not until the late 1960s that the package-holiday industry secured a leading position in the market, and so began the process which was to transform the character of the British summer holiday. For as Table 4.2 reveals, it was during the mid to late 1960s that substantial numbers of holiday-makers began to join air-package tours to the

TABLE 4.2   Air-package holidays to Western Europe, United Kingdom, 1966–78/79

Year	No. (mills)	% of all holidays to Western Europe	% of all holidays in Britain and abroad	Destination (%)		
				Spain	Italy	France
1966	1.3	36	3.6			
1971	2.9	55	8.4			
1978/79	3.5	51	7.0	46	10	9

Sources: **A. J. Burkart** and **S. Medlik**, *Tourism: Past, Present and Future*, Heinemann, 1981, p. 179; 'Holidays Abroad', *Mintel*, December 1981, p. 27

coastal resorts of Southern Europe: it shows, for example, that by 1978/79 British tourists took 3.5 million package holidays to Europe, 60 per cent of them in France, Italy and, above all, Spain. In 1971 only one-third of British adults had ever been abroad on holiday; in 1984 only one-third had not.[24] The importance of the package-holiday industry has been recognised on all sides: its critics castigate it for doing little more than satiating consumers with sunshine and chips in places like Benidorm and Torremolinos;[25] its supporters commend it for 'making a holiday abroad part of the good life, as much as television or the car are'.[26]

Yet both critics and supporters need to approach the expansion of the package-holiday industry with some caution. For while it has become common to associate the increasing popularity of holidays abroad with the increasing popularity of package tours, Table 4.2 reveals that this can be seriously misleading. For it shows that even in 1978–79, at the very end of the period, air-package tours accounted for barely 50 per cent of the holiday visits that British tourists made to Western Europe. The key to this apparent paradox is not, of course, difficult to discern. For, as was suggested above, it has always been common for tourists to travel independently as well as in groups. Indeed, it seems clear that such independent travel has become more, rather than less, common in recent years.

The growth of motor vehicle ownership was central to this, as to so many other economic and social developments in post-war Britain. Indeed, it is still not always appreciated that the car ownership rate has doubled every ten years or so since the late 1930s. For instance, whereas in 1949 there were fewer than 2 million private cars, giving 14 per cent of households access to a vehicle, twenty years later the 11 million cars in private ownership provided 60 per cent of households with the use of a vehicle of their own.[27] It was this increase, it seems, that did more than anything else to encourage independent travel. It 'gave families a new freedom of movement; not only were costs of motoring falling in relative terms, but car owners tended to perceive only the direct costs of a motoring trip, ignoring the indirect coasts *(sic)* of depreciation and wear and tear'.[28] The consequences were clear: whereas in 1951 less than 30 per cent of tourists used a car for their holiday travel, in 1981 70 per cent of them did so.[29]

The increasing use of the motor car was associated with – and helped to encourage – the growth of self-catering holidays. British holiday-makers began to take their cars across the Channel to stay in French *gîtes*, Spanish villas and other types of rented accommodation. Many more stayed in Britain, of course, looking after themselves in cottages, campsites and caravan parks. In fact, in recent years even holiday camps, recognising that tastes were changing, began to provide self-catering as well as 'serviced' accommodation.[30] Table 4.3 provides an indication of the major developments that took place in Britain during the final quarter century of the period. It shows that whereas in 1955 self-catering represented less than 20 per cent of domestic holiday accommodation, in 1979 it accounted for almost 50 per cent, with caravanning assuming a new, and major, importance. It was a remarkable transition. In 1955 some 2 million people took caravan holidays (and caravans accounted for 8 per cent of domestic holiday accommodation); fifteen years later more than 5 million people – two and a half times as many – took caravan holidays (and caravans accounted for 18 per cent of all holiday accommodation). Indeed, it has been estimated that by the mid-1970s more than 50 per cent of the British population had been caravanning at one time or other in their lives.[31]

Clearly, then, the British experience of tourism has changed dramatically since the middle of the nineteenth century. There has been both a major increase in the number (and proportion) of people participating in tourism, and significant changes in the types

TABLE 4.3 Accommodation used on main holidays of four nights or more in Britain, 1955–79 (percentages)

Year	Self-catering	Camping	Caravanning
1955	18	3	8
1965	25	4	13
1975	37	7	18
1979	47	6	18

Sources: **A. J. Burkart** and **S. Medlik**, *Tourism: Past, Present and Future*, Heinemann, 1981, p. 87; **H. Robinson**, *A Geography of Tourism*, Macdonald & Evans, 1979, p. 233

of activity that they were able, and willing, to undertake. As late as 1939 only a third of the British population took any sort of extended holiday away from home. Forty years later almost two-thirds of the population were doing so – and one person in five was holidaying abroad.[32] Certainly tourism is another form of consumption whose scholarly neglect cannot possibly be countenanced.

Surprisingly, the still underdeveloped state of tourism history proves a less serious impediment than might be expected when attempts are made to disaggregate the experiences of groups such as town dwellers, the young, the old, women and members of the upper, middle and working classes. For the underdeveloped state of tourism history may be counterbalanced, to some extent at least, by the use of oral, autobiographical and newspaper evidence, and by reference to the statistical data that have been collected in recent years by the tourist industry itself.

None the less, the association between urbanisation and tourism may not be immediately apparent. Of course, it would be difficult to overlook the fact that the demand for tourism – like that for most other forms of consumption – emanated primarily from urban areas. It was seen in Chapter 1 that the growth and redistribution of population, wealth and income tended to concentrate economic power in the towns and cities of the Midlands and South-east of England. Moreover, it is generally acknowledged that the pressures of urban living – together with reductions in working hours – meant that this economic power was used very often to participate in some form of tourism.[33] It is striking, for example, that travel agents – like building societies – appeared only in towns and suburbs above a certain size; indeed, by the end of the period the London area, with fewer than one-fifth of the country's population, housed practically one-third of its travel agents.[34]

It is easier, perhaps, to overlook the fact that urban tourists most often made for urban destinations. For whether they went for the day or stayed for a fortnight, whether they caught a train or travelled by car, the majority of tourists moved between one town and another.

Certainly the majority of day trips seem to have started and finished in urban centres. It was a pattern that was reinforced, rather than undermined, by the transport improvements that took place during the second half of the nineteenth century. For, as J. A. Patmore has pointed out, 'the railway by its very nature concentrated rather than dispersed and though it brought greatly increased freedom of movement the channels of that movement were still relatively restricted'.[35] Thus working-class and other 'excursionists' came from all over the country to the Great Exhibition of 1851.[36] Football supporters began to travel from town to town to attend league and (especially) cup matches: in 1882 two special trains carried 1,200 Blackburn Rovers supporters to the FA Cup Final in

London; in 1896 10,000 Aston Villa supporters packed into thirteen special trains to watch a cup tie at nearby Derby.[37] Still larger numbers of town and city dwellers began to take excursions to seaside resorts: they flocked from the suburbs of London to Southend, Margate, Eastbourne and Brighton; from the towns of the industrial East Midlands to Yarmouth, Cleethorpes and Scarborough; and from the textile towns and conurbations of Lancashire and the West Riding to resorts such as Southport, Morecambe and Blackpool.[38]

Nor was the fundamentally urban nature of the day trip transmogrified by the transport improvements that took place during the course of the twentieth century. It is true, of course, that the invention, and increasing ownership, of the motor car promised exciting new possibilities: 'the car brought incomparably greater freedom to recreational travel, freedom in the choice of destination, freedom in the timing of journeys, freedom to pause at a moment's whim'.[39] What is striking, however, is the restraint, rather than the abandon, with which this new-found freedom was employed. For car owners very often continued to take day trips to the towns that they, and their parents, had visited previously by train and by coach. The wife of a Preston tanker driver recalls that in the late 1950s and early 1960s she and her family regularly used their old Ford for day trips – but only to St Anne's, a small town some 12 miles or so away on the coast.[40] The author, the son of a Romford grocery buyer, remembers that during these same years his neighbour, a railway signalman, used his car for day trips, but only to Southend, Clacton or, at furthest, Walton on the Naze.[41]

The majority of more extended holidays also started and finished in urban areas. It was a pattern that was reinforced, once again, by the coming of the railways. Thus according to one geographer, 'the holiday-maker inevitably made for the nearest seaside resort: the Londoner went to Margate, Southend or Brighton, the Lancastrian went to Blackpool or Southport, and the Yorkshireman to either the East Coast or to Morecambe'. Indeed, according to this view, even in the 1970s, such holidays remained 'an ingrained habit with many; in the north of England the factory-workers make a bee-line for Blackpool, Bridlington and Whitley Bay; in London the non-professional worker goes to Brighton, Margate or Southend'.[42] There is here more than a touch of caricature. Yet it is true that even towards the end of the period, 70–75 per cent of all main holidays in Britain involved a stay by the seaside, usually in one of the larger resorts, and that a further 15 per cent or so involved visits to historic cities such as Oxford, Stratford, Edinburgh and London.[43] In the early 1950s, recalls a Lancaster factory worker, 'everybody either went to London for their honeymoon or Edinburgh'.[44] Moreover, even when British tourists travelled abroad for their holidays, they still tended to make for urban destinations: Nice, Cannes and

St Tropez on the French Riviera; Venice, Rome, Florence and other centres of classical culture; and, towards the end of the period, the urban – or urbanising – resorts of Spain's Costa Brava, Costa Blanca and Costa del Sol.[45]

The relationship between adolescence, old age and tourism is more obvious and a good deal easier to disentangle. It is clear that the elderly rarely participated in tourism to the same extent as those from other age groups. Nor is this surprising. For it was seen in Chapter 1 that many old people were forced to cope with low incomes, impaired mobility and increasing infirmity, constraints which, as can be imagined, were scarcely conducive to involvement in any form of tourism.[46] Indeed it is possible to afford their lack of involvement some limited degree of statistical precision. For it can be seen from Table 4.4 that at the end of the period the elderly were the least likely to take any type of holiday away from home: so although those aged 65 and above made up 19 per cent of the population in 1976/80, they accounted for only 12 per cent of all holidays, and no more than 6 per cent of holidays taken abroad.

However, the impediments inhibiting tourism among the elderly were becoming less severe towards the end of the period. For it was seen in Chapter 1 that a combination of demographic and material changes brought about a fundamental, and beneficial, transformation in the economic circumstances of many elderly people. 'Older people', it has been pointed out, were becoming 'wealthier, healthier and more mobile'.[47] Moreover, it was seen in Chapter 2 that the travel industry began to respond to these changes, not least by the initiatives of tour operators such as Saga, Golden Circle and Golden Days that specialised in holidays for the over 50s. These developments in demand and supply began to have their effect. For, as will be recalled from Chapter 3, the 'comparatively affluent minority of the elderly . . . spent much of their additional money on . . . services (mainly hotel and holiday expenses)'.[48] These elderly tourists looked, above all, for comfort, convenience, good weather and attractive scenery.[49] Some took advantage of out-of-season offers

TABLE 4.4   Adolescence, old age and holidays, Great Britain, 1976/80

Age	% of population	% of all holidays (1+ night)	% of all holidays abroad (1+ night)
16–24	18	21	20
25–64	63	67	74
65+	19	12	6

Sources: 'Holidays Abroad', *Mintel*, December 1981, p. 29; 'Tourism in Britain', *Mintel*, January 1981, p. 42; 'Tourism in the UK', *Mintel*, June 1978, p. 13

in Mediterranean resorts.[50] Many more relied upon coach travel, with its low prices and its 'convenience of door-to-door travel when touring, overcoming baggage and transfer problems, and courier assistance, especially in overseas travel, where the elderly avoid problems of documentation and language'.[51] In all events, it was found that by the end of the period the small minority of old people holidaying abroad spent 60 per cent more per head than holiday-makers from younger age groups.[52]

It is clear, on the other hand, that young people tended to participate in tourism to a greater extent than those from other age groups. Indeed, their participation is relatively easy to document since adolescent tourism – like almost any form of adolescent consumption – frequently gave rise to public concern and criticism. In fact, it will be apparent by now that the structural changes stimulating teenage tourism were likely to be similar to those encouraging other manifestations of so-called modern youth culture. It was seen in Chapter 1 that adolescent purchasing power began to increase significantly during the final forty years of the period, and it was shown in Chapter 2 that a number of tour companies responded by marketing their products with the teenage, and young adult consumer particularly in mind.

None the less, it is important not to make too much of these changes. For it must be recognised that throughout most of the period covered by this book many teenagers' involvement in tourism was confined to going on day trips and/or joining their families on the annual summer holiday. These, of course, were forms of consumption which generally aroused little anxiety, and about which therefore it is difficult to comment with a great deal of confidence.

It is clear, however, that day trips were of considerable importance to young people. Indeed, for many years most working-class teenagers (and children) probably relied primarily upon the excursions organised on a non-commercial basis by clubs, schools, churches and chapels. For instance, as early as 1842 an excursion train twenty-seven coaches long took more than 2,300 Sunday school pupils and teachers on a trip from Preston to Fleetwood.[53] By the turn of the century such excursions had secured a well-established place in the working-class calender. 'Sometimes we had a Sunday School treat', remembers a Bristol man, 'and were taken by tram for a day in the country – the country being one of the suburbs of Bristol, such as Ashton. And on one glorious occasion we went by horse char-a-banc to Weston-super-mare.'[54] At the same time, it became increasingly common for teenagers to go on trips with their families, a development that was encouraged, during the second half of the twentieth century, by the increasing private ownership of the motor car.[55]

However, it was when teenage boys took day trips on their own – or, worse still, with their friends – that serious anxiety was likely to be aroused. It is not difficult to imagine why. Bank holidays were always boisterous times, with the invasions of Brighton, Clacton, Southend and other resorts by 'mods' and 'rockers' during the 1960s provoking particular consternation.[56] Less publicised – but far more typical – were the petty annoyances perpetrated by teenage day trippers at seaside resorts week after week during the summer season. A 17-year-old East London boy describes how one Sunday afternoon in the early 1960s he and three friends decided to drive to Southend.

> We went to the Kursaal and started bilking the dodgem cars. You just
> jump over the fence, you see, and get in the queue; you say you've
> lost your ticket and get away with it . . . . Then we went in the bar
> and had a few drinks . . . . Then we went on the beach and Charlie
> shouted out there was a lot of bottles down there. We filled them
> with water and started throwing them about; they smashed against
> the stones . . . . Then Alan stood on the end of this pier and started
> swinging round a big tin can on a string, he was going to throw it out
> to sea, he misjudged it, instead of throwing it upwards he let go too
> late and it went straight over his shoulder, just missed this old lady.
> So we ran and jumped in the van and drove away.[57]

Moreover, by the 1960s many young people were also able to enjoy extended holidays away from their families. Indeed, the teenage holiday had a longer history than might be imagined. For it is clear that during the late nineteenth and early-to-mid-twentieth centuries large numbers of working-class and lower-middle-class teenagers attended the summer camps run by schools, churches and uniformed youth organisations. Indeed, although it is not easy to know what drew recruits to groups such as the Boys' Brigade, the Church Lads' Brigade and the Boy Scouts, it may well be that 'sport, the band and the annual camp were the activities that most attracted members and that drilling and military manoeuvres were usually regarded as tiresome concessions to authority, to be avoided wherever possible'.[58]

It also became increasingly common for young people to go on holiday with their families. It was seen earlier in the chapter that in late-nineteenth-century Lancashire, families, friends and workmates often went away together to the seaside. In fact, family holidays remained common even amidst the burgeoning, and supposedly revolutionary, youth culture of the 1960s. An 18-year-old motor mechanic from Bethnal Green explained that,

> When we go on holiday we go to a holiday camp on Canvey Island –
> my brothers, their wives, Mum and Dad, my Uncle Joe and his wife,
> Aunt Flo, and her husband who live in Hackney Road, Aunt Joan
> who lives in Cambridge Heath Road, and Aunt Margaret from
> Bishop's Way. There are only twenty-two of us this year. We're going
> to Dymchurch near Folkestone. We're going in a big Dormobile and
> we'll have four chalets and a caravan.[59]

Nor was it always easy for teenagers to break away. A Lancashire man recalls that when in 1960 he and three fellow apprentices booked to go on holiday to the Butlin's holiday camp at Pwllheli, his parents arranged – without his knowledge – to take their holiday at the same camp, at the same time. However the boys' opportunities were not curtailed completely: 'it was a big place and the lads and all the teenagers were altogether and all the families'.[60] Indeed, two recent historians of the British holiday camp report that

> many veteran campers have told us that the attraction of holiday camps for them, when they were in their teens, was precisely that, in their first holiday away from the family, parents would tolerate their going away with a group of other girls or other boys to one of the well known camps, in a way that they would never countenance for an individual. Once there they were there, of course, in and out of each other's chalets, and it was a function of the Chalet Patrols, not merely to listen for crying babies, but to ensure that the right people of the right sex were sleeping in the right places.[61]

It was also in the 1960s that teenagers, like tourists generally, began to travel abroad in significant numbers. Many young people went with their parents, of course, but others set off with their friends: they looked for – and the tour companies sought to provide – a heady combination of sunshine, alcohol and entertainment. When the marketing organisation Mintel interviewed a representative sample of 1,015 people in 1981, it inquired about the factors that they took into consideration when choosing a holiday abroad. It found, not surprisingly, that those aged between 15 and 19 placed heavy emphasis upon climate and nightlife – and virtually none upon museums and art galleries.[62] None the less, it is important not to exaggerate the extent to which young people travelled abroad with their friends. For Table 4.4 suggests that whatever financial and other advantages those aged between 16 and 24 enjoyed by the end of the period, they were no more likely than those of their parents' generation to take a holiday abroad.

However, it is really no easier to generalise about adult than about teenage tourism. Certainly, it would be a mistake to try to conflate the experiences of men and women: for whereas teenage girls probably profited as much as teenage boys from the changes that took place in this form of consumption, there seems little doubt that as they grew older women tended to gain less from these changes than men in similar social and economic circumstances. So although women of all classes benefited from the long-term trend towards more frequent, more extended and more comfortable holidays, they benefited little – if at all – from the more recent trend towards staying in self-catering, rather than serviced, accommodation.

It seems incontrovertible that as the period progressed both women and men began to share in, and contribute to, the expansion of British tourism. For day trips and holidays were essentially family activities: husbands and wives went on honeymoon together, they took their children out on day trips and, when they could afford it, they went away with their families for summer holidays at the seaside. In fact, it is striking that when detailed statistics of holiday travel first became available in the late 1940s, they revealed that women were more, rather than less, likely than men to take holidays away from home.[63]

However, the fact that women played their part in the expansion of tourism, and that tourism was fundamentally a family activity, does not mean of course that men's and women's experiences were therefore the same. There were three major differences. One was that women were far less likely than men to travel alone. For despite the attention that has been paid to the exploits of a handful of pioneering, lone lady travellers, it is important to appreciate that the overwhelming majority of women did not – and do not – travel independently. In fact, it is only very recently indeed that the travel industry has made any attempt at all to cater for the particular needs of women travelling on their own.[64]

A second difference between men's and women's experience of tourism was that wives seem to have had less say than their husbands in the selection and purchase of the family holiday. This is at once significant and somewhat surprising. It is significant in that women and men did not necessarily look for the same things in choosing a holiday. When Mintel carried out its 1981 survey into overseas travel, it discovered that male and female priorities differed in two important respects, with women setting particular store by the quality of hotel accommodation and the type of provision that was made for their children.[65] The fact that wives had less chance than their husbands to put their preferences into practice is also somewhat surprising since, as will be recalled from the previous chapter, women were apparently becoming increasingly influential in the purchase of 'gender-free' products such as holidays. The evidence with regard to tourism is, it must be admitted, fragmentary and difficult to interpret. However, although there is little firm evidence from the late nineteenth and early twentieth centuries, it does not seem unreasonable to suppose that women increased their influence over holiday selection as the period progressed. If this was so, it makes it all the more surprising to discover that even in the 1980s women seemed to exercise the power of veto, rather than the power of initiative, when it came to choosing the annual family holiday.[66]

The third difference between men's and women's experience of tourism was that women benefited a good deal more than other family members when it was decided to stay in serviced accommodation. The degree of benefit depended largely upon the social class of the family. For while being looked after in a hotel or boarding house probably meant relatively little to upper and middle-class women accustomed to relying upon domestic help, it meant an enormous amount to working-class and lower-middle-class women who were used to coping without any kind of domestic assistance. So too did staying at a holiday camp. A typical comment was this from the wife of a clerk in a dry-cleaning establishment, who worked in a biscuit factory herself:

> I like holiday camps. It is like having a second honeymoon. Arthur and I went to a little place in Wales when we were married. This is the only time I am with him for everything. This morning we had breakfast together – I have never had bacon and eggs with him in the whole year. We have such different hours: I just barely see him before tea, and then I usually have the children to look after.[67]

Such views lead inescapably to the final distinction between men's and women's experience of tourism. For if women benefited more than men from staying in serviced accommodation, they gained far less from the trend towards self-catering and other forms of independent holidaying. There could be advantages of course. For looking after oneself did not preclude the possibility of eating out, or bringing home fish and chips and Chinese take-aways. Moreover, looking after oneself meant avoiding much of the embarrassment caused by badly behaved children, and by not knowing quite how to behave in restaurants and hotels – establishments that one critic remembers bitterly as 'theatres of humiliation'.[68] For most women, however, the advantages of self-catering holidays were far outweighed by their disadvantages. For of course, the flexibility and informality of self-catering was achieved, in nearly every case, at the expense of the wife and mother who, if she was not very careful, merely exchanged one kitchen sink for another.[69]

Naturally these changes in women's – and adolescents' – experience of tourism did not occur at the same time, in the same way, among all sections of the community. For it has been seen already that the growth of tourism depended, still more than that of shopping, upon the growing purchasing power of consumers with both money and time to spare. Thus as the period progressed, the travel and holidays that had once been the prerogative of the wealthy and leisured began to be enjoyed, at least in attenuated form, by the middle class, and eventually by many members of the working class.

For several centuries prior to the period covered by this book the aristocracy alone was able to travel on anything approaching a national or international scale. Thus it was that throughout the seventeenth and eighteenth centuries young aristocrats set off on the 'grand tour' of European cities, settling down later to an annual round that included visits to their country estates, trips to spa and seaside resorts such as Bath, Harrogate and Brighton, and of course a stay in London for the duration of the 'season'.[70] However, these upper-class peregrinations were undermined, first by the Revolutionary and Napoleonic Wars of the late eighteenth and early nineteenth centuries, and then by the long-term erosion of aristocratic economic and social power that was discussed in the opening chapter of the book.[71] Those aristocrats still able to behave in 'aristocratic' ways responded, as might be expected, by ensuring that they maintained their physical and social distance from the remainder of the population. They went to weekend house parties, they took to skiing and climbing in the Alps, and they retired to the French Riviera in their old age. 'Resorts such as Blackpool and Margate were not for them; it was Deauville or Nice or some other five-star resort.'[72]

The middle class took over, and adapted, the travel and holidays that had been enjoyed by the aristocracy. Indeed it has been pointed out that 'During the nineteenth century . . . the revolution in transport – the introduction of the railway – and the emergence of a middle-class with time and money to spare for recreation, led to the growth of the modern holiday industry.'[73] Certainly the middle class made a major, and continuing, contribution to the growth of modern tourism: they took day trips, spent holidays at the seaside, went on package tours, and turned, both at home and abroad, to the flexibility of self-catering.

The association between the middle class and the day trip – like that between the day trip and the holiday industry – is not always fully appreciated. For in so far as the day trip has received any attention at all, it has tended to be regarded as a truncated, and therefore typically working-class, type of tourism.[74] In fact, it was a type of tourism which, like the summer holiday, was pioneered in its modern form by the Victorian middle class. Singly, as families, and sometimes in larger groups, they visited shops, theatres, beauty spots, historic sites and seaside resorts.[75] It was a type of tourism which retained, and with the coming of the motor car almost certainly increased, its popularity and importance during the course of the twentieth century. Singly, as families, and occasionally in larger groups, the middle class continued to visit shops, theatres, beauty spots, historic sites and seaside resorts – and began to visit new attractions such as cinemas, dance halls, shopping centres, theme parks and industrial museums.[76]

Nevertheless, it is easy to see why the middle class tends to be associated more closely with trips involving a stay away from home. In fact, middle-class adoption of aristocratic holiday habits can be discerned even before the end of the eighteenth century, as sons of the gentry began to go on the grand tour, and wealthy merchants and professionals started to spend time in the spa towns.[77] Middle-class adoption of aristocratic habits can be seen more clearly still in the early years of the nineteenth century as coastal resorts around the country began to cater for 'farmers, clergy, professional men, manufacturers, urban shopkeepers and tradesmen'.[78] Indeed, the resorts, with their promenades, assembly rooms and libraries, and rounds of concerts, balls and lectures, were modelled both physically and socially upon the longer-established and socially superior spa towns.[79] The atmosphere of these coastal resorts has been captured beautifully by F. M. L. Thompson.

> The mid-Victorian seaside resorts which grew and proliferated mainly in response to middle-class demand were, therefore, solid and sober places, comfortable but decorous and highly respectable. It was a time of propriety, of strictly segregated bathing, of bathing machines and the freezing out of bathing in the nude . . . . There were promenades for exercise, convenient for the massed Sunday church parades that were a feature of all the better-class resorts as a means of publicly establishing respectability, there were public gardens for botanical instruction, and there were piers, also for exercise and possibly with some seemly middle-brow music at the end. There were little boat-trips to explore the natural history and geology of the area, and immense quantities of shells, rock specimens, and fossils were shipped back from the Victorian seashore as witness to holiday educational achievements.[80]

However, the association between the middle class and seaside self-improvement was by no means immutable. For example, it is not usually realised that it was the lower middle class who were the first, and most loyal, patrons of the seaside holiday camps that opened between the two world wars. For as the proprietors of the camps reported in 1938, 'their visitors were not drawn from the factory floor but consisted mainly of the smaller salaried people, the black-coated worker and his family'.[81] Nor is it always recognised that for most of the period package tour operators drew their clients almost exclusively from the ranks of the comfortably-off middle class. Indeed it could scarcely be otherwise: for the trips organised by entrepreneurs such as Thomas Cook (from the 1850s) and Sir Henry Lunn (from the 1880s) were costly, time-consuming and, no doubt, socially intimidating.[82] Thomas Cook was the market leader. In the early 1870s, the cost of sending two people on the firm's six-week tour of France, Switzerland and the Rhine was £85, a sum that was equivalent to 'three to four months' salary of a senior clerk at the height of his career.[83] By the mid-1930s, Cooks was advertising a fifteen-day tour of Germany with the claim that, at £23, the trip was £8 cheaper than it would be if made independently. Yet, no matter how good the value, £23 was a sum of money that it would take a 'typical' working person practically two and a half months to earn.[84] So it was that for many years package tours remained, as they had begun, 'middle-class affairs with middle-class fares'.[86]

The middle class were also to the fore in independent travel and self-catering. For example, they were among the first to take to the countryside. Thus it has been pointed out that 'Although the bicycle brought the possibility of cheap personal mobility by the Edwardian period, clubs organizing cycling trips or country rambles were suburban and predominantly middle class.'[86] There is certainly some evidence that during the first half of the twentieth century climbing, rambling and youth hostelling proved particularly popular with lawyers, lecturers, teachers and other professional groups.[87] The middle class were also the first to travel abroad on their own. There is clear evidence that during the second half of the century tourists from both professional and non-professional backgrounds were becoming more confident and more adventurous: they took their cars abroad, they booked their own flights and accommodation, they went camping and caravanning, they rented French *gîtes* and villas in Tuscany, and some of the better off – and/or more gullible – bought villas and time-shares in the hope of maximising their independence and flexibility.[88]

This middle-class propensity for travelling and tourism may be seen in the data collected by the British Home Tourism Survey and other investigations carried out in the mid-1970s. It is clear from these data, some of which are summarised in Table 4.5, that the middle class were considerably more likely than the working class to go away on holiday, and a great deal more likely to take a holiday abroad. It is clear too that middle-class tourists had their own priorities when deciding where to go on holiday. In Britain, for example,

the proportions choosing coastal or inland locations vary between different social classes: whereas 78 per cent of the manual workers show a preference for the sea, only 69 per cent of the professional and upper-middle-class choose the coast; by contrast 21 per cent of

TABLE 4.5   Social class and holidays, United Kingdom, 1976

Social class*	% of adult population	% of holidays in Britain (4+ nights)	% of holidays abroad (1+ night)
AB	16	20	33
C1	21	23	31
C2	35	35	24
DE	28	23	12

* AB Professional and managerial groups
  C1 Skilled working class
  C2 Unskilled working class
  DE Poor and elderly

Sources: 'Tourism in the UK', *Mintel*, June 1978, p. 13

the latter but a mere 8 per cent of the former participate in country holidays where mountains and moorlands, lakes and stream are the attraction.[89]

There can be no doubt, then, that middle-class tourism has been transformed during the past two hundred years – and particularly during the past fifty or sixty years. However, it is a transformation that it is not always easy for the commentator to bring to life. So when, just after the end of our period, Frank Barrett attempted to describe the growth of tourism and what he saw as the shrinking of the planet, he drew upon the experiences of his own, obviously middle-class family:

> My grandfather's annual holiday never took him more than an hour's
> train ride from his house. My parents ventured further, but only
> as far as France. This year my annual holidays were spent on the
> Great Barrier Reef in Australia, for barely more than the price of an
> expensive package to Majorca.[90]

There can be no doubt either that working-class tourism has been transformed during the century or so that is covered by this book. For just as the middle class took over many leisure activities from the aristocracy, so in their turn the working class adopted – and adapted – many of the travel and holiday pursuits that were enjoyed by the middle class. In fact, by the end of the period working-class tourists were taking holidays which, at the beginning of the period, had been the sole, and unquestioned, prerogative of the wealthy and privileged.

Of course, not all working people made such advances. For as has been seen already it was the day trip, rather than the extended holiday, which often tends to be associated with working-class tourism. Nor is this surprising. For as the least costly and least time-consuming of all forms of travel, the day (or part-day) trip long remained the only type of tourism in which many working people were able to participate.[91]

For many years a substantial proportion of working-class day trips were organised on a highly visible, collective and/or communal basis. Excursions were run at one time or another – in one place or another – by employers, publicans, youth groups, religious bodies, friendly societies and, it seems, virtually every other type of organisation involved with the working class.[92] Indeed, it was as secretary of the South Midland Temperance Association that Thomas Cook organised his first excursion, a trip in 1841 for 570 people to travel the few miles from Leicester to Loughborough and back again.[93] In Lancashire, it was the mill-owners who took the lead. In mid-nineteenth-century Preston, for example, Horrockses and Miller sent 1,500 workers to Blackpool in 1850, Swainson and Birley 1,700 to Liverpool in 1851, and Horrockses 4,000 to Liverpool in 1860.

> The hands of the great firms would assemble at the mills in the early
> morning, and, accompanied by brass bands and bearing firm banners

aloft, march in procession through the town. They often called at the residences of the employers, serenading them (at 4.30 a.m.) with the old favourite, 'A Fine Old English Gentleman'.[94]

In other parts of the country, it was those running schools and Sunday schools that seemed to take the initiative. In early-twentieth-century Bristol, recalls one woman, her day school ran trips to Winscombe camp, while her Sunday school organised trips to Weston-super-Mare.[95] Certainly it is the communal outing – in a charabanc – that many people still seem to associate with the working-class day trip. 'For the day-trip by "chara" has been particularly taken up by working-class people,' explains Richard Hoggart.

> Every day in summer the arterial roads out of the big towns are thick with them [buses] humming towards the sea, often filled, since this is a pleasure which particularly appeals to mothers who want a short break and lots of company, with middle-aged women, dressed in their best, out on a pub, club, or street excursion . . . .
>
> If the men are there, and certainly if it is a men's outing, there will probably be several stops and a crate or two of beer for drinking on the move. Somewhere in the middle of the moors the men's parties all tumble out, with much horseplay and noisy jokes about bladder-capacity. The driver knows exactly what is expected of him as he steers his warm, fuggy, and singing community back to the town; for his part he gets a very large tip, collected during the run through the last few miles of town streets.[96]

Whatever the financial, psychological or status attractions of trips organised on a collective and/or communal basis, working people also liked to go away on their own, with their families, and with small groups of friends. The difficulty, of course, is that such outings left little evidence, and so have made little impression either upon the popular memory or upon the academic study of tourism. It is clear, however, that working people – still more perhaps than the middle class – made visits to every conceivable type of destination, by almost every conceivable type of transport. They visited friends, members of their families, fairs, markets, shops, historic sites, seaside resorts, political meetings and sporting events. They travelled on foot and, as time went by, by bicycle, train, tram, coach, motor cycle and motor car.[97] Even the most modest trip sometimes assumed a major importance in the life of the individual.

> My mother died in 1929 at Christmas and at August there was a trip and that was the first time she'd been out of Barrow. It was a railway trip and only about five shillings. I think she told everybody that she was going to Blackpool . . . . Honestly if we'd been in Fairyland she couldn't have enjoyed it better.[98]

Of course, working-class tourism was never confined to the day trip. Indeed, as working people grew more prosperous and began to benefit from the introduction of paid holidays, more and more families were able to afford to stay away from home. They followed the middle class, albeit with a time lag of some years, in visiting relatives, going to the seaside, staying in holiday camps, taking package tours, and travelling independently.

They followed the middle class to the seaside. It will be recalled from earlier in the chapter that the 1870s saw the growth of working-class seaside holidays in Lancashire (and to a lesser extent Yorkshire), a generation or more before they became common in other parts of the country. Of course, these new holiday-makers were not always welcome. For as John Walton reminds us, 'the mainstream holiday market of the early 'seventies was composed of decorous seekers after health, rest and quiet' who did not necessarily take easily to an influx of working people who 'positively enjoyed noise and bustle, and . . . drew in their wake the street vendors and fairground attractions of their home towns, filling the central streets and beach with disreputable hubbub'.[99] Some resorts fought tenacious rearguard actions: in towns like Eastbourne and Folkestone middle-class interests were entrenched so deeply 'that the great unwashed were successfully excluded by the simple expedient of refusing to permit any of the attractions demanded by trippers'.[100] On the other hand, resorts such as Blackpool, Southend, Margate, Skegness and Great Yarmouth gave themselves over almost completely to the new working-class holiday-maker. In Blackpool, for instance, 'the promenade south of Central Station was gradually engulfed by the rising tide of cheerful and uninhibited textile workers, engineers and miners'.[101] The growth of the working-class seaside holiday continued apace during the first half of the twentieth century; it will be recalled from earlier in the chapter that by the late 1930s working-class visitors to seaside resorts tended to stay, not for a day or two, but for a week or two.

> By the mid 1930s the summer movement of people to the coast had reached epic proportions. Blackpool attracted 7 million between June and September; Rhyl 2½ million; Redcar 2 million . . . . A town-planner of the period labelled the process: 'that demo-cratisation of the coast which set in with the coming of the railway'.[102]

Working people also followed the middle class to the holiday camps that opened for business between the two world wars. However, they did not follow them all that closely, for, as was seen above, it was the lower middle class, rather than the working class, who were for several years the most loyal patrons of the camps. In fact, it was not until the mid-1950s that working people began to visit the camps in sufficient numbers to be able to make them their own. But then they did so with some success. In 1973 Pradeep Bandyopadhyay felt able to report that 'the holiday camp by and large is avoided by middle-class holidaymakers'.[103] Twenty years later, Paul Theroux asked a Redcoat at the Minehead Butlin's what sorts of jobs the visitors had:

> 'Are you joking, sunshine?' he said.
> I said no, I wasn't.
> He said, 'Half the men here are unemployed. That's the beauty of Butlin's - you can pay for it with your dole money.'[104]

The working class also followed the middle class – albeit much more slowly – in taking package holidays abroad. For it was seen earlier in the chapter that during most of the period covered by this book package-tour operators drew their clients almost exclusively from the ranks of the comfortably off middle class. It was not until the 1960s, when tour operators first tried to tap the mass market, that working people began to benefit from the convenience and relatively low cost of group travel to Continental Europe. For example, betweeen 1950 and 1972 the cost of a fortnight's holiday in a southern Italian resort such as Amalfi or Salerno declined by more than 10 per cent, from £80 to £70.[105] Thus it is both surprising and unfortunate that few systematic efforts seem to have been made to discover the class background of package-tour holiday-makers. None the less, there can be no doubt that during the 1960s and 1970s increasing, and significant, numbers of working people began to take package holidays abroad. Steelworker Patrick McGeown was one early convert.

> By 1952 my wages averaged £18 weekly and I was still fit to earn them and to spend them too. Each year my wife said, 'You promised to take us to Rome' . . . . But every time she would say, 'We can't afford it, we will go next year.'
> It was 1957 before we saw Rome, and a few other famous places in Italy as well . . . .
> The tour was strenuous, possibly these affairs mostly are, and I suppose the comfort increases as the price increases. Ours was moderately priced and we had no grumbles, even if we did arrive late at our hotels with time only for a late dinner, and bed, and the prospect of a 6 a.m. rising . . . .
> I have read, and I have heard of conducted tours being condemned by superior persons. At such moments it would have been wasted time trying to convince me.[106]

Working people also followed the lead of the middle class in turning to independent travel and self-catering. Of course, their reasons for doing so were not necessarily the same; in fact, it seems likely that many working-class cyclists, walkers, campers and caravanners were motivated as much by lack of money as they were by more elevated considerations. In all events, the motives of the small minority of working people who took part in such activities during the first half of the twentieth century seem to have been extremely varied. Walter Southgate, who founded the North East London Clarion Cycling Club in 1911, recalls that their outings through the Essex countryside combined fraternity and fresh air with opportunities to meet members of the opposite sex.[107] John Nimlin, who with a group of unemployed friends formed a climbing club in Glasgow in 1930, believed that 'during the slump there were many despairing and disillusioned men who found a new meaning to life in the countryside'.[108]

The motives of the growing minority of working people taking part in such activities during the more prosperous second half of the century seem, paradoxically, to have been more fundamentally economic in origin. For the little evidence that there is suggests that they favoured self-catering, camping and caravanning, not so much for the freedom and flexibility that they offered, as for the economy and value for money that they represented. Camping and caravanning brought holidays within reach of those who otherwise would not have been able to afford them: they allowed poor families to have some sort of holiday away from home; and they enabled the better off to take several holidays a year, to travel further afield, and/or to stay away for longer periods of time.[109]

These were important advances, but they should not be exaggerated. For it was seen at the beginning of the chapter that there was – and still is – a clear correlation between income, social class and tourism, and this meant, of course, that the working class always tended to take fewer, and less expensive, holidays than the middle class. Thus Table 4.5 confirms that even in the mid-1970s, after a century and more of growth and change, working people remained considerably less likely than the middle class to go away on holiday, and a great deal less likely to take a holiday abroad.

These, and the other, developments discussed in this chapter raise issues that are of fundamental importance to the study of modern British history – and make it difficult to understand the lack of serious interest that has been shown in this form of consumption. None the less, it is clear already that the past 150 years have seen a transformation in the British experience of tourism, with major growth in the volume (and value) of tourist activity, and significant changes both in the activities undertaken and in the people able to participate in them. Such a transformation had, of course, many possible ramifications, and these will be considered in appropriate detail, and at appropriate length, in the final four chapters of the book.

NOTES AND REFERENCES

1. For general surveys, see **A. J. Burkart** and **S. Medlik**, *Tourism: Past, Present and Future*, Heinemann, 1987; **J. C. Holloway**, *The Business of Tourism*, Pitman, 1989; and **H. Robinson**, *A Geography of Tourism*, Macdonald & Evans, 1979.
2. Burkart and Medlik, *Tourism*, p. v.
3. Burkart and Medlik, *Tourism*, pp. 82–90.
4. **L. J. Lickorish**, 'UK Tourism Development: A 10–Year Review', *Tourism Management*, p. 275; Holloway, *Business of Tourism*, p. 43. Then too tourism has become associated very closely with other forms of consumption.
5. **P. Bailey**, *Leisure and Class in Victorian England: Rational Recreation and the Contest for Control, 1830–1885*, Methuen, 1978, p. 102.
6. Bailey, *Leisure and Class*, p. 114.
7. Holloway, *Business of Tourism*, p. 26.
8. **A. Mason**, *Association Football and English Society 1863–1915*, Harvester, 1981, p. 141; **J. Stevenson**, *British Society 1914–45*, Penguin, 1984, p. 387.
9. Lickorish, 'Tourism Development', p. 273.
10. Lickorish, 'Tourism Development', p. 273; Robinson, *Geography*, p. 201.
11. Holloway, *Business of Tourism*, p. 48.
12. Holloway, *Business of Tourism*, pp. 16–18.
13. Bailey, *Leisure and Class*, p. 92.
14. **J. Walvin**, *Beside the Seaside*, Allen Lane, 1978, p. 107.
15. **J. K. Walton**, *The Blackpool Landlady: A Social History*, Manchester University Press, 1978, p. 27; also pp. 33–40; **J. K. Walton**, 'The Demand for Working-Class Seaside Holidays in Victorian England', *Economic History Review*, xxxiv, 1981. **J. K. Walton**, *The English Seaside Resort: A Social History 1750–1914*, Leicester University Press, 1983.
16. Walvin, *Seaside*, p. 106. Also **J. K. Walton** and **J. Walvin** (eds), *Leisure in Britain 1780–1939*, Manchester University Press, 1983.
17. **J. A. R. Pimlott**, *The Englishman's Holiday: A Social History*, Harvester, 1977, p. 10.
18. Bailey, *Leisure and Class*, p. 72.
19. Walton, *Blackpool Landlady*, pp. 39–40.
20. **P. Bandyopadhyay**, 'The Holiday Camp', in **M. A. Smith**, **S. Parker** and **C. S. Smith** (eds), *Leisure and Society in Britain*, Allen Lane, 1973, p. 252.
21. Walvin, *Seaside*, p. 96.
22. Bandyopadhyay, 'Holiday Camp', p. 249.
23. Burkart and Medlik, *Tourism*, p. 15; Holloway, *Business of Tourism*, p. 102. See especially **P. Brendon**, *Thomas Cook: 150 Years of Popular Tourism*, Secker and Warburg, 1991.
24. **E. Royle**, *Modern Britain: A Social History 1750–1985*, Arnold, 1987, p. 266. The number of holidays of 4 nights or more taken abroad increased from 1.5 million in 1951 to 10.25 million in 1979.

25. *Guardian*, 27 December 1990.
26. Burkart and Medlik, *Tourism*, p. 32. Even when tourists did not travel and/or stay together, they did tend to holiday during the same brief period of the year. As late as the 1950s and beyond, more than 90 per cent of main holidays in Britain were taken between June and September, with well over 60 per cent crowded into the two months of July and August. See Robinson, *Geography*, pp. 230–2.
27. Burkart and Medlik, *Tourism*, p. 28.
28. Holloway, *Business of Tourism*, p. 91.
29. **P. Lavery**, *Travel and Tourism*, Elm Publications, 1987, p. 66. Also Holloway, *Business of Tourism*, p. 49.
30. **C. Ward** and **D. Hardy**, *Goodnight Campers! The History of the British Holiday Camp*, Mansell, 1986, p. 151.
31. Robinson, *Geography*, p. 234; Holloway, *Business of Tourism*, pp. 31, 98; 'Caravans', *Mintel*, January 1982, p. 26.
32. See Table 4.1; Burkart and Medlik, *Tourism*, p. 86.
33. Holloway, *Business of Tourism*, pp. 45–6.
34. Holloway, *Business of Tourism*, p. 46; Burkart and Medlik, *Tourism*, p. 169.
35. Cited Robinson, *Geography*, p. 202.
36. Brendon, *Thomas Cook*, pp. 57–63; **A. Briggs**, *Victorian People: A Reassessment of Persons and Themes 1851–67*, Penguin, 1965, ch. 2.
37. Mason, *Association Football*, pp. 146–7.
38. Walton, 'Demand', p. 251; Walvin, *Seaside*, pp. 36–9.
39. J. A. Patmore cited Robinson, *Geography*, p. 202.
40. Lancaster, Mrs R3P, p. 49.
41. Author's recollection.
42. Robinson, *Geography*, p. 224.
43. Robinson, *Geography*, p. 224; Burkart and Medlik, *Tourism*, p. 225. Lickorish, 'UK Tourism', pp. 272–3. Also Lancaster, Mr R1P, p. 33.
44. Lancaster, Mrs H5L, p. 83; also Mrs B2B, p. 46.
45. Robinson, *Geography*, pp. 274–5, 304, 318.
46. Robinson, *Geography*, p. 25.
47. Lickorish, 'UK Tourism', p. 272.
48. **M. Abrams**, 'Some Background Facts', *Journal of the Market Research Society*, **251**, 1983, p. 222.
49. 'Holidays Abroad', *Mintel*, December 1981, p. 29.
50. Lickorish, 'UK Tourism', p. 275.
51. Holloway, *Business of Tourism*, p. 89.
52. Abrams, 'Background Facts', p. 215.
53. Walvin, *Seaside*, p. 37. Also p. 97.
54. Bristol, 515276, J. Morkunas to S. Humphries, 19 September 1979; also E. T. Rich to S. Humphries, 30 September 1979; R04, p. 17; Merthyr, *Pioneer*, 20 August 1921; **C. Chinn**, *They Worked All Their Lives: Women of the Urban Poor in England, 1880–1939*, Manchester University Press, 1988, p. 41.
55. Lancaster, Mr R1P, p. 57; **P. Willmott**, *Adolescent Boys of East London*, Penguin, 1966, p. 24.
56. Willmott, *Adolescent Boys*, p. 23; **E. Hopkins**, *The Rise and Decline*

of the English Working Classes 1918–1990*, Weidenfeld & Nicolson, 1991, p. 173.

57. Willmott, *Adolescent Boys*, p. 154.
58. **S. Humphries**, *Hooligans or Rebels? An Oral History of Working-Class Childhood 1889–1939*, Blackwell, 1981, p. 134. Also **B. H. Reed**, *Eighty Thousand Adolescents: A Study of Young People in the City of Birmingham by the Staff and Students of Westhill Training College for the Edward Cadbury Charitable Trust*, Allen & Unwin, 1950, pp. 85, 91; Bristol, R04, p. 17; Lancaster, Mrs R3P, p. 81.
59. Willmott, *Adolescent Boys*, p. 70. Also **C. S. Smith**, 'Adolescence', in Smith, et al., *Leisure and Society*, p. 155.
60. Lancaster, Mr R1P, p. 32.
61. Ward and Hardy, *Goodnight Campers!*, p. 101.
62. 'Holidays Abroad', *Mintel*, pp. 29–30.
63. **A. H. Halsey**, (ed.), *Trends in British Society since 1900: A Guide to the Changing Social Structure of Britain*, Macmillan, 1972, pp. 548–9.
64. See, e.g., **J. Robinson**, *Wayward Women: A Guide to Women Travellers*, Oxford University Press, 1990.
65. 'Holidays Abroad', *Mintel*, p. 30.
66. **R. Scott**, *The Female Consumer*, Associated Business Programmes, 1976, pp. 120, 136; **R. Bartos**, *Marketing to Women: A Global Perspective*, Heinemann, 1989, p. 228.
67. Bandyopadhyay, 'Holiday Camp', p. 249.
68. Alan Bennett, cited in *Observer*, 6 October 1991.
69. Bandyopadhyay, 'Holiday Camp', p. 248.
70. **F. M. L. Thompson**, *English Landed Society in the Nineteenth Century*, Routledge & Kegan Paul, 1963, pp. 81, 104; Holloway, *Business of Tourism*, p. 24; Walton, *Landlady*, p. 14; **J. Black**, *The British Abroad: The Grand Tour in the Eighteenth Century*, Alan Sutton, 1992.
71. Thompson, *English Landed Society*, pp. 339–40.
72. Robinson, *Geography*, p. 31. Also Royle, *Modern Britain*, pp. 261–2; **M. Blume**, *Côte d'Azur: Inventing the French Riviera*, Thames & Hudson, 1992.
73. Robinson, *Geography*, p. xxvii.
74. Walvin, *Seaside*, p. 75.
75. E.g., **D. V. Jones**, *Memories of a Twenties Child*, Westwood Press Publications, 1981, p. 22.
76. Lancaster, Mr R1P, p. 59.
77. Holloway, *Business of Tourism*, p. 24.
78. Walton, *Landlady*, p. 14.
79. Robinson, *Geography*, pp. 10–11.
80. **F. M. L. Thompson**, *The Rise of Respectable Society: A Social History of Victorian Britain, 1830–1900*, Fontana, 1988, p. 290.
81. Ward and Hardy, *Goodnight Campers!*, p. 43; also pp. 42–7, 52–3; Royle, *Modern Britain*, p. 265.
82. Holloway, *Business of Tourism*, p. 27; Burkart and Medlik, *Tourism*, pp. 15–17; Stevenson, *British Society*, p. 394.
83. Thompson, *Respectable Society*, pp. 262–3.
84. *Express and Star*, 24 May 1935; *Daily Mail*, 17–18 January 1930;

J. **Benson**, *The Working Class in Britain, 1850–1939*, Longman, 1989, p. 53.

85. Thompson, *Respectable Society*, p. 262.
86. **R. Holt**, *Sport and the British: A Modern History*, Oxford University Press, 1990, p. 195.
87. Holt, *Sport*, pp. 195, 200. **I. Brown**, *The Heart of England*, Batsford, 1935, p. 81; Lancaster, Mr C8P, p. 18.
88. See, e.g., advertisements such as 'Dieppe for Whitsun', *Times*, 3 June 1930.
89. Robinson, *Geography*, pp. 226–7. Also 'Holidays Abroad', pp. 29–30.
90. **F. Barrett**, 'The Reluctant Tourist', *Independent*, 1 June 1991. Also *NOP Political Bulletin*, July 1972, p. 22.
91. **S. R. Davey**, *Recollections*, Sheffield Women's Printing Co-op, n.d., p. 45; Lancaster, Mrs H5L, p. 3.
92. Royle, *Modern Britain*, p. 264; **R. J. Waller**, *The Dukeries Transformed: The Social and Political Development of a Twentieth-Century Coalfield*, Oxford University Press, 1983, pp. 198–9.
93. Brendon, *Thomas Cook*, ch. 1; Holloway, *Business of Tourism*, p. 26.
94. **P. Joyce**, *Work, Society and Politics: The Culture of the Factory in Later Victorian England*, Methuen, 1982, p. 186.
95. Bristol, R04, p. 17. Also E. T. Rich to S. Humphries, 30 September 1979; 515276, J. Morkunas to S. Humphries, 19 September 1979.
96. **R. Hoggart**, *The Uses of Literacy: Aspects of Working-Class Life with Special Reference to Publications and Entertainments*, Penguin, 1958, pp. 146, 148.
97. E.g., Thompson, *Respectable Society*, pp. 284–6, 299–300; Walton, *Landlady*, p. 109; **J. R. Gillis**, *For Better, For Worse: British Marriages, 1600 to the Present*, Oxford University Press, 1985, pp. 296, 311; Lancaster, Mrs R3P, p. 49; Mr S9P, pp. 35–6.
98. **E. A. M. Roberts**, *Working Class Barrow and Lancaster 1890 to 1930*, University of Lancaster, 1976, p. 61.
99. Walton, *Landlady*, p. 138.
100. Thompson, *Respectable Society*, p. 291; also p. 292.
101. Walton, *Landlady*, p. 140. See **G. Cross** (ed.), *Worktowners at Blackpool: Mass-Observation and Popular Leisure in the 1930s*, Routledge, 1990.
102. Walvin, *Seaside*, p. 124. Also Robinson, *Geography*, p. 226.
103. Bandyopadhyay, 'Holiday Camp', p. 241.
104. Cited Ward and Hardy, *Goodnight Campers!*, p. 110.
105. Robinson, *Geography*, p. 27. Many working-class men probably first went abroad while on national service.
106. **P. McGeown**, *Heat the Furnace Seven Times More*, Hutchinson, 1968, pp. 173, 176–8. Also Hopkins, *Rise and Decline*, p. 182; Lancaster, Mrs P5B, p. 35.
107. Ward and Hardy, *Goodnight Campers!*, p. 15.
108. Cited Holt, *Sport*, p. 200.
109. Walvin, *Seaside*, pp. 146–7; Lancaster, Mrs C8P, p. 54; Mrs R3P, p. 84.

Chapter 5
SPORT

The history of sport has received considerably more attention than the history of tourism. Yet historians of sport, like historians of tourism, have tended to approach their subject in a somewhat partial fashion. For they too find it difficult to define the object of their study; they tend to pay greater attention to the working class than to the middle and upper classes; and they display surprisingly little interest in the relationship between the history of sport and the history of consumption.[1]

Accordingly it is the purpose of this chapter to consider the crucial – albeit still overlooked – relationship between sport and consumption. This will be done by considering the ways in which people's interest in sport influenced their behaviour as consumers: as players buying clothing, equipment and instructional material; as spectators paying for travel, refreshment and admission to events; as enthusiasts purchasing books, magazines and newspapers; and as gamblers visiting bookmakers and betting shops, and having a weekly flutter on the football pools.

This chapter, like the others in this part of the book, is divided into two. The first, briefer, section considers the major changes that have taken place nationally in the consumption of sporting goods and services; the second, considerably longer, section examines the differing experiences of those living in particular parts of the country, and of elderly, adolescent, female, and aristocratic, middle-class and working-class consumers. It will be argued that there have been three major developments: a major increase, and reorientation, in the amount spent playing sport; and substantial increases in the amounts spent watching, and gambling on sporting events.

However, once again such claims are easier to make than they are to substantiate satisfactorily. For it is much more difficult to define sport than it is tourism or shopping. Many scholars have attempted to differentiate sport from games, leisure and recreation. John Bale, for example, seeks to confine his discussion of sport

110

to 'institutionalised contests involving the use of vigorous physical exertion, between human beings or teams of human beings'.[2] Such a definition, he explains,

> allows us to consider sport at different levels of commitment, from professional to recreational, but excludes *(a)* the so-called 'field sports' in which the physical prowess is more or less restricted to the animal; *(b)* activities like bowls which is barely physical and chess which is almost wholly cerebral (despite being regarded as a sport in the Soviet Union); *(c)* mountaineering which may be physical but in which the competition is rather against the environment than other human beings; and *(d)* swimming with one's family on Sunday morning or on a summer holiday, or jogging around the block, neither of which can be regarded as competition – the essence of modern mass and top-level sport.[3]

Yet such exclusions appear unduly restrictive. For a definition of sport that excludes everything from field sports to bowls, mountaineering, jogging and recreational swimming seems likely to impede, rather than facilitate, a study of the relationship between sport and consumption. Thus the definition of sport adopted in this chapter is considerably wider than that proposed by John Bale. It follows Tony Mason in describing sport more loosely – but it is believed more helpfully – as 'a more or less physical, strenuous, competitive, recreational activity. It will usually, but not always, be in the open air and might involve team against team, athlete against athlete, or the clock.'[4] It is a definition that encompasses not just field sports, mountaineering, jogging and swimming, but individual sports like golf, squash and athletics and team games such as cricket, Rugby and soccer.

Armed with this definition, it is possible to attempt to determine the major changes that have taken place in consumer spending on sporting goods and services. It is clear, of course, that there has been a major increase in participant expenditure on sport. Unfortunately the scale of the increase cannot be measured with any precision. For it is impossible to identify and isolate – let alone quantify – the amount of money that sportsmen and women spent on the myriad of goods and services available to them. There were clothing, equipment, rule books and instructional material to buy; club membership and match fees to find; specialist coaching to hire; and travel and refreshments to pay for.[5] Thus it must be emphasised that the estimates of participant expenditure that are presented in Table 5.1 rest upon somewhat insubstantial foundations. The figures for 1914 need to be approached with particular caution: they have been calculated by multiplying recent estimates of participation in four major sports (golf, tennis, soccer and angling) by contemporary estimates of direct expenditure per participant, and multiplying the product by four (on the basis that in 1979 these four sports

TABLE 5.1   Participant expenditure on sport, United Kingdom, 1914–79/81

Year	Total		Per head of population*		Per participant	
	£ million (at current prices)	*In real terms (1914= 100)*	*£ (at current prices)*	*In real terms (1914= 100)*	*£ (at current prices)*	*In real terms (1914= 100)*
1914	13.2	100	0.3	100	4.3	100
1979/81	990.0	374	18.0	281	35.0	41

* Population: Great Britain

Sources: 'Sports Clothing and Footwear', *Retail Business*, January 1983, pp. 17, 19; Table 5.2

accounted for just over a quarter of participant expenditure on sporting goods and equipment).

Provided that the basis of the 1914 figures is borne in mind, Table 5.1 provides a useful – and original – guide to the major changes that have taken place in participant expenditure on sport. It shows that there has been an enormous growth in consumer spending (at least when measured at constant prices). It suggests that between 1914 and 1979/81 aggregate expenditure increased seventy-five times; expenditure per head of population increased fifty-six times; and expenditure per participant increased eight times. However, it goes without saying that such figures need to be adjusted in order to take account of changes in the cost of living. When this is done, it can be seen that the rates of growth were far less dramatic than they appear at first sight. It seems that between 1914 and 1979/81 real aggregate expenditure increased just three and three-quarter times; real expenditure per head of population increased barely two and three-quarter times; whilst real expenditure per participant declined by more than a half. (Indeed it transpires that at the end of the period the 'typical' Briton was spending just £18 a year on playing sport – compared, it will be recalled, to nearly £90 on taking holidays, and more than £1,300 on doing the shopping.)

The decline in real expenditure per participant is particularly difficult to explain. For as Table 5.2 shows, the years since the First World War have seen the reorientation, as well as the growth, of participant expenditure. Since this reorientation involved a rise both in the popularity of expensive sports (such as golf and tennis) and in the cost of fundamentally inexpensive sports (such as athletics, angling and soccer), it would lead, one might suppose, to the growth, rather than the decline, of real expenditure per participant. How then is the decline to be explained? The key to the paradox lies, it seems, in

TABLE 5.2   Participant expenditure (at current prices) on golf, tennis, soccer and angling, United Kingdom, 1914–79/81

Year	Golf		Tennis		Soccer		Angling	
	£ mill	£ per part- icipant	£ mill	£ per part- icipant	£ mill	£ per part- icipant	£ mill	£ per part- icipant
1914	1	15	1	10	0.4	1	1	5
1979/81	127	127	45	60	46	29	44	11

Sources: **R. Holt**, *Sport and the British: A Modern History*, Oxford University Press, 1989, p. 126; **J. Lowerson**, 'Angling' in **T. Mason** (ed.), *Sport in Britain: A Social History*, Cambridge University Press, 1989, pp. 20–1; **J. Lowerson**, 'Golf', in Mason (ed.), *Sport*, pp. 188–9; **T. Mason**, *Association Football and English Society 1863–1915*, Harvester, 1980, pp. 32, 89; **T. Mason**, 'Football', in Mason (ed.), *Sport*, p. 150; 'Sports Clothing and Footwear', *Retail Business*, January 1983, p. 19; **H. Walker**, 'Lawn Tennis', in Mason (ed.), *Sport*, pp. 249, 256–7.

a combination of statistical bias and historical misunderstanding: the undue emphasis that Table 5.1 gives to early twentieth-century golf and tennis; and the fact that in these early years of the century the relatively small number of upper- and middle-class enthusiasts playing sport spent a good deal more money than is generally appreciated. It was calculated in 1899, for instance, that the average club golfer spent some £25 a year on his (or her) hobby – a sum that it would have taken even a well established male clerk nearly three months to earn.[6]

Whatever the merits of such an explanation – and whatever the demerits of Tables 5.1 and 5.2 – it is clear that the past hundred years or so have seen a substantial increase in participant expenditure on sport. It is an increase that underlines the importance of the relationship between sport and consumption – and undermines, in its turn, the common contention that the British have become a nation of spectators.[7]

This is not to deny that the past hundred years have also seen a substantial increase in the amount of money spent on watching sport. However, once again the scale of the increase cannot be gauged with any accuracy, for it is impossible to identify, and quantify, the many goods and services on which the paying public chose to spend its money. There was the admission charge to find; a programme, travel and refreshments to pay for; as well sometimes as a badge, scarf, rosette or rattle to buy. Indeed it must be emphasised that the figures for spectator spending presented in Table 5.3 rest, still more than those for participant spending in Tables 5.1 and 5.2, upon strikingly insecure foundations. They have been calculated

TABLE 5.3 Spectator expenditure on sport, England and Wales, *c.* 1895–1980

Year	Total		Per head of population		Per spectator	
	£ mill (at current prices)	In real terms (1914= 100)	£ (at current prices)	In real terms (1914= 100)	£ (at current prices)	In real terms (1914= 100)
1895	1.96	100	0.06	100	0.31	100
1950	9.04	150	0.21	114	0.10	11
1980	99.04	201	1.98	131	2.0	35

Sources: **J. Bale**, *Sport and Place: A Geography of Sport in England, Scotland and Wales*, Hurst, 1982, p. 76; **A. H. Halsey**, *Trends in British Society since 1900: A Guide to the Changing Social Structure of Britain*, Macmillan, 1972, p. 561; **E. Hopkins**, *The Rise and Decline of the English Working Classes 1918–1990: A Social History*, Weidenfeld & Nicolson, 1991, p. 262; **T. Mason**, *Association Football and English Society 1863–1915*, Harvester, 1980, pp. 143, 150; **T. Mason**, 'Football', in **T. Mason** (ed.), *Sport in Britain: A Social History*, Cambridge University Press, 1989, pp. 152, 165; **K. A. P. Sandiford**, 'English Cricket Crowds during the Victorian Age', *Journal of Sport History*, **9**, 1982, pp. 16–17; **J. Williams**, 'Cricket', in Mason (ed.), *Sport*, p. 121; information from Robin Phillips.

by multiplying the (reasonably reliable) estimates of attendances at two major spectator sports (cricket and football) by the (rather less reliable) estimates of average admission charges to these sports, and multiplying the product by two (on the basis that in 1982 these two sports accounted for just over 50 per cent of attendances at the country's major sporting events).[8] Thus it must be borne constantly in mind that because Table 5.3 considers only one element of spectator expenditure, it underestimates, much more than Tables 5.1 and 5.2, the importance of the relationship between sport and consumption in modern British society.

None the less, the evidence brought together in Table 5.3 makes it possible to discern the most significant changes that have taken place in spectator spending. It shows quite clearly that there has been a major growth in expenditure (when measured at constant prices): between 1895 and 1980 aggregate expenditure increased fifty times; expenditure per head of population increased thirty-three times; and expenditure per spectator increased six-and-a-half times. Once again, of course, these figures need to be adjusted in order to take account of increases in the cost of living. Once again, the revised figures reveal rates of growth far less dramatic than they appear at first sight: they show that between 1895 and 1980 real aggregate expenditure doubled; real expenditure per head of population increased by just 30 per cent; while real expenditure per spectator declined by approximately two-thirds.

The decline in real expenditure per spectator, like that in real expenditure per participant, seems rather difficult to explain. However, on this occasion too the decline is probably exaggerated by the way in which the statistics have been compiled. Because Table 5.3 is based solely upon changes in attendances/admission charges at cricket and soccer, it does not reflect either the (probably more rapidly) rising cost of admission to sports such as golf, tennis and motor racing or the (certainly more rapidly) rising cost of travelling to and from fixtures as spectator sports of all kinds became organised on a regional, national and international basis.[9]

Notwithstanding such statistical limitations, the evidence presented in Table 5.3 remains of considerable interest. It underlines yet again the importance of the relationship between sport and consumption, and it appears to undermine almost completely the belief that the British have become a nation of spectators. For it suggests that at the end of the period the typical Briton was spending £2 a year to watch sport – as opposed to £18 a year to play it.

However, the belief that the British have become passive, rather than active, consumers of sport receives powerful reinforcement when attention is directed towards spending on other sports-related goods and services. For sport has been used to sell an enormously wide variety of products. Those interested in sport could buy specialised books, magazines and periodicals, and purchase toys, models and pictures of their heroes and (occasionally) heroines. They could select their newspaper reading, radio listening and television viewing on the basis of their sports coverage, and gamble, of course, on the results of horse races, football matches and most other sporting events. Those interested in sport were also able to purchase any number of goods and services which, although having no immediate sporting connection, were endorsed – and supposedly used – by leading sports personalities.

The list of products that sport has been used to sell seems to extend almost endlessly, and to embrace virtually every sector of the modern British economy. However, there is space here to consider just two of the many forms of consumption to which these products have given rise: reading and gambling. It must be recognised, therefore, that the discussion which follows considers some, but by no means all, consumer expenditure on sports-related goods and services.

Sport has been used for well over a hundred years to sell books, magazines, periodicals and newspapers.[10] Of course, it is impossible to calculate in any precise way the extent to which sports coverage determined the public's choice of daily and Sunday papers, and thus the proportion of spending on newspapers that should be considered in a study of the relationship between sport and consumption.

However, it is easy to show (as in Table 5.4) that the newspaper-buying public spent large, and growing, sums of money on newspapers that devoted large, and sometimes growing, amounts of space to the coverage of sport. Sport, it has been pointed out, 'remains a predictable and considerable part of most national and local newspapers.'[11] It is also easy to show that the British public spent large, and growing, sums of money on newspapers that specialised exclusively in sport. Football always seems to have dominated, with the Saturday evening sports editions ('The Pink', 'The Buff' and so on) assuming a secure, almost cherished, role in the provincial working-class weekend; they became, so it has been claimed, 'as much a part of the cultural scene as the gas lamp and the fish and chip shop.'[12] Indeed, as one young clerical worker pointed out just after the Second World War, 'There are plenty of self-classed sportsmen whose sole sport is buying the evening papers to read the result.'[13]

However, spending on newspapers – and other sports-related products – pales almost into insignificance when set alongside the British public's apparently insatiable appetite for gambling on the results of sporting events. This, of course, is a peculiarly complex subject with which to deal. It is difficult to distinguish between gambling on sporting and non-sporting events. It is difficult to decide whether it is more useful to measure gambling by gross cost/turnover (the amount of money staked) or by net cost (the amount of money staked less any winnings). It is difficult, above all, to assess the true extent of an activity which has been criticised, marginalised and deemed, in many forms, to be illegal.[14] Yet it remains a fundamental paradox of gambling history that such disapproval, illegality and elusiveness seem to have encouraged, rather than deterred, scholarly (and other) attempts at quantification.

TABLE 5.4   Newspaper circulation/coverage of sport, 1937/39–1968/75

Year	Times		Daily Mail		Daily Mirror	
	Circ'n (mill)	% of news space devoted to sport	Circ'n (mill)	% of news space devoted to sport	Circ'n (mill)	% of news space devoted to sport
1937/39	0.21	21	1.51	36	1.37	36
1947/51	0.25	16	2.25	33	4.57	24
1968/75	0.40	14	2.10	34	5.03	53

Sources: **D. Butler** and **J. Freeman**, *British Political Facts 1900–1968*, Macmillan, 1969, p. 284; **J. Tunstall**, *The Media in Britain*, Constable, 1983, p. 124.

TABLE 5.5 Turnover of gambling on sport, Great Britain, 1914–77

Year	Total		Per head of population	
	£ mill (at current prices	In real terms (1914= 100)	£ (at current prices)	In real terms (1914= 100)
1914	100	100	2.5	100
1931	350	309	7.8	275
1977	4,090	205	75.3	151

Sources: 'Gambling', *Mintel*, November 1978, p. 47; **R. McKibbin**, 'Working-Class Gambling in Britain 1880–1939', *Past and Present*, **82**, 1979, p. 152; **J. Stevenson**, *British Society 1914–45*, Penguin 1984, p. 384.

The figures presented in Table 5.5 have been compiled by taking the most reliable – or it might be truer to say, the least unreliable – estimates of gambling turnover, and reducing them by a third (on the basis that in 1978 betting on horse-racing, dog-racing and football matches accounted for 63 per cent of recorded turnover).[15] Whatever their limitations, the resulting figures are of considerable value in seeking to understand the complex relationship between sport and consumption. They show quite clearly how turnover has grown. They suggest that between 1914 and 1978 the amount of money (at current prices) spent gambling on sporting events increased forty times, with spending per head increasing thirty times. They suggest too that the amount of money (in real terms) spent gambling on sport slightly more than doubled, with real spending per head increasing by almost exactly 50 per cent. Nor is this all. For the figures presented in Table 5.5 can also be used to compare gambling with the other forms of sporting consumption that have been considered in this chapter. When this is done, it emerges conclusively that the amount of money spent gambling on sport has always been many times larger than the amount spent playing it and watching it. This means that at the end of the period, for example, the 'typical' Briton was spending £75 a year gambling on sport – compared, it will be recalled, to £18 a year playing it, and £2 a year watching it. Gambling constitutes 'an enormous market', concluded a marketing survey of 1978, and 'should continue to be a major element in the leisure society of the 1980s.'[16]

It is clear then that in Britain, and no doubt elsewhere, the history of sport and the history of consumption have become intimately entwined. For as entrepreneurs in all sectors of the economy came to recognise, people's interest in sport could be, and often was, an important determinant of their behaviour as consumers.

Naturally, different consumers responded in different ways. Accordingly, the remainder of this chapter is devoted to a more detailed consideration of the behaviour of identifiable, albeit often overlapping, groups of consumers: those living in particular parts of the country; the young and the old; women; and members of the upper, middle and working classes.

It will probably come as little surprise to learn that those living in different parts of the country tended to behave rather differently in their consumption of sporting goods and services. Thus it is fortunate that there have been more – and more interesting – studies than might be expected into the historical geography of sport.[17] In fact, by using these studies, together with those produced in recent years by marketing groups such as Mintel, it can be shown quite clearly that the money that consumers spent playing, watching and gambling on sport needs to be – and can be – disaggregated and examined both locally and regionally.

It is not always appreciated, for example, that participant spending on sport, like spending on shopping and tourism, tended to be concentrated in the South and South-east of England. That such geographical concentration should sometimes go unremarked is not, in fact, all that surprising since several very well known sports had their heartlands in Wales and Scotland.

The Welsh were more likely to play Rugby union – and presumably to spend money doing so – than those living in other parts of Great Britain. Thus it has been discovered that already in the 1890s the South Wales valleys were criss-crossed with dense networks of local clubs: Pontypool and district, for instance, had the Ironsides, the United Friends, Tranch Rovers, Ponymoil Wanderers, Talywain Red Stars and many more besides.[18] The Principality remained a hotbed of club Rugby: it was found, for example, that in the early 1980s Dyfed and Gwent boasted one club per 4,000–4,500 people, compared to fewer than one club per 26,000 of the British population as a whole.[19] So it appears to be more than mere hyperbole to suggest that in Wales, or at least in South Wales, the game of Rugby union became 'the one great pastime of the people'.[20]

The Scots were more likely to play golf – and to spend money doing so – than either the Welsh or the English. Indeed it has been pointed out more generally that the pattern of golf club/golf course location represents 'a classic example of a mis-match between population and provision. Most facilities are found where fewest people live.'[21] Certainly, Scotland has always been very well provided for. It was reported in 1982, for instance, that 'In Scotland today there are about 400 golf courses and 630 clubs for a population of under 5.5 million while in England the respective figures are just over 1,000 and 1,300 for a population of about 46 million.'[22] It follows, not very surprisingly, that the Scots were also more likely than the Welsh or the English to spend money on golfing equipment. When *Mintel* interviewed a group of just over 1,000 people in 1981, it discovered that whereas 21 per cent of the Scottish sample owned golf clubs (and 5 per cent had bought some in the previous year), only 8 per cent of those living in England owned clubs (and only 2 per cent had bought some during the preceding year).[23]

None the less, it remains true that those from the South and South-east of England were generally more likely than those living elsewhere to spend money playing sport.[24] It is well known, at least among historians of leisure, that major sports like cricket can trace their roots to Southern England; that innovations such as synthetic athletics tracks, and public squash courts and skating rinks had their origins in the capital; and that sports such as soccer, squash and tennis remained particularly popular in the South of the country.

Squash, tennis and other racket sports have always been played most – and involved most expenditure – in the urban and suburban areas of Central and South-east England. Indeed, for many years the West End of London contained the heaviest concentration of squash-playing facilities in the country: in the late 1930s and early-mid 1940s districts such as Knightsbridge and Piccadilly contained more than 20 per cent of all the courts in the country. In fact, even when the game's popularity grew so rapidly during the 1960s and 1970s, the major centres of English squash-playing remained concentrated in Kent, Surrey and Greater London.[25] Tennis, too, remained primarily a Southern English game. In 1979/81 London and the South-east of England contained 22 per cent of all the regular tennis players in Britain, compared to just 6 per cent in Scotland and 3 per cent in Wales; in London and the South of England a third of individuals and/or households possessed a tennis racket, compared to no more than a quarter in Great Britain as a whole.[26] Thus squash, tennis and other racket sports became concentrated in South-central England, and became identified with what John Bale describes as 'part of a life-style which defines a kind of outer-metropolitan popular culture.'[27]

In much the same way, cricket began, and has remained, a sport that (with the striking exception of Yorkshire) is played most often in the Southern counties of England. It has been calculated, for example, that both in the early nineteenth century and in the late twentieth century the four South-eastern counties of Kent, Essex, Surrey and Sussex each contained more than the average number of cricket clubs per head of population.[28] It was found in 1981 that those living in London and the South of England were twice as likely as the Scots – and more likely even than those from Yorkshire and the North-east – to have bought, or have been given, a cricket bat of their own.[29]

It is not nearly so usual to associate soccer with the South of

England. For it is Scotland, Merseyside, Tyneside and Wearside that we tend to think of as the hotbeds of the national game. But this is to confuse watching with playing. What evidence there is suggests very strongly that soccer has been played more in the South than in the North – and more, it should be added, in rural and suburban areas than in large urban centres. The best evidence comes from the very end of the period. It was found in 1982 that over a quarter of all football clubs in England and Wales were clustered in Greater London and the Home Counties. It was discovered, more surprisingly still, that the highest proportions of males (aged between 11 and 40) playing football were to be found in the South rather than the North of the country.

> Figures for London (13.4 per cent) and the south-east (11.1 per cent) contrast with those of places like Tyne and Wear (6.1 per cent), Durham (8.4 per cent) and Lancashire (6.2 per cent). Such seedbeds of modern professional football are more like rural Devon (6.7 per cent) in terms of the percentages of the male population who actually play the game.[30]

It seems to be more generally understood that expenditure on watching sport has tended to be concentrated, along with professionalism, in Scotland, the Midlands and especially the North of England. Of course, London, the Home Counties and South Wales offered attractions of their own. For many years Crystal Palace and Wembley Stadium played host to important – and expensive – athletic meetings, soccer internationals, FA cup finals, and the finals even of such an archetypally 'Northern' game as Rugby league.[31] Horseracing, too, was concentrated in the South-east of England, with courses such as Ascot, Epsom, Newbury and Goodwood forming a ring to the south of the capital.[32] Thus at the end of the period the South-east of England accounted for 22 per cent of all race meetings, 23 per cent of all days' racing, and practically 50 per cent of the most important races.[33] Rugby union never became a major spectator sport, being regarded by both administrators and enthusiasts alike as a game to be played rather than watched. However, this was not quite so true in Wales where the strength of the club system meant, for instance, that 'nearly 13 per cent of the adult population paid to watch rugby in 1974, compared with the national figures of 2.8 per cent.'[34]

None the less, it was in Scotland, the Midlands and the North of England that those interested in sport were most likely to pay to watch. It was only in Scotland that it was possible to watch minority sports like curling, skiing or, of course, the highland games.[35] It was really only in the North of England that it was possible to watch games like crown green bowling or (with the exception of cup finals) Rugby league. The latter was one of the most regionally concentrated of all British sports, its professional clubs clustered in West Yorkshire and Greater Manchester, with outposts in Cumbria, Cheshire and Merseyside. The attempts that were made to transplant the game to other parts of the country ended invariably, and apparently inevitably, in failure and retrenchment.[36]

It was in the North of England that professional soccer first took root. The Football League was made up originally of twelve Northern (and Midland clubs); for many years its headquarters was in Preston 'and even at the end of the period it had only moved as far south as Lytham St Annes.'[37] It was in the North of England, the Midlands and Scotland that matches attracted the largest crowds. All but one of the 10,000 plus crowds identified for the years 1875–79 were in Glasgow; and most of the clubs capable of drawing large attendances at the end of the nineteenth century were to be found in Manchester, Liverpool, Newcastle, Sheffield, Glasgow and Birmingham.[38] Little has changed. For as was seen above, it is areas such as Scotland, Merseyside, Tyneside and Wearside that we continue to associate with professional football. Indeed, it has been found even in the past twenty years that both the proportion of the adult population attending matches and the proportion of consumer spending on entertainment that is devoted to watching soccer tends to decline as one moves from the North to the South of the country.[39]

It is a great deal more difficult to disaggregate gambling on a national and/or regional basis. None the less, it does appear that gambling on sport – like watching sport (and like many other forms of gambling) – has been most common in Scotland and the North of England. This regionalisation of gambling was encouraged, though not of course determined, by the regionalisation of spectatorship. For in many sports it was possible, and usual, to place a bet without going anywhere near the event upon which the wager depended. Horse racing was a case in point. So although off-course cash betting was illegal between 1853 and 1961, it was legislation which proved, in the words of John Stevenson, 'more remarkable for its breach than its observance'.[40] With racing becoming 'the sport of punters who rarely saw a race', betting could, and did, take place anywhere in the country.[41] However, it took place more often in the North than in the South. For example, when *Mintel* carried out a detailed investigation into gambling at the end of the period, it discovered that the proportion of the population betting on horse-racing was some 15 per cent higher in Scotland, Yorkshire and the North-east of England than it was in Great Britain as a whole.[42]

Football was another sport on which it was possible, and usual, to bet without witnessing the events upon which the wager depended. None the less, the football pools too appear to have been most popular in the North of the country. 'The idea of asking interested parties to forecast the results of several given matches for a small stake and in the hope of winning a big prize seems to have originated within the sporting press' published, and circulating, in the Midlands and North-west of England.[43] It was particularly in these parts of the country, suggests the qualitative and quantitative evidence alike, that large numbers of people continued to bet (small amounts of money) on the football pools. The Pilgrim Trust reported in 1938 that

> The extent to which the interests and indeed the whole lives of so many of the Liverpool unemployed centre round the pools must be seen to be believed. The queues at Post Offices filling in coupons, the number of 'guaranteed systems' for correct forecast on sale in Liverpool's poorest districts, the periodicals containing nothing but pool analyses, the dirty and torn sports columns of the papers in Public Libraries, with the rest of the paper untouched (apart from advertisements of vacant jobs), are some measure of the strength of the interest.[44]

Fifty years later *Mintel* interviewed 1,000 adults 'in order to monitor the level of consumer gambling activity' in the late 1970s. It discovered that those living in the North of England were 10 per cent more likely, and those living in the South of England 10 per cent less likely, than the average Briton to gamble on the football pools: 'the pull of the more old-fashioned activities, such as football pools . . . seems to get weaker as one moves southwards.'[45]

It is clear then that sport, like tourism and shopping, possesses a geography as well as a history. It is a geography that, once again, has important implications for the study of consumption; for it helps to reveal, and explain, the ways in which those living in different parts of the country differed in their consumption of the many sporting goods and services that were available to them.

Age exercised a more obvious – and more profound – impact than geography upon the consumption of sporting goods and services. However, in the absence of detailed scholarly studies, it can be tempting to oversimplify the relationship between age and consumption. It seems plausible to suggest that the younger the consumer, the more he (and sometimes she) was likely to spend on playing and watching, and that the older the consumer, the more he (and sometimes she) was likely to spend on reading and gambling. In fact, the relationship between age and consumption is not quite so straightforward. For although young people certainly played and watched a good deal more sport than their elders, they did not necessarily spend a great deal more money in doing so.

The relationship between age and consumption is straightforward in so far as the physical demands of sports such as athletics, boxing, football, rowing, Rugby and tennis tended to confine participation to the young and the active. Mass-Observation found in 1948 that 'Active participation in sport is roughly twice as common amongst people between 16 and 24 as among people in the 25 to 44 age group.'[46] *Mintel* found in the mid 1970s that participation in athletics, Rugby and football peaked between the ages of 15 and 24 (with 8 per cent of the age group taking part in athletics, 9 per cent playing Rugby and 19 per cent playing football). It was discovered, in fact, that in each of these three sports the participation rates of those aged between 15 and 24 equalled, or exceeded, the rates of all other age groups combined.[47]

The relationship between age and consumption is less straightforward in so far as the participation of the young did not necessarily involve them in any direct expenditure. Children of school age were generally able – and required – to join in sports such as athletics, cricket, football, netball, rounders, Rugby or swimming without (them or their parents) having to worry too much about the cost.[48] Young people of all ages proved adept at improvisation. They found places in which to swim, discovered open spaces on which to play their matches, and collected the materials with which to make their bats, balls, stumps and goal posts: 'it was football down the back street with a couple of coats put down as goal posts. Played with any old tennis ball or any ball we could get really'.[49]

In fact, in low-cost sports such as athletics, cricket and football it was possible for young people to progress to a surprisingly high level without incurring any significant outlay. Of course, stories extolling the exploits of young men wearing only plimsolls and ordinary clothes are the stuff of which both boyhood memories and sporting legends seem to be made. Yet such stories are not without a certain foundation in fact. Indeed, as *Mintel* pointed out in the mid 1970s, football remained 'perhaps the best example of a major sport with a relatively limited equipment market . . . . Half the participants in football spend less than £10 per annum which helps explain both its popularity and its relative insignificance in the sports equipment market.'[50]

The relationship between age and consumption is complicated still further by the growing tendency for young people to use sports clothing and footwear for purposes other than those for which they were originally intended. For in recent years it has become common for children and adolescents, whether or not they participated in sport, to wear track suits, tennis shirts, football jerseys and especially running shoes as fashion accessories. 'There is a growing trend for sportswear to be used as leisurewear', concluded *Retail Business* rather wearily in 1983.[51] Indeed, as *Mintel* went on to explain, 'Many millions of people dress at the weekend in sports clothing, even though they have never played a game seriously in their lives.'[52]

These are complex issues with which to deal. They mean that the relationship between age, participation and consumption remains, and is likely to remain, impossible to quantify in any precise fashion;

for while many young sportsmen and women did not purchase specialised sportswear, a growing number of non-participants began to do so towards the end of the period.

The relationship between age, spectatorship and consumption is at once more, and less, difficult to ascertain. It is more difficult in that little is known about the ages of those attending sporting events; it is less difficult in that adult admission charges did not vary according to age – so that it can at least be assumed that there was generally a direct, albeit incomplete, correlation between attendance and consumption.

The ages of those attending sporting events have attracted surprisingly little scholarly (or other) attention. Indeed, even major spectator sports such as cricket, Rugby and racing have received only the most cursory consideration. It was found that in the mid-1960s, for example, 'attendance at boxing and wrestling matches, like that at greyhound and horse racing, tended to be highest amongst single men aged 19 to 22 years'.[53] Fortunately, football is the one sport whose crowds, because of their size and occasional violence, have been considered in a certain amount of detail. Even so, difficulties remain. Tony Mason reports that Victorian and Edwardian observers could not agree which age group was most likely to attend football matches. He turns to the only hard data available, that provided by the Ibrox disaster of 1902 in which some 550 spectators were injured and killed. He comes to the cautious conclusion that 'If the Ibrox figures are an accurate reflection it would suggest that the 16–39 age group usually provided most of the crowd at a football match with a significant minority in their forties.'[54] Richard Holt suggests that the age structure of football crowds changed significantly with the spread of working-class prosperity during the second half of the twentieth century. 'The car might need a running repair; the wife would want a "drive" in the country or, at least, a lift to the shops. Spectator sport could be followed from home on a winter's afternoon and older men increasingly chose to do this.'[55]

It is difficult then to generalise about the ages of sport's paying customers. But what evidence there is suggests that it was generally young (and perhaps single) men between their late 'teens and late thirties who were most likely to watch professional sport, and most likely therefore to spend money on admission, travel and refreshments.

It was this same age group – and not the elderly – who were most likely to spend money betting on sporting events. Unfortunately, evidence about the relationship between age, sport and gambling is patchy in the extreme. Yet once again, what evidence there is suggests that young adults were particularly active. In 1947 Mass-Observation questioned 1,600 people in London, Birmingham, Blaina, Exmoor, Middlesbrough, New Earswick and York about their gambling; it was found that those aged between 25 and 40 were considerably more likely to gamble on dog-racing, horse-racing and the football pools than either the young (those aged between 16 and 25) or the middle-aged and elderly (those aged over 40).[56] Forty years later *Mintel* 'decided to repeat previous research in order to monitor the level of consumer gambling activity'. It found from its questioning of 1,000 adults that 'There is a fairly wide spread of age in gambling, with adults from 20 to 64 indulging quite heavily.' However it discovered that while the football pools now had 'an ageing profile', horse-racing continued to 'appeal quite strongly to younger adults'.[57]

Thus the relationship between age and the consumption of sporting goods and services is by no means as straightforward as it appears at first sight. For, whereas it is true that the young were most likely to spend money playing and watching sport, it is not the case that the elderly were most likely to spend money gambling on sport. In so far as it is possible to generalise, it seems reasonable to conclude that the most active consumers of nearly all types of sporting goods and services were young, male adults in their late teens, twenties and thirties.

It follows, and goes almost without saying, that women have been involved far less than men in the consumption of sporting goods and services. For wherever they lived and whatever their age, women spent far less than men on playing, watching, reading about and gambling on sport. As feminist scholarship, marketing analysis and common-sense observation all make clear, sport in Britain remained, as it always had been, primarily a male – not to say a masculine – preoccupation.

Certainly, women spent a great deal less money than men on playing sport. This was not because they participated in less expensive sports, or spent less on those sports in which they did participate. It was simply that they took part so much less. Indeed, throughout most of the period it was only upper-class and middle-class women who enjoyed the combination of money, time and confidence that was required in order to be able to participate.

Upper-class women often joined enthusiastically in field sports such as beagling, fishing, fox-hunting and stag-hunting.[58] Middle-class women sometimes joined – with more or less enthusiasm – in a much wider range of activities. Many, if not most, well-brought-up schoolgirls learned to play team games like cricket, hockey, lacrosse, netball and rounders.[59] A minority continued to play after leaving school, but it was more usual for those interested in sport to take up pursuits such as golf, swimming, tennis or, in later years, squash and jogging.[60] These, and most other, sports had their adherents – many of whom were skilled, enthusiastic and prepared to spend a good deal of money on their hobby. Yet they never comprised more than a small, albeit growing and sometimes highly visible, minority of those participating in sport.

Golf and tennis were the only two sports to achieve lasting popularity among middle-class women. Neil Tranter has shown, for example, that 'Of the 31 golf clubs known to have existed in central Scotland between 1891 and 1900, at least thirteen contained significant numbers of female members.'[61] John Lowerson has argued more generally that, although 'The initial growth of golf had been powerfully anti-feminine as the game offered men yet another escape from domestic demands . . . women encroached early . . . producing a grudging but very segregated acceptance.'[62] The game remained expensive and socially exclusive. It was found in the mid-1960s, for example, that even in managerial and professional families no more than 5 per cent of women played golf on a regular basis.[63]

Tennis became popular with young middle-class women. For as Richard Holt has pointed out rather mischievously, 'Learning to play tennis well enough to make a pair for mixed doubles became an *art d'agrément*. Gentle athleticism went hand in hand with feminine adornment with the wayward shots of the daughters coming to rest in the flower beds from which mothers and aunts would cut blooms for the house.'[64] It was always a highly sociable game. The number of clubs affiliated to the Lawn Tennis Association grew from some three hundred at the turn of the century, to 1,000 or so in 1914, more than 3,000 in the late 1930s, and getting on for 4,000 in 1960.[65] In Scotland, and presumably elsewhere, the early clubs made determined, and sometimes successful, efforts to recruit women and so maintain a desirable balance between their male and female members.[66]

It was important – and could be expensive – to be turned out correctly. Certainly there was never any shortage of advice on what to wear. Within a few years of the game's introduction in the early 1870s, one ladies' magazine recommended that its readers wear a 'large straw hat of the coal-scuttle type', 'a cream merino bodice with long sleeves edged with embroidery; skirt with deep kilting, over it an old-gold silk blouse-tunic with short wide sleeves and square neck'.[67] As the game developed, tennis-wear became less elaborate, but more specialised: by the 1930s, for instance, provincial department stores were advertising separate outfits to be worn when playing and when travelling to and from matches. Even the so-called 'sexual revolution' of the 1960s did little to change the stores' emphasis upon fashion rather than function: as Wolverhampton's leading department store explained in 1964, its 'Ladies Tennis Wear' was 'pretty enough to make any girl take up the game'.[68]

Yet not very many did so. For while female participation in – and expenditure on – sport has increased over the past hundred years, it has not increased very fast or very far. Just before the end of the period *Mintel* conducted 'consumer research, with a sample of 2,200 adults, into sporting habits and expenditure' across the United Kingdom. It sought first to assess the level of participation in ten major sports: athletics, fishing, golf, riding, badminton, squash, tennis (and cricket, football and Rugby). It found that only 2 per cent of the women in the sample played golf and only 7 per cent played tennis; it transpired, in fact, that after a century and more or rapid, and supposedly deep-seated, economic, social and cultural change, 82 per cent of the women in the sample 'had not taken part in any of the sports in the last year'.[69]

Given such low levels of participation, it is not surprising that women of all classes probably spent as much money watching sport as they did playing it. Yet still they spent far less than men: for not only did they attend fewer matches than their husbands, sons and brothers, but in the early years of the period they sometimes paid far less for doing so.

Unfortunately, women spectators have been still more neglected than women participants, and therefore the discussion which follows should be treated with considerable caution. None the less, it does appear that during the early years of the period women joined sporting crowds more often than is usually acknowledged. It has been claimed that in nineteenth-century Scotland, for instance, women 'figured prominently among the crowds at all the major spectator sports except for soccer and probably quoiting'.[70] Indeed, it has been suggested that 'In view of the often vast size of the crowds they attracted, the other major spectator sports of the age – boat racing, Highland games and amateur athletics gatherings, and horse-racing – must also have drawn substantial numbers of female onlookers.'[71]

South of the border, soccer too attracted considerable numbers of female spectators. Tony Mason reports that until the mid-1880s ladies were often admitted free to games, but that this did not long survive the advent of professionalism: for instance, the privilege was abolished at Preston in 1885 following an Easter Monday game at which some 2,000 ladies were said to have been admitted without paying.[72] Of course, women continued to attend matches, but in modest, and relatively declining, numbers. Thus when their presence was noticed, it tended to be remarked upon in enthusiastic, not to say exaggerated, terms. It was claimed in January 1930, for example, that large numbers of supporters were travelling to London to watch games in the third round of the FA cup: 'many of them being women, who in these days of emancipation, understand and enjoy the great winter game just as much as do their menfolk.'[73] The reality was a good deal more prosaic. In the mid-1960s only 4 per cent of women watched football regularly – and football, along with cricket and swimming, was the most popular of all spectator sports with women.[74] Paying to watch sport of any kind remained, as it always had been, primarily and overwhelmingly, a masculine preoccupation.

Gambling was rather different. For as John Hargreaves has pointed out, although sport generally is 'an area of cultural life which is dominated by the presence of men . . . if more passive forms of involvement, like . . . gambling are taken into account, women come into the picture on a more equal footing with men.'[75] In all events, it seems that women, like men, have always spent much more gambling on sport than playing or watching it. It is sometimes possible to use the evidence of informed contemporaries. Ross McKibbin cites a conversation that took place at the turn of the century between a social investigator and a newspaper-seller from the Manchester working-class district of Ancoats.

'Why do these women show such eagerness to buy the noon edition?'
'Sporting,' said the newsagent.
'How sporting? Do they bet?'
'Good heavens, man, it's all they live for.'
'And all newsagents in the neighbourhood do a good noon-edition trade?'
'Yes,' said the newsagent.[76]

It is also possible to turn to the evidence afforded by the marketing surveys that were carried out towards the very end of the period. Thus in 1978 *Mintel* reported relatively modest levels of female gambling, with 2 per cent of women betting on dog-racing, 12 per cent on horse-racing, and 15 per cent on the football pools.[77]

Moreover, women have always spent less than men. There is disappointingly little evidence from the first half of the period, but it is striking that the surveys carried out by Mass-Observation in 1947 and by *Mintel* in 1982 both produced remarkably similar results. They confirmed that women gambled less often (and less heavily) than men on sporting events: they were about two-thirds as likely to bet on horse-racing, between a half and two-thirds as likely to bet on the football pools, and between two-fifths and two-thirds as likely to bet on dog-racing.[78]

There can be no doubt, then, that there was, once again, a clear correlation between gender and consumption. For whatever the impact of broader economic and social developments, women have always involved themselves far less than men in the consumption of sporting goods and services: they spent a great deal less on playing and watching, and a good deal less on gambling.

There was a correlation too between class and consumption. For as Tony Mason has pointed out, 'Sport cannot escape the economic and social divisions of British society.'[79] So just as the different classes tended to behave differently as shoppers and tourists, so too they tended to behave differently in their consumption of sporting goods and services.

Members of the aristocracy had the time, the money and the inclination to pursue a leisured lifestyle, a way of life that often included a seemingly insatiable interest in expensive, and socially exclusive, forms of sport. Young aristocrats were taught at public school to box and row, and to play team games like Rugby and cricket. The middle-aged turned to 'para-military' pursuits such as hunting, shooting, fishing and archery; to golf; and sometimes to climbing or yachting.[80] The costs could be enormous. For example, at the Longleat estate of the Marquess of Bath, expenditure under the game account alone rose from some £400 in 1810, to over £2,500 in 1856, and £3,000 and more a year throughout the final two decades of the century.[81]

Aristocrats of all ages – and both sexes – enjoyed watching the sports in which they were interested. Indeed, their social season involved watching rowing at Henley, yachting at Cowes, cricket at Lords, and racing at Ascot, Epsom and Goodwood.[82] Moreover, many aristocrats enjoyed gambling on the sports that they played and watched. In fact, some individuals let their enjoyment run away with them completely.

> Thus the fourth and last Marquess of Hastings, the 'King of Punters', who was accustomed to start the day with a breakfast of mackerel bones cooked in gin, went rapidly to his ruin and death following the notorious Derby of 1867, selling his Scottish estates to the Marquess of Bute for £300,000 to pay his creditors.[83]

Naturally, few, if any, members of the middle class were able to pursue their sporting interests with such abandon. But many middle-class men – and a few middle-class women – turned to sport with some alacrity, and thus became major consumers of a wide, and growing, range of sports-related goods and services.

The middle class devoted more of its sports-related expenditure to playing than to watching. A small minority joined in such socially exclusive activities as hunting, shooting and fishing. Although they managed to do so much more cheaply than the aristocracy, they still incurred considerable, and generally increasing, costs. So when it was maintained at the turn of the century that hunting was 'most assuredly' not an expensive sport, it was explained that 'an initial outlay of £140 and an annual expenditure of £80 should cover all the out-of-pocket expenses of any man of moderate weight, well carried to hounds, three days a fortnight.'[84]

The majority of middle-class sportsmen and women turned, of course, to less exclusive, and less expensive, pursuits. They enjoyed, and initially dominated, sports like athletics, cycling and cricket that were to become popular with all classes in society. Cricket was a particular favourite. For example, in 1841 eight middle-class Lancastrians formed a cricket club: 'Sixty-eight of the seventy-one members . . . have been identified, all drawn from non-manual occupations as one might expect of members of a club who often played on a Tuesday, had their own insignia and wore straw hats.'[85] Forty years later cricket in the Stirling area of Scotland displayed a similar, albeit less narrow, social distribution: a third of the players whose occupations can be identified came 'from small business, clerical groups, the liberal professions, and the landed, though . . . the unskilled were under-represented, comprising only 6.8 per cent of the 177 cricketers traced.'[86] This relationship between the middle class and cricket survived only in an attenuated form. *Mintel* found in the late 1970s and early 1980s that, whereas 'In general, participation in sports is biased towards . . . upmarket people . . ., cricket seem[s] to have more evenly based support'.[87] However, it suggested, not very surprisingly, that it was 'upmarket' cricketers who remained the most likely to spend money on their sport: the organisation's survey of over a thousand adults revealed, for instance, that those from middle-class households were more than twice as likely as those from working-class backgrounds to own a cricket bat of their own.[88]

Middle-class sportsmen (and women) also turned to sports like Rugby, tennis, squash and golf that were too expensive, too time-consuming and/or too socially exclusive to become popular with the working class. The class basis of Rugby union is well known. For as Eric Dunning and Kenneth Sheard point out in their study, *Barbarians, Gentlemen and Players*, 'the twentieth-century expansion of Rugby Union appears to have formed part of the long-term trend towards class-exclusiveness in British sport which started in the 1890s when all but a handful of public schools turned from soccer to Rugby Union.'[89]

The class exclusivity of golf was, if anything, even more apparent. For in England and Wales, if not in Scotland, virtually all those who joined golf clubs, and the vast majority of those who played on public courses, came from middle-class backgrounds. Moreover, conspicuous expenditure seems to have been a critical feature of the club game. It was not just that there were membership subscriptions to pay, green fees to meet, and clubs and balls to buy. There were special clothes to purchase, accessories to obtain, match fees to find, perhaps lessons to pay for, and certainly drinks to be bought in the bar when the round itself was finished.[90] Such costs were – and were intended to be – beyond the reach of the majority of the population. It was estimated at the turn of the century that the average club golfer spent just over ten shillings a week on the game – a sum equivalent to almost half the income of a working man in full employment.[91] It was found at the end of the period that although 'the average enthusiast spent less than £10 per year on his sport . . . this still amounts to a very substantial, if fragmented, market': 10 per cent of the players interviewed spent between £50 and £99 a year on the game, with 2 per cent spending between £100 and £499. Golf, it was claimed, 'is the major sport as far as equipment is concerned'.[92]

The middle class devoted much less of its sports-related expenditure to watching. However, once again it is impossible to be precise. For while middle-class enthusiasts attended fewer events than those from other groups, they tended both to patronise highly publicised occasions and to pay more than spectators from the working class. Thus many middle-class enthusiasts liked nothing better than to watch the professional (or quasi-professional) versions of the games that they played themselves. Rugby players headed for Murrayfield and Twickenham, golfers flocked to tournaments like the British Open and the Ryder Cup, while tennis players made their annual pilgrimage to Wimbledon where they struggled for centre-court tickets, and consumed 'prodigious amounts of food and drink'.[93]

Yet cricket it was that acquired the most secure hold over middle-class sports-lovers. There seems little doubt, for example, that 'large cricket audiences in the Victorian age were composed mainly of upper and middle class persons.'[94] Indeed, it has been pointed out that 'Towards the end of the century, the various county committees catered to the Victorian obsession with order and degree by segregating the classes. The modern cricket headquarters included members' pavilions, balconies, grand stands, and open areas – each denoting, through price and usage, a certain social status.'[95] The middle-class love of cricket continued. A Mass-Observation study conducted in 1948 found, for example, that clerical workers were more interested than manual workers in watching the game.[96] A government survey carried out in the mid 1960s concluded that

> Attendance at cricket matches is very much higher amongst the junior non-manual (21 per cent compared with 14 per cent for the whole male sample) . . . . The especial interest in cricket displayed here by the junior non-manual group corresponds with their unusually high rate of regular *active* participation in this game that we remarked on earlier.[97]

None the less, it is not very often appreciated that the middle class, like other classes, devoted most of its sports-related expenditure, not to playing or watching, but to gambling. Of course, respectability, secrecy and shame make middle-class gambling a particularly difficult form of consumption with which to deal. However, what little evidence there is suggests that middle-class gamblers were more likely to bet on horse-racing than other sports, with the possible exception of football. It was reported by Mass-Observation in 1947 that gamblers on horse-racing were to be found disproportionately among supervisory and administrative workers and other members of the middle class.[98] It was reported by *Mintel* in the late 1970s and early 1980s that although 'The AB class have comparatively low levels of participation in all the major types of betting other than playing cards', 14 per cent of AB's – one person in seven – bet regularly on horse-racing.[99]

Thus the correlation between class and consumption becomes increasingly clear. For as players and gamblers, though less as spectators, the middle class became, and remained, major consumers of the growing number of sporting products that were being produced in the modern British economy.

The correlation between class and consumption becomes visible too in the ways in which working people behaved as players, spectators and gamblers. However, once again some caution is necessary. For it is not as easy as it appears to disaggregate, and evaluate, working-class consumption of sports-related goods and services. It is essential to avoid, in particular, the temptation of assuming either that high levels of involvement necessarily generated high levels of consumption, or that high levels of aggregate consumption were associated with – and caused by – high levels of individual consumption. For it was obviously possible for the very size of the working class to translate low levels of individual consumption into high, and economically and socially significant, levels of aggregate consumption.

Such cautions are especially apposite when considering working-class participant consumption. None the less, it would be a mistake to allow such concerns to conceal the leading role that working men (though rarely women) played in many kinds of sport. Working-class men provided the overwhelming majority of participants in sports such as angling, athletics, boxing, cricket, pigeon-racing, Rugby league and soccer.[100] Neil Tranter suggests, for example, that in the late nineteenth and early twentieth centuries, 'Skilled and semi-skilled manual workers supplied nearly a third of all central Scotland's athletes, around a half of all its anglers and cricketers and almost three-quarters of all its footballers and quoiters.'[101] The social and marketing surveys carried out during the second half of the twentieth century suggest that little changed during the following fifty years. Thus it was found in 1969 that in many sports there remained 'a sharp divergence in the socio-economic characteristics of players', with the national sport, soccer, 'being predominantly the game of manual workers'.[102]

However, as has been seen already, many of the sports popular with working people could be, and were, pursued at remarkably little cost. Anglers sometimes made do with little more than a home-made rod and line; footballers often played without proper shirts, shorts, socks or shinpads; whilst cricketers frequently relied upon their clubs to provide them with everything from bat and ball to pads, stumps, sightscreens and scoreboard.[103] Other sports popular with working people seemed to offer manufacturers and retailers still slimmer prospects of stimulating consumer spending. In fact, the compilers of one marketing survey carried out in the midst of the jogging boom of the 1970s decided to exclude athletics 'mainly because of the limited amount of individual consumer expenditure on equipment'.[104]

It is here, of course, that the distinction needs to be drawn between individual and aggregate expenditure. For with a million or more footballers taking to park and playing field every weekend in winter, the football boot market alone was worth £23 million a year at the end of the period.[105] With hundreds of thousands, and later millions, of anglers setting off each Saturday and Sunday 'encumbered with tackle of various kinds', 'Fishing may not be a glamorous sport but it is a good steady market from the manufacturers' point of view.'[106] The cumulative spending of these working-class (and other) sportsmen had its effect: it was estimated that by the mid-1970s, for example, the United Kingdom market for sports equipment (excluding clothing) was worth approximately £120 million a year.[107]

None the less, working people devoted a relatively high proportion of their sports-related expenditure to watching, rather than playing, sport. However, once again, any attempt at statistical precision seems completely unattainable: for although working-class supporters attended in much greater numbers than those from other classes, they tended to pay less when doing so. There were all sorts of ways to cut costs. They walked to the match, stood rather than sat, sat in cheap rather than comfortable seats, did not buy a programme, did without refreshments, and when all else failed made do with watching other supporters on their way to watch. The Pilgrim Trust reported in the 1930s that,

> On a Saturday afternoon, when an important League match is on, the unemployed men in Liverpool turn out and gather along the streets where the crowds go up by foot, tram, bus or motor car to watch it. To watch a match is in itself a second-hand experience and the unemployed man . . . has to make do with this substitute for it.[108]

Of course, supporters in huge numbers did pay to watch the sports they enjoyed. They crammed into pubs and small halls to watch boxing and wrestling.[109] They flocked to local race courses, and later to (even more local) greyhound stadiums. 'Dog-racing had much to offer the working man', explains Wray Vamplew; 'meetings were held in the evenings after his work was over; the tracks were within walking distance or a short bus ride of tens of thousands of people; and the excitement was perhaps more intense than in horse racing as races were held every quarter of an hour or so.'[110]

Yet, just as cricket acquired a secure hold over middle-class enthusiasts, so it was soccer that attracted, and sometimes obsessed, working-class sports-lovers. 'There is no doubt', concludes Tony Mason, 'that by 1915 the majority of the spectators who went to watch professional football matches were working class in origin, occupation and life style.'[111] There is no doubt either that working people continued to make up the great majority of football crowds. For although there is some dispute among sports historians as to whether or not more unskilled workers attended matches between the wars, there is no disagreement as to the fundamentally working-class composition of the crowds. Indeed, whatever the widening of support brought about by England's success in the 1966 World Cup, football crowds ended the century, as they began it, overwhelmingly working-class in occupation and lifestyle.[112] The spending of the crowds was of considerable significance: it was reported that in 1980 English football supporters paid practically £50 million in order to watch league matches alone.[113]

However, it will come as little surprise to learn that the working class, still more than the middle class, devoted most of its sports-related expenditure to gambling. Moreover, as might be expected, the quantity and quality of the evidence relating to this form of consumption varies considerably. It is at its weakest for the beginning of the period when it was undermined by a curious combination of middle-class superiority and working-class respectability and/or defensiveness; it is at its strongest towards the end of the period when leisure industry entrepreneurs sought to understand what they recognised to be a vast, and highly lucrative, market.[114]

At all events, the evidence is quite strong enough to show that working people gambled regularly on the sports that they most enjoyed watching: horse racing, dog racing and football. As Andrew Davies puts it, 'Sport was a major preoccupation in working-class life', and during the first half of the twentieth century, 'popular sports were all closely bound to gambling. From the 1900s, new forms of mass betting, especially the football pools, which developed a national framework in the interwar period, more than compensated for the decline of gambling on cruel sports.'[115] Ross McKibbin believes it safe to suggest that by the late 1930s, 'the majority of the working class bet fairly regularly, perhaps as much on horses as on the pools', and that 'the very poorest bet least and that the skilled working classes bet most'.[116]

Such generalisations seem to apply with as much force to the post-war, as the pre-war, working class. For example, Mass-Observation suggested in the late 1940s that gambling on the dogs and the pools was predominantly a working-class interest, with skilled artisans particularly active.[117] *Mintel* reported in the late 1970s and early 1980s that betting on horse-racing, dog-racing and the football pools remained predominantly working-class activities, though most common now among the skilled and semi-skilled: 'Two thirds of adults gamble at sometime or other during the year . . . . In class terms it is the C1 and C2 groups who have the highest levels.'[118] However, expenditure was modest, with more than three-quarters of all C1 and C2 respondents claiming – or admitting to – spending of less than one pound a week.' The report concluded rather gloomily that,

> Increased wealth is not likely to lead to a proportionate rise in spending on gambling. The socio-economic profile of those who take part in gambling is somewhat down-market, which is not a good indication for long-term prospects. However all this is relative and there is no doubt that the size of the gambling market will 'remain substantial, even though there will not be growth in real terms.[119]

Whatever the long-term prospects, the size of the gambling market confirms, yet again, how strange it is that neither historians of sport nor historians of consumption have displayed any real interest in the relationship between these two important aspects of modern economic and social life. Accordingly, it has been the purpose of this chapter to begin to remedy this deficiency. It has been shown that, although the relationship between sport and consumption is more complicated than it appears at first sight, it is possible to identify certain key ways in which people's interest in sport influenced their behaviour as consumers. It has been shown that as players, as spectators and as gamblers, those interested in sport became active, and often enthusiastic, consumers of the sporting and sports-related goods and services that were made available to them. It is to the implications of these, and other, forms of consumption that attention will be directed in the following, final section of the book.

NOTES AND REFERENCES

1. For valuable general surveys, see **R. Holt**, *Sport and the British: A Modern History*, Oxford University Press, 1989; **T. Mason**, *Sport in Britain*, Faber & Faber, 1988; **T. Mason** (ed.), *Sport in Britain: A Social History*, Cambridge University Press, 1989.
2. **J. Bale**, *Sport and Place: A Geography of Sport in England, Scotland and Wales*, Hurst, 1982, p. 2, italics removed.
3. Bale, *Sport*, p. 2.
4. **T. Mason**, 'Introduction', in Mason (ed.), *Sport*, pp. 4–5. Also Holt, *Sport*, p. 10.
5. Nor can it be assumed that such expenditure was an addition to, rather than a substitute for, expenditure on watching, reading about

and gambling on sport. See **T. Mason**, *Association Football and English Society 1863–1915*, Harvester, 1980, p. 176; **S. G. Jones**, *Sport, Politics and the Working Class: Organised Labour and Sport in Interwar Britain*, Manchester University Press, 1988, pp. 50–52, 141.
6. **W. J. Ford**, 'Cricket', in **F. G. Aflalo** (ed.), *The Cost of Sport*, Murray, 1899, p. 277; **J. Lowerson**, 'Golf', in Mason (ed.), *Sport*, p. 189.
7. E.g., Mass-Observation, 3045, 'A Report on British Sport', 1948, p. 12.
8. **E. Hopkins**, *The Rise and Decline of the English Working Classes 1918–1990: A Social History*, Weidenfeld & Nicolson, 1991, pp. 261–2. Cf. **G. H. Gallup**, *The Gallup International Public Opinion Polls: Great Britain 1937–1975*, Random House, 1976, II, p. 578.
9. **N. Fishwick**, *English Football and Society, 1910–1950*, Manchester University Press, 1989, p. 52.
10. See, for example, 'General and Special Interest Magazines', *Retail Business*, August 1982, pp. 37–8; **S. Shipley**, 'Tom Causer of Bermondsey: A Boxer Hero of the 1890s', *History Workshop*, Spring 1983, pp. 37, 50; **J. Williams**, 'Cricket', in Mason (ed.), *Sport*, p. 123; **M. Clapson**, *A Bit of a Flutter: Popular Gambling and English Society c. 1823–1961*, Manchester University Press, 1992, pp. 34–5, 38–9; **W. Vamplew**, 'Sport and Industrialization: An Economic Interpretation of the Changes in Popular Sport in Nineteenth-Century England', in **J. A. Mangan** (ed.), *Pleasure, Profit, Proselytism: British Culture and Sport at Home and Abroad 1700–1914*, Cass, 1988, pp. 14–15.
11. Mason, 'Introduction', p. 3.
12. Mason, *Football*, p. 193. Also pp. 187–95; **I. Jackson**, *The Provincial Press and the Community*, Manchester University Press, 1971, p. 118; Holt, *Sport*, pp. 306–10; Fishwick, *English Football*, pp. 94–100.
13. Mass-Observation, 3141, 'Report on Sport', 1949, p. 13.
14. 'Gambling', *Mintel*, February 1982, p. 33.
15. 'Gambling', *Mintel*, November 1978, p. 47.
16. 'Gambling', *Minetel*, 1978, p. 53.
17. See especially Bale, *Sport and Place*, and **J. Bale**, *Sports Geography*, Spon, 1989.
18. Holt, *Sport*, p. 153.
19. Bale, *Sport and Place*, p. 63.
20. Cited Holt, *Sport*, p. 250.
21. Bale, *Sport and Place*, p. 130.
22. Bale, *Sport and Place*, p. 128.
23. 'Sports Equipment', *Mintel*, April 1981, pp. 45, 48.
24. E.g., Mass Observation, 3045, p. 8.
25. Bale, *Sport and Place*, pp. 103–5; 'Sports and Games Equipment, Part 2', *Retail Business*, December 1982, p. 22.
26. 'Sports and Games Equipment', p. 21; 'Sports Equipment', *Mintel*, p. 45.
27. Bale, *Sport and Place*, p. 106.
28. Bale, *Sport and Place*, pp. 68–75.
29. 'Sports Equipment', *Mintel*, p. 45.

30. Bale, *Sport and Place*, p. 48; also pp. 45–9.
31. Mason, *Football*, p. 141; **J. Crump**, 'Athletics', in Mason (ed.), *Sport*, pp. 47–8.
32. Bale, *Sport and Place*, p. 144.
33. Bale, *Sport and Place*, pp. 144, 146. For speedway, see pp. 135–7.
34. Bale, *Sport and Place*, p. 67. Also Holt, *Sport*, p. 106.
35. Bale, *Sport and Place*, pp. 159–60. **N. L. Tranter**, 'Sport and the Economy in Nineteenth and Early Twentieth Century Scotland: A Review of Recent Literature', *Scottish Historical Review*, April 1989, p. 61.
36. **E. Dunning** and **K. Sheard**, *Barbarians, Gentlemen and Players: A Sociological Study of the Development of Rugby Football*, Martin Robertson, 1979, p. 228; Bale, *Sport and Place*, p. 59; Holt, *Sport*, p. 189.
37. Mason, 'Football', p. 178.
38. Mason, *Football*, pp. 138–43; Tranter, 'Sport', p. 63.
39. Bale, *Sport and Place*, p. 32.
40. **J. Stevenson**, *British Society 1914–45*, Penguin, 1984, p. 384.
41. Holt, *Sport*, p. 182.
42. 'Gambling', *Mintel*, 1982, p. 43.
43. Mason, *Football*, pp. 181-2.
44. Cited Stevenson, *British Society*, p. 386.
45. 'Gambling', *Mintel*, 1978, pp. 50–51. Cf. 'Gambling', *Mintel*, 1982, p. 43.
46. Mass-Observation, 3045, p. 7.
47. 'Sports Equipment', *Mintel*, p. 55.
48. See, for example, Merthyr, *Pioneer*, 10 September 1921; **S. Garrett**, *All Abroad for Acocks Green: A True Story*, *passim*; **T. D. Golding**, *The Brum We Knew*, p. 22.
49. Lancaster, Mr R3B, p. 18. Also Merthyr, *Pioneer*, 21 May 1921; **N. James**, *A Derbyshire Life*, Postmill Press, 1981, p. 15; Mason, *Football*, p. 82; **C. Forman**, *Industrial Town: Self Portrait of St Helens in the 1920s*, Granada, 1979, p. 192; **P. McGeown**, *Heat the Furnace Seven Times More*, Hutchinson, 1968, p. 29.
50. 'Sports Equipment', *Mintel*, pp. 54–6. Also **D. Scott** and **C. Bent**, *Borrowed Time: A Social History of Running: Salford Harriers 1884–1984*, Salford Harriers, 1984, p. 28; Fishwick, *English Football*, p. 5.
51. 'Sports Clothing and Footwear', *Retail Business*, January 1983, p. 18.
52. 'Sports Equipment', *Mintel*, July 1977, p. 54.
53. **K. K. Sillitoe**, *Planning for Leisure*, HMSO, 1969, p. 130. Also Mass-Observation, 3045, p. 9.
54. Mason, *Football*, p. 158. Also Holt, *Sport*, p. 160.
55. Holt, *Sport*, p. 335. Cf. Sillitoe, *Planning*, pp. 130, 237.
56. Mass-Observation, 2538, 'Preliminary Synopsis of Report on Gambling', 1947, p. 7.
57. 'Gambling', *Mintel*, 1978, pp. 50, 52.
58. **N. L. Tranter**, 'Organized Sport and the Middle-Class Woman in Nineteenth-Century Scotland', *International Journal of Sports History*, **6**, 1989, p. 36.

59. **K. E. McCrone**, *Sport and the Physical Emancipation of English Women 1870–1914*, Routledge, 1988, pp. 59–61.
60. See, e.g., McCrone, *Sport*, pp. 154–91; Holt, *Sport*, pp. 117–34; Mason, *Sport*, pp. 7–13.
61. Tranter, 'Organized Sport', p. 37.
62. Lowerson, 'Golf', pp. 204–5.
63. Sillitoe, *Planning*, pp. 126–7.
64. Holt, *Sport*, p. 126.
65. Holt, *Sport*, p. 126; **A. H. Halsey**, *Trends in British Society since 1900: A Guide to the Changing Social Structure of Britain*, Macmillan, 1972, p. 562.
66. Tranter, 'Organized Sport', p. 38.
67. Holt, *Sport*, p. 127.
68. *Express and Star*, 13 June 1964; also 9 May 1935.
69. 'Sports Equipment', *Mintel*, p. 55. Also Mass-Observation, 3045, p. 7; 3141, p. 2.
70. Tranter, 'Organized Sport', p. 38.
71. Tranter, 'Organized Sport', p. 39. Also McCrone, *Sport*, p. 153, n. 63; **W. Vamplew**, 'Horse-racing', in Mason (ed.) *Sport*, p. 218.
72. Mason, *Football*, p. 152. Also **K. A. P. Sandiford**, 'English Cricket Crowds in the Victorian Age', *Journal of Sports History*, Winter, 1992, p. 16.
73. *Express and Star*, 11 January 1930. Cf. Mass-Observation, 3045, p. 9; Fishwick, *English Football*, p. 123.
74. Sillitoe, *Planning*, p. 239.
75. **J. Hargreaves**, *Sport, Power and Culture: A Social and Historical Analysis of Popular Sports in Britain*, Polity, 1986, pp. 103–4.
76. **R. McKibbin**, 'Working-class Gambling in Britain 1880–1939', *Past and Present*, **82**, 1979, pp. 166–7. Also Fishwick, *English Football*, p. 123.
77. 'Gambling', *Mintel*, 1978, p. 51.
78. Mass-Observation, 2538, p. 6; 'Gambling', *Mintel*, 1982, p. 42; Clapson, *Flutter*, p. 47.
79. Mason, *Sport*, p. 82. Also pp. 7, 78–81, 83–7.
80. **S. G. Checkland**, *The Rise of Industrial Society in England 1815–1885*, Longman, 1964, p. 97; Vamplew, 'Horse-racing', p. 228; Holt, *Sport*, pp. 25, 54–6.
81. **F. M. L. Thompson**, *English Landed Society in the Nineteenth Century*, Routledge & Kegan Paul, 1963, p. 138. Also pp. 97, 147.
82. Holt, *Sport*, pp. 66, 114–5; Vamplew, 'Horse-racing', p. 218; **W. Vamplew**, 'The Sport of Kings and Commoners: The Commercialization of British Horse racing in the Nineteenth Century', in **R. Cashman** and **M. McKernan** (eds), *Sport in History: The Making of Modern Sporting History*, University of Queensland Press, 1979, p. 318.
83. **D. Cannadine**, 'Aristocratic Indebtedness in the Nineteenth Century: The Case Re-opened', *Economic History Review*, **30**, 1977, p. 629.
84. Aflalo, *Cost of Sport*, p. 150. For shooting, see pp. 1-31; for fishing, pp. 71–86; for climbing, pp. 352–5.
85. Holt, *Sport*, p. 72, drawing upon **M. A. Speak**, 'Social Stratification

and Participation in Sport in Mid-Victorian England with Particular
Reference to Lancaster, 1840–70', in Mangan (ed.), *Pleasure*, p. 50.

86. Holt, *Sport*, p. 154.
87. 'Sports Equipment', *Mintel*, 1977, pp. 51–7.
88. 'Sports Equipment', *Mintel*, 1981, pp. 45–53.
89. Dunning and Sheard, *Barbarians*, p. 235.
90. Lowerson, 'Golf', pp. 194–5, 198, 200–1, 210–11; **I. Brown**, *The Heart of England*, Batsford, 1935, pp. 70–71.
91. Aflalo, *Cost of Sport*, p. 289; **J. Benson**, *The Working Class in Britain, 1850–1939*, Longman, 1989, p. 53.
92. 'Sports Equipment', *Mintel*, 1977, p. 52; also pp. 56–7.
93. Walker, 'Lawn Tennis', in Mason (ed.), *Sport*, p. 265. Also Lowerson, 'Golf', pp. 210–12; **G. Williams**, 'Rugby Union', in Mason (ed.), *Sport*, pp. 325–6.
94. Sandiford, 'Cricket Crowds', pp. 18–19.
95. Sandiford, 'Cricket Crowds', p. 17.
96. Mass-Observation, 3045, p. 10.
97. Sillitoe, *Planning*, p. 131.
98. Mass-Observation, 2538, p. 7. See Clapson, *Flutter*, pp. 60–1.
99. 'Gambling', *Mintel*, 1982, p. 43.
100. See, for example, **J. Mott**, 'Miners, Weavers and Pigeon Racing', in **M. A. Smith**, **S. Parker** and **C. S. Smith (eds)**, *Leisure and Society in Britain*, Allen Lane, 1973; Lowerson, 'Angling'; in Mason (ed.), *Sport*, p. 83; Dunning and Sheard, *Barbarians*; **J. Lowerson**, 'Brothers of the Angle: Coarse Fishing and English Working-Class Culture, 1850–1914', in Mangan (ed.), *Pleasure*.
101. Tranter, 'Sport and the Economy', p. 66.
102. Sillitoe, *Planning*, p. 125.
103. 'Earwig', in Merthyr *Pioneer*, 30 July 1921; Lowerson, 'Angling', p. 38.
104. 'Sports Equipment', *Mintel*, 1977, p. 54. Also p. 51; 'Sports Equipment', *Mintel*, 1981, p. 54; Lowerson, 'Angling', pp. 12, 38.
105. Mason, *Football*, p. 163.
106. 'Sports Equipment', 1977, p. 54. Also Lowerson, 'Angling', pp. 12, 14, 20–1, 38–9.
107. 'Sports Equipment', *Mintel*, 1977, pp. 51–2. Also Lowerson, 'Angling', p. 12.
108. Cited Mason, *Football*, p. 148. Children tried to get in without paying. See **T. Golding**, *The Brum We Knew*, p. 71; Brown, *Heart of England*, p. 112; **M. Hartley**, 'Football and the Working Class: A Study of Aston Villa Supporters, 1919–1939', BA disssertation, University of Wolverhampton, 1992, p. 15.
109. Shipley, 'Tom Causer', pp. 43–7.
110. **W. Vamplew**, *The Turf: A Social and Economic History of Horse Racing*, Allen Lane, 1976, p. 69. Also pp. 134–6; Vamplew, 'Horse-racing', pp. 216–7; Jones, *Sport*, p. 47.
111. Mason, *Football*, p. 150. See also **S. Tischler**, *Footballers and Businessmen: The Origins of Professional Soccer in England*, Holmes & Meier, 1981, ch. 7.
112. Holt, *Sport*, pp. 332–3. Also Mass-Observation, 3045, p. 10.

113. Mason, *Football*, pp. 152, 165.
114. 'Gambling', *Mintel*, 1977; 'Gambling', *Mintel*, 1982.
115. **A. Davies**, 'The Police and the People: Gambling in Salford, 1900–1939', *Historical Journal*, **34**, 1991, p. 89.
116. McKibbin, 'Gambling', pp. 155–6.
117. Mass-Observation, 2538, p. 7.
118. 'Gambling', *Mintel*, 1982, pp. 41, 44.
119. Ibid. pp. 41, 44.

Part Three

CONSEQUENCES

Chapter 6

THE CONSOLIDATION OF NATIONAL IDENTITY?

It is becoming increasingly clear that there is a relationship between consumption and national identity. It has been said that in eighteenth-century North America the growth of consumer society was a major cause of, and vehicle for, the growth of American national consciousness.[1] It has been claimed that in the first half of the nineteenth century, popular culture in Britain was 'an explosive mixture of regional elements and class rivalries', but that 'In the second half spectacle defused it for a time and in the process created mass advertising and, for the first time, a truly national commodity culture'.[2] Indeed it has been suggested that during the twentieth century 'the spread of mass consumerism' contributed to 'the creation of a more uniform "mass society", which in spite of its regional and social differences had common sources of information and similar awareness.'[3]

Such arguments are difficult either to sustain or refute. For neither material nor ideological developments are easy to identify, and it is tempting, as always, to find what one is looking for. It must be clear already from this study how hard it is to decide when, and to what extent, Britain became a consumer society; and it can be seen in many other studies how hard it is to determine when, and to what extent, the British people became aware of their national identity.[4] Nor is this all. For if it is hard to identify the course of material and ideological developments, it is more complicated still to disentangle the relationship between them. It is difficult to show that changes in consumption were a cause, rather than a consequence, of changes in national awareness; and it is no easy matter to trace in detail the ways in which people's behaviour as consumers did, or did not, influence their attitudes towards the country in which they lived. It remains difficult, above all, to distinguish consumption from other influences upon people's attitudes: the schools in which they were taught; the youth groups in which they enrolled; the communities in which they lived; the churches in which they worshipped; and the wars in which they fought.

None the less, it appears indisputable that there was a relationship of some sort between consumption and national identity. For, to put it at its most simple, activities like shopping, sport and tourism involved consumers in making choices, on a daily, weekly and annual basis, between products that emanated – and were known to emanate – from particular parts of the world: Britain, Europe, Asia, the Empire/Commonwealth, Latin America and North America.

Accordingly, it is the aim of this chapter to attempt to disentangle the relationship between consumption and national identity. It will be argued that the relationship was fundamentally contradictory. For, on the one hand, it seems that the British experience of consumption helped to forge a consciousness of, and some pride in, being British. On the other hand, it appears that it also helped to foster other forms of consciousness: an awareness of, and pride in, belonging to the Empire/Commonwealth; being English, Welsh or Scottish; and being from a particular region or locality.

These are complex issues. Yet there really cannot be any doubt that in certain respects at least the British experience of consumption did encourage a consciousness of, and quite often a pride in, British national identity. For in so far as changes in shopping, tourism and sport had an effect, they tended to maintain or increase, and certainly not to decrease, consumers' consciousness of the country to which they belonged.

Shopping was the most common, as well as the most important, of all forms of consumption, and it tended very often to maintain and/or increase consumers' awareness of being British. Certainly, there is abundant evidence to show that throughout the period covered by this book retailers of all types acknowledged, and attempted to exploit, what they perceived to be their customers' sense of national identity.

Whenever and wherever they operated, retailers seeking to stress quality and exclusivity referred, almost routinely, to the non-British origins of many of the products that they sold. High-class shopkeepers liked to stress, for example, that their linen came from Ireland, their cigars from Egypt, their leather from Spain, their fashions from France. Indeed, some sought to associate themselves more directly with what was seen as the style and sophistication of France. Alison Adburgham reports, for instance, that by the second half of the nineteenth century, Burlington Arcade in the West End of London was home to shops with names such as the 'French Glove House' and 'Madame Marion, Artiste in Artificial Flowers'. . . . Next door there was Madame Parsons, British to the core no doubt, but Madame by courtesy and convention like most milliners and corsetières.'[5] Such courtesies and conventions were not confined to desirable districts of the capital, for in cities, towns and suburbs across the country fashion-shop proprietors continued for many years to trade under French names, and/or to turn themselves into honorary Frenchmen and women.[6]

Nor were such devices the prerogative of traditional retailers selling luxury products. For it is not always appreciated that several of the new, late nineteenth-century retailers who prospered by stressing low cost and easy availability also endeavoured to emphasise the non-British origins of their products. Thus one or two of the new department stores and food multiples traded under names that drew immediate attention to their overseas connections: even before the First World War there were 'Bon Marché' department stores in both Brixton and Liverpool,[7] while the Home and Colonial Stores and the River Plate Fresh Meat Company each had more than four hundred branches in towns and cities across the country.[8]

However, it was by advertising the British origins of their products that mass-market retailers (and their suppliers) revealed most vividly their belief in the power of British national identity. In fact, their ingenuity knew few bounds. Late-nineteenth-century advertisers saw particular possibilities in that most potent of national symbols, the Royal Family. With or without their subjects' consent, they displayed the Royal Warrant, printed royal testimonials, juxtaposed pictures of royalty alongside those of their products, and tried to involve members of the Royal Family in their publicity stunts: in 1887, for example, Thomas Lipton attempted to present Queen Victoria with a 5-ton cheese on the occasion of her Golden Jubilee.[9] Twentieth-century entrepreneurs were no less inventive. Indeed, the production of royal souvenirs became almost an industry in its own right. For example, in the months before the Coronation of 1937 the Town Clerk of Oxford (and presumably other places) 'was bombarded with advertising from commercial manufactures for commemorative pottery, blotters, covers for souvenir programmes, photographs of the Royal Couple for outside display, floats and balloons for children's parties.'[10]

Both nineteenth- and twentieth-century advertisers saw that war too could be turned to their advantage. Thus Pears' soap greeted the 1884 invasion of the Sudan with an advertisement explaining that if it had done nothing else, 'it has at any rate left the Arab something to puzzle his fuzzy head over, for the legend PEARS' SOAP IS BEST, *inscribed in huge white characters on the rock which marks the farthest point of our advance towards Berber*, will tax all the wits of the Dervishes of the Desert to translate'.[11] Fifteen years later, during the Boer War, the manufacturers of Vinolia soap attempted to help soldiers' dependants – and of course their own sales – by opening a 'Transvaal War Fund' which received a halfpenny for every bar of soap sold.[12] Not surprisingly, the so-called 'total' wars of the twentieth century afforded still greater possibilities. It has been said that during the early months of the First World

War 'there was a notable concentration on "Britishness", coupled with attempts to exploit the widespread anti-German feeling': the Maypole Dairy Company, for instance, announced proudly that its margarine was made out of nuts captured from German ships.[13] It has been found that during the Second World War, 'In almost every kind of advertisement, patriotic symbolism abounded in forms ranging from idealised servicemen and gallant British housewives to caricatures of Hitler'.[14] There were many devices: Cadburys, for instance, promised shoppers that 'Blackouts won't get you down – once you've bought a tin of Peace-time Sleep' with Bourn-vita.[15]

Twentieth-century advertisers discovered several other ways of appealing to the public's sense of national identity. Those promoting Dominion products sought to present them as British. 'Why buy foreign butter?', they asked in 1935: Australian butter 'is better value and British'.[16] Those promoting British products drew attention to the deleterious consequences of purchasing foreign goods. 'Help to find employment for our own people', shoppers were urged in the mid 1930s: buy Moonraker Condensed and Sweetened Milk.[17] More and more, however, advertisers felt able to appeal to a generalised national identity that appears all the more potent for its lack of specificity. Thus during the 1930s, Cadbury's explained that it used 'Milk from British farms only'; Aspro adopted the slogan, 'British to the Core'; while Vauxhall Motors claimed to embody 'All That Is Best in British Motoring'.[18] In fact, for many years the motor trade continued to wrap itself in the Union Jack: 'Drive the flag', motorists were urged in 1980 – buy an Austin Morris.[19]

Of course, such an examination of retail advertising strategies in no way exhausts the discussion of the relationship between shopping and national awareness. For it is one thing to show that retailers (and manufacturers) sought to appeal to shoppers' sense of national identity; it is quite another to show that they were successful in their efforts. Moreover, it is essential to distinguish between the impact that consumption had upon shoppers' awareness of being British and the impact that it had upon their pride in being British. However, when this is done, two broad conclusions may be drawn.

It is clear that in so far as there was a relationship between shopping and national identity, the former reinforced the latter. For it seems incontrovertible that retailers' emphasis upon the foreign and/or British origins of their products maintained or increased, rather than decreased, shoppers' consciousness of their British national identity. Unfortunately, the empirical evidence is less conclusive than one would wish. Nevertheless, there is a good deal of impressionistic material, and a small amount of social survey data, to confirm that by the mid-twentieth century shoppers of all types were making a connection between consumption and national identity. A Gallup poll survey of 1939 revealed that 46 per cent of respondents attempted to discover whether the products they were purchasing had been made in Britain.[20] A National Consumer Council report published in 1980 concluded that 'a majority of consumers say that they would like to know the country of origin of the goods that they buy.'[21]

It is less clear that shopping reinforced a pride in, as opposed to an awareness of, British national identity. Indeed, to some extent consumers believed that overseas products were superior. It is well known that many upper- and middle-class shoppers displayed a preference for foreign goods in general, and for French goods in particular.[22] It is less well known that other shoppers also came – albeit cautiously and selectively – to display a preference for foreign products. For example, by the end of the period, Japanese electrical goods enjoyed an enviably high reputation: 'I think with hi-fi and so on I would tend to go for Japanese because they seem to have got a very good name for reliability and quality. A lot of the British stuff doesn't look quite as nice either.'[23]

None the less, what evidence there is seems to suggest that on the whole shopping tended to reinforce – or at least to act as a vehicle for – British feelings of superiority. Some shoppers tried to avoid Jewish stores: 'Let those who buy things from them cheap try bloody working for 'em', exclaimed one embittered Londoner in 1938.[24] Others did not like the way that overseas visitors behaved when out shopping. 'Don't mention bloody foreigners to me', complained one harassed Second World War consumer. 'Pushing lot of devils. They go into shops and paralyse the shopkeepers. They just sail in and say I want a lb. of this and lb. of that and get [it].'[25] Other consumers used shopping as a means of expressing their dislike of particular foreign regimes: the Axis powers during the Second World War, and countries such as Chile, Israel and South Africa during the 1960s and 1970s. The Gallup poll survey carried out in 1939 revealed that the respondents who tried to find out whether the goods they were buying had been made in Britain, used the information they obtained to boycott those produced in Germany, Italy and Japan.[26] However, most shoppers seemed to exhibit a less ideological, more broadly based preference for British products. Some people remained suspicious of almost any new food, whether foreign or not.[27] Others were more discriminating. The Consumer Council report of 1980 discovered, for example, that 'several mothers recognise that T-shirts and cheap clothing from Hong Kong will probably be of inferior quality and will not wear/wash as well as the UK equivalent'. However, the report concluded on a cautious note.

> Consumers feel that if there is a choice between two identical products – one foreign and one British – they will select the latter, but that is as far as patriotism goes . . . . 'Buying British', if not a thing of the past, is being regarded now as a luxury that not all can afford to indulge in.[28]

Tourism was a less common form of consumption than shopping, and so exercised a less pervasive, albeit much more direct, impact upon consumers' sense of national identity. The crucial development was the growth of overseas travel which, it has been seen, proved so marked a feature of late-twentieth-century tourism. Such travel tended to reinforce tourists' consciousness of being British, as well, very often, as bolstering their pride in being so. However, the discussion of these changes is particularly difficult: the evidential problems are still more daunting than in the case of shopping; while in so far as scholars and other commentators have considered the social and cultural consequences of tourism, they have usually directed their attention towards the repercussions for host, rather than visitor, communities.[29]

None the less, it is clear that the relationship between tourism and British national identity was closer than it appears at first sight. For it is not always appreciated that domestic travel, like foreign travel, could sometimes draw upon, and reinforce, a sense of, and a pride in, being British. Even day trips sometimes functioned in this way. Almost any visit to a museum, art gallery, botanical garden, zoo or safari park provided a glimpse, however slight, of British history and/or the world beyond Britain's shores. Thus one turn-of-the-century guide suggested that a visit to Southend-on-Sea would be of particular value in educating 'the finished product of an East End board school' for it would instil in him (or her) 'national sentiments and national pride'.[30] Almost any visit to a national or regional exhibition like the Great Exhibition of 1851, the Manchester Art Treasures Exhibition of 1857, the British Empire Exhibition of 1924, the British Industries Fair of 1936, the Glasgow Empire Exhibition of 1938, or the Festival of Britain of 1951 provided a view, however partial, of Britain's position in the world.[31] When William Thackeray saw the 'miscellaneous objects' at the Great Exhibition, he wrote that,

> These England's triumphs are,
> The trophies of her bloodless war.[32]

When historian Eric Hopkins recalled the Festival of Britain, he remembered it as 'a kind of middle-class celebration of British achievement'. It was described, he recalls, as "all Heal let loose", a reference to the fashionable furniture store in Tottenham Court Road.[33]

Even taking the annual family holiday in this country sometimes drew upon, and bolstered, consumers' sense of national identity. Of course, for many years foreign travel was beyond the reach of the vast majority of the population: the only decision to be made was whether to do without a holiday, or to take a holiday in Britain. However, with the advent of cheap air travel and low-cost package tours during the 1960s, consumers were faced with a further decision to make: to do without a holiday, to take a holiday in Britain or to holiday abroad.[34] In these circumstances, even the rejection of foreign travel could be significant. For whether the decision to holiday in Britain was made on grounds of cost, convenience or fear of the unknown, it involved a comparison of what Britain and countries like France, Italy and (especially) Spain were able to offer to the tourist.

It goes almost without saying that foreign travel drew upon, and reinforced, much more directly tourists' sense of national identity (and/or sense of the familiar). Travelling abroad could not but sharpen tourists' understanding of what it meant to be British. Some tourists were delighted with what they discovered on the Continent. Lancashire steel worker Patrick McGeown, remembers vividly his first holiday abroad in 1957.

> I loved Italy, the bright air so lovely to breathe and so lovely to live
> in, and so different from the gas fumes and dust of the melting shop.
> I puzzled over the fact that men still died in such wonderful places,
> and since that was true then how account for the fact that I in my
> atmosphere had lived at all.[35]

Venturing further afield, other tourists experienced feelings only of superiority.

> Except for wearing funny hats and being crisscrossed with camera
> straps and conglobulating in a close mass, a group of tourists
> politically resembles a collective British milord of the nineteenth
> century. Tourists behold the foreign destitute, scrutinise their rags
> and note their terrible food, observe their ramshackle dwellings and
> acquaint themselves with their ignorance and superstition, not with
> outrage or even pity, but with satisfaction.[36]

Whether or not they liked what they found when they left this country, even the most unobservant of tourists could scarcely fail to recognise that things were different abroad. For example, in 1950, Essex factory worker Joseph Halliday took his wife to Holland where he had been asked to referee an Anglo-Dutch soccer match. The trip was a revelation, 'a big interlude', as he put it, in a 'small life'. In Rotterdam they visited Crooswijk cemetery 'where wreaths were laid on graves of R.A.F. airmen'.

> A method of burial, peculiar to us, was noticed here. Whereas
> our dead are laid horizontal, in Holland they are placed vertical,
> undoubtedly saving much space. With the inscriptions, too, there were
> also encased photographs of the dear departed.[37]

However, for many men it was sport, as much as tourism or shopping, that played a central role in determining their sense of national identity. It is a role which, much more than tourism or shopping, has attracted considerable scholarly and popular attention.[38] Of course, such interest has its dangers as well as its benefits, for it makes it easy to exaggerate the intimacy of the relationship between sporting consumption and British national awareness. Thus some caution is certainly necessary. It is essential, above all, to realise that British national identity cannot be used as a generic term to encompass all the forms of national identity found within the British Isles; it is essential to recognise that there was – as there is – a difference between British, English, Welsh and Scottish national identities. When this is done, it can be seen that the consumption of sporting goods and services did relatively little to foster British – as opposed to English, Welsh and Scottish – feelings of national awareness.

Moreover, not all forms of sporting consumption were equally important in the fostering of British national identity. It is difficult to see that the playing of sport had much effect at all. It is true that grandiose claims were sometimes made for the relationship between sporting participation, national character and national pride: for example, when Lord Rosebery presented the FA cup in 1897 he said he was sure that football helped to bring out those 'splendid characteristics of the British race – stamina and indomitable pluck'.[39] However, such sentiments were probably always confined to a rather narrow section of the male population. ('I do not think "playing for one's side" develops . . . true patriotism', maintained a housewife and occasional teacher just after the end of the Second World War.[40]) Indeed, even proponents of the view that participation in sport helped to foster national awareness made no reference at all to the expenditure that playing involved. For in their view, it was participation, not consumption, that was the crucial determinant of national awareness.

In so far as there was a relationship between the consumption of sporting products and feelings of British national identity, it was to be found, not in participation but in spectatorship. For there is no doubt that watching sport (together with reading about it, and gambling on it) was much more influential than playing it. John Hargreaves places particular emphasis upon the role of the media.

A sense of unity conferred by the feelings of belonging to the nation, cutting across class, ethnic, gender and other loyalties, is, perhaps, the very linchpin of a hegemonic system, and the media are, arguably, the most important institution reproducing national identity today. Since the 1950s especially, with the expansion of TV coverage of international events, media sport has increasingly provided opportunities for people to identify with the nation through sport.[41]

It is not difficult to show that both national sporting occasions and British involvement in international competition relied upon, and helped to foster, a sense of British national awareness. It has been pointed out that 'Coverage of the great annual sporting occasions, such as the Cup Final, the Derby, the Oxford and Cambridge Boat Race, etc., tends to convey a sense of a national way of life'.[42] The Cup Final is the clearest example. Coming to London offered supporters the opportunity of visiting the heart of the Empire/Commonwealth, joining in quasi-religious communal singing, and (from 1914 onwards) seeing a member of the Royal Family present the cup to the captain of the winning team. Whatever Britain's economic, political or moral decline, here was an occasion which, it was claimed, had no rival anywhere in the world.[43]

It has been pointed out, too, that British involvement in international competition assisted in the fostering of British national identity. Once again, John Hargreaves draws attention to the power of the media. It is, he argues,

> in coverage of international events in which 'we' compete against foreigners that 'Britishness' [constitutes a conventional reference point] signifying membership of a unique community, sharing a common, valued and specific way of life, which supersedes or takes precedence over all other loyalties and identities.[44]

It was a view shared, perhaps rather surprisingly, by the Labour government of 1975.

> Success in international competition has an important part to play in national morale . . . in the sporting world the pinnacle of achievement is to represent one's country . . . . The government feels it right to give special encouragement to sportsmen and women capable of performing at international level and expect clubs and other bodies to give priority to international calls over local interests.[45]

However, it is here that considerable caution is called for. For as any sports enthusiast knew, national teams in the most popular British spectator sports – football, Rugby and cricket – represented not Great Britain but England, Wales and Scotland. Nevertheless, interest in following British teams did have a certain limited impact on British national awareness. The Olympic Games provide the best illustration, since almost from the outset, England, Wales, Scotland (and Northern Ireland) competed together as a single nation-state rather than as three (and four) separate countries.[46] 'British athletes competing at the first modern Olympic Games in 1896 did not do so as part of a national team. In 1900 and 1908 they did, and from 1912, participation at the Games was open only to members of national teams.'[47] However, this is not the end of the matter. For the fact that British Olympians competed together as a single team does not mean that public interest in their performances generated a large volume of consumer expenditure; and it certainly does not mean that the expenditure that was generated was a cause, rather than a consequence, of British national consciousness.[48]

Thus the relationship between sport and British national identity – like that between shopping and national identity, and tourism and national identity – remains irritatingly elusive. The evidence is fragmentary, its interpretation contentious. None the less, some generalisation does now appear to be possible. It seems clear that, as was suggested at the beginning of the chapter, the British people's experience of consumption did something at least to foster a consciousness of, and a certain pride in, their British national identity.

However, as was also pointed out at the beginning of the chapter, the British people's experience of consumption helped to foster other forms of consciousness. It did a little to encourage international and imperial/Commonwealth awareness; it did a good deal to foster English, Welsh and Scottish consciousness; and it did a considerable amount to reinforce regional and/or local identities. Accordingly, it is to a consideration of these further forms of consciousness that the remainder of the chapter will be devoted.

The first of these forms of consciousness can be dealt with very briefly, for there is really no evidence to suggest that changes in consumption had an impact upon feelings of international co-operation. Thus, despite the growth of multinational firms, the internationalisation of trade, and the globalisation of branding and advertising that occurred during the course of the twentieth century, there are few, if any, indications that shopping or the consumption of sporting products did anything at all to foster feelings of international co-operation. There were, of course, constant claims that international sport provided a possible avenue towards international peace and brotherhood; but there were no suggestions, it seems, that this was a movement that changes in consumption might help to promote.[49] There are some claims, it is true, that tourism had a part to play. 'It may be', suggests John Urry, 'that tourism can in a rather inchoate way develop "international understanding"'. He draws particular attention to the growth of the package tour industry.

> The shift in public attitudes in Britain towards a pro-Europeanism in the 1980s is difficult to explain without recognising that some role is played by the European tourism industry and the way in which huge flows of visitors have made Europe familiar and unthreatening.[50]

It is a plausible enough argument, but one that remains unproven and clearly requires a great deal of further empirical investigation.

The second form of supra-national consciousness, imperial/Commonwealth awareness, requires rather more detailed examination. For there is some evidence that changes in consumption were related to, and probably had an impact upon, attitudes towards the Empire in general, and the white Dominions in particular. Certainly, consumption was a key element of 1930s' economic nationalism (and supra-nationalism). It was seen earlier in the chapter that during these years a number of manufacturers and retailers sought to promote Dominion products as British. It needs to be emphasised that this was part of a much wider movement.

> Well before the Ottawa agreements in 1932 and the deliberate turn to imperial preference Britain's overseas trade was becoming increasingly autarkic: in the 1930s imports from the colonies and the Dominions doubled. The promotion of tea as the national beverage, the British Empire Exhibition at Wembley in 1924 (an event comparable, in its effect on public opinion, to the Great Exhibition of 1851) and the activities of the Empire Marketing Board all helped to encourage the notion of imperial self-sufficiency.[51]

Established in 1926, the Empire Marketing Board sought 'to make Empire buying a national habit'.[52] 'The Empire today is our best market', explained Emu Australian Wines at the end of the decade: for whereas in 1927 the average Australian spent almost £10 on British goods, the average European spent only about twelve shillings.[53]

Such devices did not long survive the Second World War. However, it is not always appreciated that in post-war Britain tourism began to take over from shopping as a vehicle for Dominion loyalties. There were two crucial developments. The first was the large-scale emigration that had been taking place since early in the nineteenth century to the so-called lands of white settlement. It was a movement that showed few signs of abating: it has been estimated, for example, that between 1946 and 1948 nearly 15,000 United Kingdom citizens settled in New Zealand, more than 36,000 emigrated to Australia, and more than 100,000 to Canada.[54] The result was that there remained in Britain a large, and growing, number of families with relatives in the Dominions. The second development allowing tourism to serve as a vehicle for the expression of Dominion loyalties was the growth during the 1960s of cheap (or at least cheaper) charter flights to several far-flung corners of the Commonwealth. Thus it was that for some consumers at least tourism began to take over from shopping as a means of reinforcing imperial/Commonwealth ties and loyalties.[55]

However, it was sport, as much as shopping or tourism, that encouraged male consumers to maintain an affinity with countries such as Australia, New Zealand (and South Africa). It is not difficult to point to a number of well-known and successful imperial sporting institutions. The British Empire (later Commonwealth) Games were first held in Canada in 1930, and thereafter 'took their place alongside other displays of imperial achievement, custom, and industry at the periodic inter-war Empire exhibitions.'[56] Test matches in Rugby and cricket, which had been established towards the end of the nineteenth century, were keenly – and sometimes bitterly – contested, and came to constitute what Richard Holt has called 'the real stuff of Dominion sport.'[57]

It is a good deal more difficult to show a correlation between interest in such events, the consumption of sporting products, and feelings of imperial/Commonwealth identity. However, some links can be discerned. Cricket tests in particular attracted large crowds, considerable gate receipts, substantial spending on travel and refreshments, and a very great amount of media coverage. Already by the late 1870s and 1880s, test matches against the Australians were drawing crowds of well over 30,000, and their results were being interpreted, in some quarters at least, in terms of imperial genetics. So when the Australians won at Lords in 1878, their victory was greeted as one 'all of our own flesh and blood'. Their success was our success: 'we welcome their prowess cheerfully as a proof that the old stock is not degenerating in those far-off lands'.[58] Foreigners, it was felt, could never understand such imperial ties. K. S. Inglis claims, for instance, that 'In 1899 colonials and Englishmen enjoyed telling each other a story in which Kruger shakes with fright as (*sic*) the news that a contingent of Australian soldiers is on the way to South Africa: "And I hear that Eleven of them have defeated all England!"'[59] Such attitudes never completely disappeared. Almost fifty years later, towards the end of the Second World War, the Chancellor of the Exchequer, R. A. Butler decided to exempt cricket from entertainment tax on the grounds that it occupied 'a special place among sports, not only as forming a part of the English tradition, but as a common interest helping to bind together the various countries of the Commonwealth'.[60]

This mention of the English (as opposed to the British) tradition leads naturally to a consideration of other non-British forms of consciousness, and especially those associated with England, Wales and Scotland. As might be expected, the relationship between consumption and these forms of national identity is no easier to unravel than those between consumption and the forms of national consciousness that have been considered above. However, it will be argued, and with some confidence, that shopping and sport played a considerable part in maintaining an awareness of, and a loyalty to, the three countries that together constituted Great Britain.

Shopping was certainly of considerable importance.[61] Encouraged, no doubt, by Queen Victoria's apparently insatiable enthusiasm for the Highlands of Scotland, some English retailers, both traditional and modern, began to specialise in products from north of the border. For example, the first Scotch Wool Shop opened in Greenock in

1881: the enterprise proved successful and expanded, so that by 1910 the chain had more than two hundred, and by 1939, more than four hundred branches. Most retailers did not, of course, specialise to such an extent, but contented themselves with drawing attention to their clan tartans, their Harris tweeds, their Shetland jumpers, their Scots porridge, and, of course, their Scotch whisky.[62] It was more usual for manufacturers and retailers to draw attention to the Englishness of their products. For although few, if any, retailers, specialised explicitly in English goods, many, if not most, sought to emphasise the indigenous origins of their product range. Indeed, the term 'English', like 'British', came to be employed as a generalised symbol of quality which, as was observed above, is all the more telling for its lack of specificity. It could be, and was, used to sell virtually anything: retailers and their suppliers advertised everything from 'English pork' sausages, to 'Olde English' marmalade, 'England's Glory' matches, 'Strictly English' tailoring and 'English Electric' cookers.[63]

Tourism was less important, but it too played a part. Indeed, it could scarcely be otherwise. For just as the growth of international travel fostered a sense of British national identity, so the growth of long-distance domestic travel helped to foster an awareness of the differences between England, Wales and Scotland. In fact, even absurdly short-distance travel sometimes had an effect. 'Thank God I'm back in good owd England', said Suffolk farm worker John Edmunds after returning home from his one and only trip (of 6 miles) beyond the parish of his birth.[64] Long-distance travel usually raised consumers' consciousness of the British Isles in more orthodox ways. Indeed, even towards the very end of the period, tourists of every age and background continued to be surprised at the striking contrasts that confronted them when travelling between England, Wales and Scotland.[65]

Sport was a great deal more important in fostering English, Welsh and Scottish identities. None the less, too much should not be made of the relationship between participant consumption and national identity. All that can be said with any certainty is that particular sports became associated with particular nations (cricket with England, Rugby union with Wales, and soccer with Scotland); and that every schoolboy was supposed to want to play football for England, Wales or Scotland – not for Great Britain.[66]

It was spectator consumption that was important – especially when, as in the case of Scottish soccer and Welsh Rugby, watching and playing tended to become mutually reinforcing. It has been pointed out that 'The growth of international competition, particularly since the 1950s, provides regular opportunities now for the expression of varying shades of nationalist sentiment, from the patriotism of the respectable, law-abiding English working class, to Scottish . . . and

Welsh nationalism and to the xenophobia of the football hooligan.'[67] For it will be recalled from earlier in the chapter that national teams in the most popular spectator sports represented, not Great Britain, but England, Wales and Scotland. Anybody who saw Wales and England play Rugby at Cardiff Arms Park, or England and Scotland meet at Murrayfield, would appreciate the intensity of the relationship between sport and national identity.[68] Anybody who followed soccer would know that England, Scotland and Wales ran their own separate league and cup competitions, and that England-versus-Scotland games were among the most competitive in the international calendar. As Tony Mason explains, football performed a central role 'in the cultural life of the Scots, becoming the main medium of expression of a dislike of England and the English'.

> The annual international between the two countries gave the smaller, poorer nation the opportunity to show its dominant neighbour that the British national game was played best of all by the Scots . . . . The biannual visit to London for the Scotland-England international has seen many of these expressions of national feeling from 1913, when the *Manchester Guardian* described the Scottish supporters as demonstrating 'racial defiance' with their chants of 'Scot-land Scot-land' and the *Daily Express* match report was headlined 'Scots looters repelled', to 1977 when the celebrations of the Silver Jubilee of Queen Elizabeth II coincided with a rise in support for nationalist politics and a 2–1 Scottish victory at Wembley. At the end of the game the pitch was invaded and the goalposts pulled down.[69]

There is one further form of consciousness that needs to be considered. For consumption had an impact not only upon international, imperial and national loyalties, but upon those that were based, more narrowly, around region and locality. It is a relationship that, for all its importance, can easily be overlooked if too much emphasis is placed upon the growth of mass production, the spread of national advertising and the creation of a national commodity culture.

Shopping, tourism and sport all had some effect. Retailers, for example, were keen to stress the regional and/or local origins of their products when they believed that this would help to stimulate sales. It was those selling food who were always most active in this respect. Indeed, the list of regional and local specialities sold in British shops appears almost endless: Devon cream, Dundee cake, Worcester sauce, Bakewell tarts, Burton beer, Cornish pasties, Eccles cakes, Whitby oysters, and cheeses from Cheshire, Lancashire, Leicestershire and Wensleydale.[70] Then, too, cities such as Bristol, Leeds, Newcastle and Norwich became regional centres of consumption. 'Let us first dispose of a myth', exhorts Bill Lancaster. 'Newcastle is not an industrial city . . . . Newcastle's primary functions over the last two centuries have been commerce and consumption.'[71]

Tourism had a more obvious effect. For it was difficult to travel even a relatively short distance in England, Wales or Scotland without becoming aware of the survival and strength of regional diversity. Indeed, it was precisely to experience such diversity that day-trippers and holiday-makers took to their travels. Blackpool, it has been claimed, became associated with 'a distinctive brand of northern populism . . . forging an image of "the people of the North" as sharing a no-nonsense, down-to-earth, practical regional spirit'.[72] Yet the impact of tourism upon regional/local consciousness was highly unpredictable. For tourism of any kind could generate resentment as well as satisfaction, conflict as well as understanding. John Field describes some of the petty – and not so petty – indignities to which tourists in Folkestone were subjected during the 1960s.

> I worked for two years on the buses, and I detested tourists . . . . So you took your quiet and petty revenge. Older conductors would come into the staff café . . . bragging about the day's short-change tricks. Usually the sums involved were quite small, but sometimes it would be a matter of a pound or so – large enough to cast a brief silence over the card game at the corner table. Others would exult over a misdirection, or a rumour that some Midlanders had been beaten up for calling fishermen 'fairies'.[73]

However, it was sport that proved of particular importance in reinforcing regional and local loyalties. For sport was all about identifying, competing against, and trying to beat one's opponent, an opponent who, in both individual and team games, was increasingly likely to come from another part of the country.[74] Even participation (and the expenditure to which it gave rise) probably had some limited effect: it has been suggested, for instance, that the many competitions organised by angling clubs and federations probably did something to perpetuate regional ties and loyalties.[75]

Yet once again, it was spectatorship (and the expenditure to which it gave rise) that proved of greatest potency. Rugby league is perhaps the most obvious example, for, as was seen in the previous chapter, the game was confined almost exclusively to the counties of Yorkshire and Lancashire. According to a Yorkshire correspondent of the *Daily Mail*, 'Those who talk about "race decadence" and "a C3 nation" would alter their views if they toured the area where Rugby League holds sway.'[76] According to playwright Colin Welland,

> In south-west Lancashire, babes don't toddle; they sidestep. Queuing women talk about 'nipping round the blindside'. Rugby league provides our cultural adrenalin. It's a physical manifestation of our rules of life, comradeship, honest endeavour, and a staunch, often ponderous, allegiance to fair play.[77]

None the less, it is soccer that provides the most telling illustration of the relationship between consumer expenditure and regional and local loyalties. For as John Hargreaves has pointed out with some distaste, 'Football culture, both traditionally and in its latter-day version, is stridently male chauvinist, sporadically violent and is the focus of fierce local patriotism.'[78] Such partisanship was deep-seated, and Tony Mason's discussion of its origins cannot be bettered. 'Professional and semi-professional teams seem to have developed first in those towns in Lancashire and the midlands which were industrial and urban but relatively settled.'

> In such circumstances it would not be surprising to find a growing identification with place emerging among both middle and working classes. Football can be seen both to contribute to this and to benefit from it. It benefits from it in that if there already exists this sense of identification with place then any organisation which takes the name of the town has a good chance of attracting support particularly if it is competing with similar institutions in other places and especially if it succeeds in such competition.

However, there was more to it than this, for as Mason goes on to explain, 'the football team can also contribute to the intensity or diffusion of this local consciousness and particularly among working people.'

> Nor does this happen only among those working people who regularly watch its matches. Regular matches, local newspaper coverage, conversations with people who do watch, all these help to buttress notions of being from Bolton or Blackburn, Bury or Sheffield, Nottingham or Derby.[79]

Such local consciousness was one of the roots upon which football hooligans were able to draw. Indeed, many commentators have re-marked, in their different ways, upon the 'nationalism, racism and general ethnocentricity' of the modern hooligan. 'To him, Englishness [Scottishness and Welshness], manliness and belonging to one's local community are all of a piece and when the chips are down the essence of these qualities is the willingness and ability to fight for them.'[80] 'Oxford Boys we are here', they chanted: 'shag your women, drink your beer'; 'You're gonna get your fuckin' heads kicked in', they greeted visiting supporters. Thus as a young Arsenal fan explained, 'All the North Bank care about is their team and the other [visiting supporters'] end and that's all there is to it.'[81] Such attitudes reached their apogee (or nadir) during the miners' strike of 1984–5 when London fans visiting clubs on the coalfields taunted the home supporters by waving £5 and £10 notes at them. The link between consumption, sport and regional identity could hardly be made more vividly.

It is not often that relationships between consumption and regional, national and other forms of consciousness manifest themselves quite so explicitly. Nonetheless, it does now appear possible to offer certain, reasonably secure, generalisations about the relationship between consumption and national identity. It seems clear that the relationship was indeed contradictory. For although consumption played some part in fostering British national consciousness, it also helped to reinforce other forms of identification – especially with the Dominions, with England, Wales and Scotland, and with particular regions and localities. Indeed, this is the type of contradiction that will recur time and again in subsequent chapters as an attempt is made to understand the consequences of the rise of the so-called consumer society.

NOTES AND REFERENCES

1. **T. H. Breen**, '"Baubles of Britain": The American and Consumer Revolutions of the Eighteenth Century', *Past and Present*, **119**, 1988, esp. pp. 75–7, 103–4.

2. **T. Richards**, *The Commodity Culture of Victorian Britain: Advertising and Spectacle, 1851–1914*, Verso, 1991, p. 251.

3. **J. Stevenson**, *British Society 1914–45*, Penguin, 1984, p. 468. Also **T. R. Nevett**, *Advertising in Britain: A History*, Heinemann, 1982, p. 84; **R. Samuel**, 'Introduction: Exciting to be English', in **R. Samuel** (ed.), *Patriotism: The Making and Unmaking of British National Identity*, Routledge, 1989, I, pp. xxxii–xlii. The relationship between consumption and national identity also manifested itself politically. Consider, for example, the anxieties and struggles over the corn laws in the 1840s, foreign competition in the 1880s and 1890s, tariff reform in the 1900s and imperial preference in the 1930s.

4. For general discussions, see Samuel, *Patriotism*, 3 vols; **R. Colls** and **P. Dodd** (eds), *Englishness: Politics and Culture 1880–1920*, Croom Helm, 1987.

5. **A. Adburgham**, *Shops and Shopping 1800–1914: Where, and in What Manner the Well-Dressed Englishwoman Bought her Clothes*, Barrie & Jenkins, 1989, p. 107; also pp. 104, 245–7.

6. As I write this, in Wolverhampton in 1992, the 'Ladies' Wear Shops' section in the local *Yellow Pages* contains, *inter alia*, several boutiques, a 'Parisian Lady' and a 'Nous L'Avons'.

7. Adburgham, *Shops*, pp. 169, 194.

8. **M. J. Winstanley**, *The Shopkeeper's World 1830–1914*, Manchester University Press, 1983, p. 142; **J. Burnett**, *Plenty and Want: A Social History of Food in England from 1815 to the Present Day*, Routledge, 1989, p. 127.

9. Nevett, *Advertising*, p. 97; Richards, *Commodity Culture*, ch. 2; **L. de Vries**, *Victorian Advertisements*, John Murray, 1968, pp. 32, 58, 80.

10. **A. De Filippo**, 'King, Country and Empire: Working Class Patriotism in Oxford, 1935–1939', M A dissertation, University of Warwick, 1992, pp. 61, 66. Also Lancaster, Mrs L2L, pp. 19–20; **T. Golding**, *The Brum We Knew*, pp. 95–6.

11. **de Vries**, *Victorian Advertisements*, p. 12.
12. *Daily Mail*, 9 January 1900; *Wolverhampton Chronicle*, 15 November 1899. Also Nevett, *Advertising*, p. 98. Similar funds were opened by 'Old Flag' cigarettes and 'Fuller's American Confectioners'. See *Daily Mail*, 16–17 January 1900.
13. Nevett, *Advertising*, p. 141; also pp. 142–3, *Daily Herald*, 4 April 1919.
14. Nevett, *Advertising*, p. 169.
15. **G. Dyer**, *Advertising as Communication*, Methuen, 1982, p. 51.
16. *Express and Star*, 14 May 1935; also 14 February 1933.
17. *Express and Star*, 24 May 1935. Also Dyer, *Advertising*, p. 47.
18. *Express and Star*, 13 January 1930; also 22 May 1935; *Daily Mail*, 15, 16, 18, 23 January 1930; *Daily Herald*, 1 April, 6 November 1919; *Daily Sketch*, 13 December 1941.
19. *Express and Star*, 11 January 1980; *Bristol Evening Post*, 3 March 1952.
20. **G. H. Gallup**, *The Gallup International Public Opinion Polls: Great Britain 1937–1975*, Random House, 1976, p. 19.
21. **A. Foster**, 'Country of Origin Marking: The Consumer's View', *Retail & Distribution Management*, March–April 1980, p. 48.
22. Adburgham, *Shops*, p. 33. Also Burnett, *Plenty*, pp. 70–4.
23. Foster, 'Country', p. 47.
24. Mass-Observation, A12, 'Anti Semitism Survey', 1938, p. 32; also pp. 2, 42, 46.
25. Mass-Observation, 697, 'Feelings about Foreigners'.
26. Gallup, *Gallup Polls*, p. 19; Mass-Observation, A12, p. 13.
27. **R. Roberts**, *The Classic Slum: Salford Life in the First Quarter of Century*, Penguin, 1973, p. 116; **E. Roberts**, *A Woman's Place: An Oral History of Working-Class Women 1890–1914*, Blackwell, 1984, p. 159; Burnett, *Plenty*, p. 312; **R. A. Hawkins**, 'The Pineapple Canning Industry during the World Depression of the 1930s', *Business History*, **31**, 1989, pp. 54–5.
28. Foster, 'Country', p. 48.
29. **J. Urry**, *The Tourist Gaze: Leisure and Travel in Contemporary Societies*, Sage, 1990, pp. 56–9.
30. **J. K. Walton**, *The English Seaside Resort: A Social History, 1750–1914*, Leicester University Press, 1983, pp. 223, 225.
31. See, e.g., **C. McArthur**, 'The Dialectic of National Identity: The Glasgow Exhibition of 1938', in **T. Bennett**, **C. Mercer** and **J. Woollacott** (eds), *Popular Culture and Social Relations*, Oxford University Press, 1986.
32. **A. Briggs**, *Victorian Things*, Penguin, 1990, p. 61. See also *Bristol Advertiser*, 18 January, 22 February 1936; **A. Briggs**, *Victorian People: A Reassessment of Persons and Themes 1851–67*, Penguin, 1965, ch. 2; Richards, *Commodity Culture*, ch. 1.
33. **E. Hopkins**, *The Rise and Decline of the English Working Classes 1918–1990: A Social History*, Weidenfeld & Nicolson, 1991, p. 111. Also Gallup, *Gallup Polls*, p. 234.
34. Gallup, *Gallup Polls*, pp. 5, 159, 177, 330, 459, 461.
35. **P. McGeown**, *Heat the Furnace Seven Times More*, Hutchinson, 1968, p. 177. Also Gallup, *Gallup Polls*, p. 330.

36. **A. Klimowski**, 'The Quest for Reality', *Guardian*, 18 October 1990.
37. **J. Halliday**, *Just Ordinary, But . . . An Autobiography*, The Author, 1959, p. 223.
38. E.g., **R. Holt**, *Sport and the British: A Modern History*, Oxford University Press, 1989, pp. 203–79; **T. Mason**, *Sport in Britain*, Faber & Faber, 1988, p. 112.
39. **T. Mason**, *Association Football and English Society 1863–1915*, Harvester, 1981, p. 225. Also Holt, *Sport*, p. 95; Mass-Observation, 3141, 'Report on Sport', pp. 8, 12.
40. Mass-Observation, 3141, p. 9.
41. **J. Hargreaves**, *Sport, Power and Culture: A Social and Historical Analysis of Popular Sports in Britain*, Polity, 1986, p. 154.
42. Hargreaves, *Sport*, p. 154. Also *Oxford & Cambridge Centenary Boat Race*, Oxford/Cambridge University Boat Clubs, 1929; **S. G. Jones**, *Sport, Politics and the Working Class: Organised Labour and Sport in Interwar Britain*, Manchester University Press, 1988, p. 54.
43. *Sunday Worker*, 6 January 1929. Also Mason, *Football*, pp. 240, 244, n. 15; Holt, *Sport*, p. 269; 'Sport in War-Time', *Mass-Observation Weekly*, 3 May 1940; **N. Fishwick**, *English Football and Society, 1910–1950*, Manchester University Press, 1989, p. 138.
44. Hargreaves, *Sport*, p. 154. Also **A. Goldberg** and **S. Wagg**, 'It's Not a Knockout: English Football and Globalisation', in **J. Williams** and **S. Wagg** (eds), *British Football and Social Change: Getting into Europe*, Leicester University Press, 1991, pp. 239–41.
45. Hargreaves, *Sport*, p. 191.
46. Holt, *Sport*, pp. 273–4.
47. **J. Crump**, 'Athletics', in **T. Mason** (ed.), *Sport in Britain: A Social History*, Cambridge University Press, 1989, p. 67.
48. Holt, *Sport*, p. 274.
49. Gallup, *Gallup Polls*, p. 371.
50. Urry, *Tourist Gaze*, p. 58.
51. Samuel, 'Introduction', p. xxiii. See De Filippo, 'King, Country and Empire', p. 67.
52. *The Times*, 2 June 1930. See **S. Constantine**, 'Bringing the Empire Alive: The Empire Marketing Board and Imperial Propaganda, 1926–33', in **J. M. Mackenzie** (ed.), *Imperialism and Popular Culture*, Manchester University Press, 1986.
53. Advertisement in *Daily Mail*, 25 January 1930. See Constantine, 'Empire Alive', p. 216. Also Mass-Observation, A9, 'Interim Report on Margarine Survey', 1938, p. 2.
54. **G. F. Plant**, *Oversea (sic) Settlement: Migration from the United Kingdom to the Dominions*, Oxford University Press, 1951, p. 158. None the less, in 1948, 17 per cent of a sample interviewed could name no part of the British Empire, and 3 per cent believed that the United States was a British colony, *Daily Graphic*, 2 November 1948; *Daily Mail*, 21 December 1948.
55. The relationship between tourism (and sport) and 'New Commonwealth' ties and loyalties was, of course, a great deal more complicated.
56. Holt, *Sport*, p. 234.

57. Holt, *Sport*, p. 226. Also Mason, *Sport*, p. 87; **B. Stoddart**, 'Cricket's Imperial Crisis: The 1932–33 MCC Tour of Australia', in **R. Cashman** and **M. McKernan** (eds), *Sport in History: The Making of Modern Sporting History*, University of Queensland Press, 1979, pp. 126–7.

58. **K. S. Inglis**, 'Imperial Cricket: Test Matches between Australia and England 1877–1900', in Cashman and McKernan (eds), *Sport*, pp. 165–6. Also **K. A. P. Sandiford**, 'English Cricket Crowds during the Victorian Age', *Journal of Sport History*, **9**, 1982, p. 10.

59. Inglis, 'Imperial Cricket', p. 173.

60. Mason, *Sport*, p. 87.

61. See **D. E. Allen**, *British Tastes: An Enquiry into the Likes and Dislikes of the Regional Consumer*, Hutchinson, 1968.

62. Adburgham, *Shops*, pp. 70–8, 191; Samuel, 'Introduction', p. xxxi. It was claimed that in Glasgow, Jewish retailers sometimes gave themselves Scottish names. Mass-Observation, A12, p. 46. Also McArthur, 'Dialectic'.

63. E.g., *Daily Mail*, 23 January 1930; *Daily Herald*, 16 November 1940; *Bristol Evening Post*, 7 March 1952; *Express and Star*, 13 June 1955; 3, 9 June 1965; **M. J. Wiener**, *English Culture and the Decline of the Industrial Spirit, 1850–1980*, Penguin, 1981, pp. 76–7.

64. **J. Benson**, *The Working Class in Britain, 1850–1939*, Longman, 1989, p. 131.

65. Author's recollection.

66. **G. Williams**, 'From Popular Culture to Political Cliché: Image and Identity in Wales, 1890–1914', in **J. A. Mangan** (ed.), *Pleasure, Profit, Proselytism: British Culture and Sport at Home and Abroad 1700–1914*, Cass, 1988; *NOP Political Bulletin*, April 1972, p. 13; Holt, *Sport*, pp. 236–7, 246–66; **H. F. Moorhouse**, 'On the Periphery: Scotland, Scottish Football and the New Europe', in Williams and Wagg (eds), *British Football*.

67. Hargreaves, *Sport*, pp. 107–8.

68. Hargreaves, *Sport*, p. 155.

69. Mason, *Football*, p. 179.

70. E.g., *The Times*, 2 June 1930; *Daily Mail*, 31 December 1940; *Picture Post*, 22 December 1945.

71. **B. Lancaster**, 'Newcastle – Capital of What?', in **R. Colls** and **B. Lancaster** (eds), *Geordies: Roots of Regionalism*, Edinburgh University Press, 1992, p. 55.

72. **T. Bennett**, 'Hegemony, Ideology, Pleasure: Blackpool', in Bennett, Mercer and Woollacott (eds), *Popular Culture*, p. 135; also pp. 142–5.

73. **J. Field**, 'The View from Folkestone', in Samuel (ed.), *Patriotism*, II, p. 5.

74. E.g., **H. Taylor**, 'Sporting Heroes', in Colls and Lancaster (eds), *Geordies*.

75. Lowerson, 'Angling', in Mason (ed.), *Sport*, p. 30.

76. 'J. R. H.' to *Daily Mail*, 18 January 1930.

77. Cited Bale, *Sport and Place*, p. 55. *NOP Political Bulletin*, September–October 1971, p. 17.

78. Hargreaves, *Sport*, p. 106. Also Fishwick, *English Football*, p. 97.

79. Mason, *Football*, p. 234. Also **J. Bale**, 'Playing at Home: British

Football and a Sense of Place', in Williams and Wagg (eds), *British Football*, pp. 135–6; **R. J. Holt**, 'Football and the Urban Way of Life in Nineteenth-century Britain', in Mangan (ed.), *Pleasure*, esp. pp. 72–83.

80. Hargreaves, *Sport*, p. 108. Also **J. Williams**, 'Having an Away Day: English Football Spectators and the Hooligan Debate', in Williams and Wagg (eds), *British Football*.

81. Holt, *Sport*, pp. 230, 236.

Chapter 7

THE CREATION OF YOUTH CULTURE?

It has been clear for many years that there is a relationship between consumption and youth culture. Indeed, it seems to be accepted that the relationship, which had always been close, became increasingly intimate during the course of the twentieth century. It is claimed by some commentators that the period between the wars 'was probably the first time that a substantial number of teenage wage-earners in Britain found themselves with a significant amount of money to spend on leisure.'[1] It is claimed much more commonly that the years following the Second World War saw consumption play a key role in the creation of a distinct, distinctive and highly visible youth culture.[2] Thus in his classic study, *Teenage Consumer Spending in 1959*, Mark Abrams concluded that

> the quite large amount of money at the disposal of Britain's average teenager is spent mainly on dress and on goods which form the nexus of teenage gregariousness outside the home. In other words, this is distinctive teenage spending for distinctive teenage ends in a distinctive teenage world.[3]

Here was one group, it seems, that took to consumption with a vengeance.

In fact, the relationship between consumption and youth culture – like that between consumption and national identity – is considerably more complex than it appears at first sight. It has been seen several times already in this study how hard it is to decide when, and to what extent, young people became independent consumers. It can be seen in many other studies how hard it is to decide whether, and to what extent, young people became members of 'a distinctive teenage world'.[4] Nor, of course, is this all. For once again, it is difficult to distinguish between cause and effect, to decide in this case whether changes in consumption were a cause, rather than a consequence, of changes in youth culture. It is difficult to distinguish consumption from all the other influences acting upon young people's behaviour and attitudes: the families in which they were brought up; the schools in which they were taught; the friends with whom they spent their spare time.

None the less, the relationship between consumption and youth culture sometimes seems to be complicated unnecessarily. For example, according to one – unusually clear – statement of sub-cultural theory, young people's consumption was 'a response to the gaps and contradictions in the set of *ideas* that young people are offered (by parents, by the media, by the teenage consumption industry, by the state) as a way of *making sense of their marginality*'.[5] Non-sociologists would probably put it rather more simply: they would suggest, perhaps, that young people turned to activities such as shopping, sport and tourism because they saw them, in part at least, as ways of defining, and expressing, their distinctiveness, a distinctiveness both from the children's world that they were leaving and from the adult world that they were entering.

It is the aim of this chapter to consider the validity of such views, to disentangle – and perhaps demythologise – the relationship between consumption and youth culture. It will be argued that the relationship was rather more straightforward than that between consumption and national identity. It will be shown that while young people's use of consumption helped to forge a number of small, but highly visible, youth sub-cultures, it also served to foster a more broadly based, albeit far less visible, culture that, transcending youth, came to embrace many, if not most, of the teenage population.[6]

Certainly, it would be difficult to ignore the fact that over the past hundred years or so a succession of youth groups – from hooligans to hippies, from students to skinheads – turned to consumption as an important means of defining and expressing their distinctiveness from the remainder of society. It was among such groups that consumption manifested itself most visibly – and, of course, most contentiously.

Nevertheless, the consumption of certain groups of middle-class teenagers does sometimes seem to be overlooked. Nor perhaps is it difficult to see why, for groups like students and hippies tended to be both few in number and constrained in their spending.

Students were a case in point. For they were atypical both in their numbers and in their spending. Throughout most of the period covered by this book, university (and other) students comprised but a tiny minority of young people: between 1900 and 1938/39 the number of full-time students in higher education increased remarkably little, from 25,000 (1.2 per cent of those aged between 18 and 21) to 69,000 (2.7 per cent of those in the age group). It was not until the Robbins Report of 1963, the expansion of teacher training, and the creation of the polytechnics and new universities that the number of students began to climb at all significantly: from 216,000 (8.5 per cent of the age group) in 1962/63, to 534,000 (13.3 per cent) in 1980/81.[7]

This increase in student numbers changed student spending, but did not make it a great deal more typical. For although young people from less privileged (and therefore less atypical) backgrounds began to enter higher education in somewhat greater numbers, they modified – rather than overturned – traditional patterns of student consumption. They were more likely to live at home, and a great deal more likely to be short of money. So it was that walking in the Lakes tended to give way to InterRailing around Europe; that May balls were superseded by Saturday evening hops; and sports jackets were replaced by duffle coats and donkey jackets. As Roy Hattersley recalls, he and his fellow Hull University students 'believed – from the depth of our duffle-coats, corduroy trousers and long, striped scarves – that sartorial rebellion was the hallmark of integrity.'[8]

Hippies were still more atypical consumers. For although they comprised probably the most distinctive of all 1960s middle-class sub-cultures, it has been estimated that by the end of the decade there were no more than fifty serious communal groups in existence throughout the whole of Great Britain.[9] The hippies' rejection of the adult world involved, it has been pointed out, the adoption of alternative 'ways of growing up – play not work, drugs not drink, communes not marriage.'[10] Yet as these examples suggest, their rejection of a conventional way of life did not entail the complete abandonment of all forms of consumption. For hippies, like students, modified – rather than totally rejected – traditional patterns of consumption, spending a good deal of what money they had on the purchase of products such as music and drugs, rather than fashion and furniture.[11] Thus hippies too used consumption – and non-consumption – as a means of defining and expressing their particular view of the world.

Working-class youth groups tended to be a good deal more visible. This was not only because they were larger and there were more of them, but because they set so much store by dressing (and behaving) in distinctive, and often threatening, ways. Thus what is so striking is that, however much the members of these groups wished to challenge adult society, it was consumption that they used as the vehicle with which to mount their challenge.

Such groups had a surprisingly long history. Scholars like Stephen Humphries, Geoffrey Pearson and Paul Thompson point to the 'symbolic provocation' of the street gangs, provocation to which middle-class adults reacted with such anxiety in the years before the First World War.[12] 'Look at them well', exhorted the *Daily Graphic* at the turn of the century.

> The boys affect a kind of uniform. No hat, collar, or tie is to be seen. All of them have a peculiar muffler twisted around the neck, a cap set rakishly forward, well over the eyes, and trousers very tight at the knee and very close at the foot. The most characteristic part of their

uniform is the substantial leather belt heavily mounted with metal. It is not ornamental, but then it is not intended for ornament.[13]

However, most students of youth culture concentrate their attention upon the working-class groups that emerged so spectacularly in the years following the Second World War. Here again, consumption was central to the challenge that they mounted. Indeed, the first of these groups, the 'teddy boys' of the early 1950s, derived their name from their adoption – and adaptation – of Edwardian upper-class clothing. They wore tight 'drainpipe' trousers, drape jackets with velvet collars, bootlace ties, brightly coloured socks and thick crêpe-soled shoes known as 'brothel creepers'.[14] Such proletariatisation of upper-class dress was neither cheap nor, it has been claimed, a mere stylistic flourish: it expressed, it is explained, 'both the reality and the aspirations of the group'.

> Despite periodic unemployment, despite the unskilled jobs, Teds, in common with other teenagers at work during this period, were relatively affluent . . . . Teds thus certainly had money to spend and, because it was practically all they had, it assumed a *crucial* importance. Much of the money went on clothes: the teddy boy 'uniform'.[15]

The groups that followed the teddy boys, the mods and rockers of the 1960s, and the skinheads and punks of the 1970s, all continued to set great store by the use of consumption.[16] The mods provide by far the clearest example of such consumption-related rebellion. Indeed, according to some rather over-enthusiastic commentators, this small group of semi-skilled and white-collar workers from London and the South-east of England assumed a key role in the economic and social development of post-war Britain. They were, claims Mike Brake, 'the pioneers of consumerism, inspiring Mary Quant and Carnaby Street.'[17] This, of course, is to exaggerate. Yet although it is absurd to suggest that the mods were the precursors of post-war consumerism, they certainly did assume considerable symbolic importance; they became, as Brake himself suggests, 'a symbol of affluent teenage consumption'.[18]

In fact, it is the symbolism of the mods that repays particular attention. For the mods, like the teds before them, took conventional, inoffensive products (and practices), and gave them new meanings that made them unacceptable and threatening. 'Thus the scooter, a formerly ultra-respectable means of transport was appropriated and converted into a weapon and a symbol of solidarity. Thus pills, medically diagnosed for the treatment of neuroses, were appropriated and used as an end-in-themselves'.[19] Thus the traditional bank holiday trip to the seaside was transformed into a wonderful opportunity to claim public space, fight rockers, alarm holiday-makers and enrage the authorities.[20]

It is not difficult to see then why so much attention has been lavished upon the small minority of teenagers who became members of these highly visible youth groups and sub-cultures. However, considerable caution is necessary, for most young people were, of course, neither students nor hippies, neither teds nor mods. Indeed, some social scientists specialising in youth culture have had the grace to admit that when they and their colleagues 'turn their eyes on the adolescent, they somehow forget their own youth.'

> And so their reason falls prey to the recurring moral panics which surround young people: drug orgies, football hooliganism, mugging, mods and rockers, Hell's Angels, rock festivals, truanting, student unrest, ban the bomb, cosh boys, teddy boys, skinheads, drop-outs, venereal disease, glue-sniffing, vandalism etc., etc., etc.[21]

The fact is that most young people, boys as well as girls, working-class as well as middle-class, rebelled a good deal more cautiously than a litany of such panics would lead one to suppose. The great majority of young people spent more time in their bedrooms or at church youth clubs than they did at rock festivals or on the football terraces.[22] The great majority of young people managed to get through their teenage years without becoming involved in anything that could remotely – or at least reasonably – be described as deviant or delinquent behaviour.[23]

Accordingly, it is the aim of the remainder of the chapter to consider the consumption of this, the – relatively silent – majority of young people. It will be argued that most young people's experience of consumption – or at least of shopping, tourism and sport, the three activities at the core of this study – proved of considerable, and increasing, importance in reinforcing and strengthening the generational awareness of the teenage population. For consumption it was that provided a standard against which many, if not most, young people began to compare themselves; consumption it was that provided an ideal to which many, if not most, young people sought to aspire.

Shopping became of central importance: young people's experience of this, the most common form of consumption tended to reinforce their sense both of being young and of belonging to a distinct, albeit often rather inchoate, youth culture. For whether they shopped with their parents, by themselves, or with their friends; whether they bought the same products as other consumers, or purchased those created specifically for the youth market, the result tended to be much the same: they found that their activities very often brought them into conflict with parents, shopkeepers and other members of the adult world.

Shopping with parents was fraught with difficulties, and frequently resulted in – more or less thinly disguised – disagreement and resentment. Nor perhaps could it be otherwise. For as they grew older, middle-class daughters disliked being expected to accompany their mothers on regular weekend expeditions to local dress shops and department stores.[24] As they grew older, children of all classes – and both sexes – resented the control that accompanying parents were able to exercise over the products that they bought. The author of this book remembers – only too vividly – the embarrassment of going shopping with his mother to buy short trousers when he was a young teenager in Romford during the late 1950s.[25] Stef Pixner remembers – just as vividly, it seems – the embarrassment of going shopping with her mother in North London at much the same time.

> On Saturdays I go with Mum to the market in Camden Town, and the Coop department store they have there . . . . As I get older, though, I don't want to spend Saturdays with her any more. It gets tiresome, and I feel sulky. *Mummy thinks I am very moody and hoity-toity, but she treats me as if I'm so young.*[26]

If shopping with parents brought the most acute embarrassment, shopping alone, or with friends, brought other difficulties, many of which served, once again, to set the young apart from those older than themselves. It was seen earlier in this volume that as the period progressed young people's – more or less reluctant – involvement in family food shopping gave way to a – normally much more enthusiastic – involvement in buying consumer goods for themselves. The result was that by the 1950s, if not before, going shopping on a Saturday seems to have become part of many girls' (and to a lesser extent boys') regular weekly routine. Indeed, it was in the local high street, looking at the latest fashions, choosing a new dress, buying a hit record, or crowding into a coffee bar, that many young people came to feel, however fleetingly, that they, like those they read about in newspapers and magazines, were members of the new, consumerist and highly distinctive youth culture.[27]

This sense of distinctiveness was reinforced by the reactions of many adults to teenage spending. Shopkeepers were sometimes rather suspicious of young people shopping alone – and were often highly suspicious of those shopping together in groups.[28] Then too, parents were frequently critical of the products that their children brought home from their shopping expeditions. In fact, the oral and autobiographical evidence contains surprisingly few examples of such disputes, but it seems reasonable to suppose that they became more common as teenage spending became more powerful, and adult concern more pronounced. Thus in his fascinating study of Campbell Bunk, Islington, between the wars, Jerry White cites several graphic instances of working-class girls quarrelling bitterly with their mothers over the buying of clothes. May Purslowe and her mother were, White explains, constantly at loggerheads. 'Mrs Purslowe had taken it on herself to clothe May out of the money the girl handed over [from her wages]. But her mother's choice of couturier was restricted to totters' barrows in Campbell Road and the Fonthill Road rag shop.' May Purslowe takes up the story.

> And this one particular day I said to her, 'I'm not giving you all my money, I'm gonna buy my own clothes.' And we went to Chapel Street, Islington market, and I bought a velvet skirt and a blouse. And when I came home, washed meself, dressed to go out, she says to me, 'And where do you think *you're* going?' I said, 'Well, I'm going out.' So she says, 'Oh are you? And she did no more, she tore all these clothes off me.[29]

No doubt, when readers of this book recall their own teenage years they will remember similar, if perhaps less violent, disputes with their parents over the clothes, tapes, magazines and records that they bought while out shopping with their friends. As a columnist in one provincial newspaper remarked rather coyly in 1964, at the height perhaps of popular concern about teenage consumption, 'Mother and daughter cannot worship at the same shrine.'[30]

It seems clear, then, that shopping assumed a considerable, and growing, significance in the fostering of youth culture. Indeed, it is no exaggeration to suggest that the relationship between shopping and young people is fundamental to a proper understanding of the rise of the so-called consumer society. For as consumption and youth culture became more closely entwined, it was in the high street that their embrace was to be found at its most intimate and most influential.

Tourism never assumed the same significance as shopping in the fostering of youth culture. Nor can this come as any real surprise. For it has been seen already that during most of the period covered by this book young people had relatively little experience of tourism, and that what experience they did have tended to be confined to day trips and/or holidays taken, not with friends, but with members of their family. It was not, it seems, until the final twenty to thirty years of the period that tourism began to reflect, and/or stimulate, young consumers' sense both of being young and belonging to a distinctive youth culture.

Day trips were long taken in family groups. In fact, the spread of car ownership during the 1950s and 1960s probably tended, at least at first, to keep families together on their days out. For example, the son of a co-operative store manager from Preston remembers that although he and his family never went away on holiday together, his great uncle owned a car and used to take them out on day trips to places such as Blackpool, Chester Zoo and the Lake District.[31]

Holidays too were long taken in family groups. Indeed, for many years holidays were, if anything, still more family-orientated than day trips. For not only did young people who went on holiday usually go away with their parents, they often went to stay with aunts, uncles, grandparents, or friends of the family. It has been explained already that it became increasingly common for young people of all classes to go on holiday with their families, and that such family holidays remained common even during the burgeoning, and some would say revolutionary, youth culture of the 1960s. It must be stressed too that it remained surprisingly common for young people to spend their holidays with their relatives. Two examples, taken almost at random from Barrow-in-Furness during the late 1940s and 1950s, will serve to illustrate the resilience and importance of such forms of tourism. A middle-class respondent recalls that, apart from one family holiday in a London hotel, her holidays as a girl consisted of occasional brief visits to family friends, one visit to an aunt in Ireland, and a number of summers spent with her grandparents.[32] A working-class respondent recalls that the only holiday he ever had when a boy was going to Bolton to see his father's parents.[33]

The growth of more commercialised forms of travel and accommodation did surprisingly little to undermine the family basis of the British summer holiday. In fact, the organisers of the new forms of mass tourism – holiday camps, caravan parks, camp sites and package tours – sought primarily, and sometimes exclusively, to attract visitors in family groups. Holiday camps provided facilities popular with young families; caravan parks promised their clients 'the perfect family holiday'; and package-tour operators did their best to appeal to families by offering discounts for children, and organising play schemes and baby-sitting/listening services.[34]

The family nature of British tourism was not, of course, necessarily welcomed by teenagers condemned, as they often saw it, to spend their holidays, as well as the rest of the year, trapped within the confines of the nuclear family. Many young holiday-makers attempted, more or less successfully, to assert their independence by distancing themselves, both emotionally and physically, from their parents and siblings. Sulking was common, and struggles for autonomy the source of many arguments. It will be recalled that when a Lancashire apprentice and three of his friends booked a holiday at Butlin's in Pwllheli in 1960, his parents arranged to stay at the same camp, at the same time. However, it will be recalled too that his attempt at independence was not entirely in vain: 'it was a big place and the lads and all the teenagers were altogether and all the families'.[35] Thus family holidays, like family shopping, often reminded teenagers, yet again, that they were young and belonged to – or aspired to belong to – a youth culture that was different from, and in some respects antagonisitic to, that of their parents.[36]

Nevertheless, the family nature of British tourism should not be exaggerated. There was also a long history, it will be recalled, of teenagers (and younger children) going away, semi-independently, in the care of adults other than their parents: they took day trips, and went on camping and other holidays organised by a whole number of religious, educational, uniformed and other special interest groups.[37] There was a long history, too, of teenagers going away on day trips and holidays independent both of parents and of adults acting *in loco parentis*. Seen in this light, the bank holiday battles between mods and rockers that erupted during the 1960s should be viewed perhaps as the culmination, rather than the beginning, of adult anxiety over teenage tourism.[38] Seen in this light, the delights promised by package-tour operators such as Club 18–30 should be viewed as the continuation, in warmer and more exotic locations, of the oppportunities for independence, romance and entertainment offered by the holiday camps immediately before and after the Second World War.[39]

It seems clear then that by the end of the period covered in this book tourism had assumed some significance in the fostering of youth culture, although it would be an exaggeration to suggest that the relationship between tourism and young people attained anything like the same importance as that between shopping and young people. However, it would not be unreasonable to maintain that as consumption and youth culture became more closely entwined, so seaside and other resorts – from Blackpool to Benidorm, from Margate to Majorca – became associated more obviously with young consumers spending money, enjoying themselves, and asserting their independence.

Sport was less important than tourism and shopping – and less important than might be expected – in the fostering of youth culture. In fact, the disjunction between sport, consumption and youth culture is difficult both to describe and to explain. It has been shown already that even though young people played, and probably watched, more sport than those from other age groups, this did not necessarily involve them in the additional expenditure that might be anticipated. It will be shown here that even when young people did spend money on their sporting interests, this did not necessarily strengthen their sense of being young and/or of belonging to a distinctive youth culture. Sport, it must be remembered, often served as a bridge, as well as a barrier, between the generations.

Young people played, watched (and sometimes gambled on) sport in the company not only of their peers but also of the adults whose lives intersected with theirs. Thus the majority of young people playing football, Rugby, cricket, rounders or netball on an organised basis probably did so in teams run by (and using pitches and equipment provided by) teachers, employers, clergymen and youth-club leaders.[40] The minority of young people who pursued their sporting interests to a higher level almost invariably played alongside (and were coached and supported by) enthusiasts older than themselves. Indeed, one turn-of-the-century observer of working-class life in the industrial North remarked that 'when play is organized for youths of a particular age it is common for those of a higher age to lie and cheat in order to join', both to get a game and to try to make sure of winning.[41]

The relationship between such participation, consumption and youth culture remains difficult to disentangle. Sometimes, of course, the involvement of adults led, as with tourism and shopping, to resentment and rejection. It has been found, not very surprisingly, that secondary schoolgirls tended to view with suspicion the sexual orientation of their games teachers, and to regard the entire physical education curriculum as 'unfeminine, irrelevant and childish'.[42] However, it has also been found, again not very surprisingly, that 'considerably fewer schoolboys develop hostility to PE as compared with girls', and that although 'Most adult males give up participation in active sport as they grow older . . . they will not give up being participants in the sports culture which is so important a feature of male bonding at all levels.'[43] So it seems that whether or not young sportsmen spent much on their clothing and equipment, the fact that they played with adults meant that they were inculcated, more than non-participants, into an adult culture that stressed hard work, fair play, social drinking and male bonding.[44] It was only towards the very end of the period, when the distinction between sporting goods and fashion goods became blurred, that participation, consumption and youth culture became inextricably, albeit rather misleadingly, interrelated.

However, this emphasis upon the cross-generational nature of participation must not be allowed to obscure the fact that towards the end of the period a growing, though still modest, number of young consumers began to watch (and sometimes gamble on) sport in the company of others of their own age. Unfortunately, football is the only activity about which it is possible to generalise with any confidence at all. It has been seen, for example, that the age structure and behaviour of football crowds began to change in the years following the Second World War. Until the 1940s and 1950s young supporters tended to go to matches with their fathers, and stand on the terraces with spectators of all ages. A Manchester City supporter remembers that at Maine Road

> it was a very mixed crowd. There were a lot of old blokes, and women, even some elderly women. You all stood there together. You knew everybody. You never saw 'em between games. But we always stood in roughly the same place and we knew the forty or fifty people around us 'cos they were always there.[45]

The situation began to change during the 1960s.[46] It is important, of course, not to confuse, and conflate, the behaviour of the hooligans with that of the majority of young and peaceable, if highly vocal, supporters. None the less, it does seem that changes were afoot; fewer teenagers went with their fathers to matches, and were prepared to meet up with the 'old blokes'. More and more, it appears, young spectators began to meet their friends in the pub, go together to the match, and join up with other young supporters at particular 'ends' of the ground.

> Sustained by the self-confidence and greater autonomy provided by the new youth cultures and buoyed by the nationalistic excess inspired by the England World Cup success of 1966, 'the lads' began to establish the Saturday afternoon rituals which quickly attracted aspiring 'hard cases' from the housing estates and city neighbourhoods.[47]

'We're gonna win the football league again', they chanted; 'You're gonna get your fuckin' heads kicked in'.[48]

Such changes were more important than they may appear. For although most young people never went near a football ground, it became fashionable to take an interest in the sport, and important for working-class (and to some extent middle-class) youths who wished to retain credibility with their friends to participate in the Saturday afternoon rituals; they had a drink, went to the match, had a few more drinks, and bought a football special on the way home. Once again, the 1960s were of key significance. For this was the decade during which England won the World Cup; this was the decade during which football spectatorship, and the consumption associated with it, assumed a considerable importance in young people's, as well as in working people's lives.[49]

The relationship between sport, gambling and youth culture also seems to have changed, to some limited extent, during the 1960s. However, it is important to exaggerate neither the scale nor the consequences of this transformation. For both before and after the 1960s, most teenagers showed relatively little interest in gambling on sport (or indeed on anything else): it will be recalled, for example, that although the evidence about young people's betting is extremely patchy, it suggests that they gambled far less than those in their twenties and thirties.[50] Moreover, both before and after the 1960s, many, if not most, teenagers probably learned about gambling from members of their immediate family. They took bets to the local street bookmaker, they went with their father to the nearest greyhound track; and they helped, or at least watched, their parents fill in the pools coupon each Monday or Tuesday evening.[51]

Yet some change did occur. There was an increasing tendency, it appears, for those teenagers who did gamble to do so alone or with friends of their own age. It was a change that was made possible by a combination of structural and legislative developments. The growth of larger, more heavily capitalised, more convenient – and above all more anonymous – forms of gambling made it easier for young people to gamble whether or not they had their parents' approval.[52] The passing of the Betting and Gaming Act of 1960 had much the same effect: for it led, so it seemed, to the opening of betting shops in every town and village in the land.[53] Such developments notwithstanding, it is difficult to sustain the argument that betting on sport became, or ever had been, part of a distinctive youth culture. Betting on sport remained, as it always had been, part of a distinctive, but a much broader and largely working-class culture.

Thus the impact of these changes should not be exaggerated, and the relationship between sport, consumption and youth culture should not be simplified unduly. However, some generalisation is now possible. It appears that by the end of the period sport generally had assumed some limited importance in the fostering of youth culture. For if nothing else, it had become fashionable for boys and young men to follow football, and fashionable for young people of both sexes to wear track suits, trainers and other types of sports clothing.

The evidence that has been presented in this chapter points to a number of clear, and apparently uncontentious, conclusions. It suggests, above all, that there was a significant, and growing, relationship between consumption and youth culture, so that by the 1960s young people seemed to be among the most active, enthusiastic and independent of all consumers. More and more, it seems, young people shopped, travelled and watched sport with their own money, in their own way, in their own time. More and more, it seems, such consumption became an integral part of a new and distinctive teenage culture that appeared, to some commentators at least, almost to transcend region, gender and class.

None the less, the relationship between consumption and youth culture was less straightforward than it appeared to some observers. It is true, of course, that the evidence produced in this chapter, as in the book as a whole, considers only three forms of consumption: shopping, tourism and sport. Such a focus, valuable though it is, can prove particularly misleading in the study of youth culture; for it ignores several forms of consumption, such as reading, drinking, dancing and going to the cinema, which had long been of equal, if not greater, importance to large numbers of young people.[54] Thus it should be borne constantly in mind that the evidence presented in this chapter tends, if anything, to underestimate the intimacy of the relationship between consumption and youth culture.

That said, the evidence produced in this chapter points to two broad, convincing and important conclusions regarding the relationship between consumption and youth culture. It shows that peer-group pressure and parental pressure were not necessarily mutually antagonistic; and that the cohesiveness of consumption was in no way able to transcend the divisiveness of region, gender and class. It confirms, in other words, that consumption did not create a distinct and distinctive youth culture.

NOTES AND REFERENCES

1. **D. Fowler**, 'Teenage Consumers? Young Wage-Earners and Leisure in Manchester, 1919–1939', in **A. Davies** and **S. Fielding** (eds), *Workers' Worlds: Cultures and Communities in Manchester and Salford, 1880–1939*, Manchester University Press, 1992, p. 150.
2. See, e.g., **S. Frith**, *The Sociology of Youth*, Causeway Books, 1984, p. 8; **D. O'Sullivan**, *The Youth Culture*, Methuen, 1974, pp. 7, 10–11.
3. **M. Abrams**, *Teenage Consumer Spending in 1959 (Part II): Middle Class and Working Class Boys and Girls*, London Press Exchange, 1961, p. 5. Also **P. Willmott**, *Adolescent Boys of East London*, Routledge & Kegan Paul, 1966, p. 15; **J. McGuigan**, *Cultural Populism*, Routledge, 1992, pp. 90, 92; **H. Gilbert**, 'Growing Pains', in **L. Heron** (ed.), *Truth, Dare or Promise: Girls Growing Up in the Fifties*, Virago, 1985, pp. 45–6; **B. Osgerby**, '"Well, It's Saturday Night an' I Just Got Paid": Youth, Consumerism and Hegemony in Post-War Britain', *Contemporary Record*, **6**, 1992.
4. See, e.g., Frith, *Sociology*, pp. 1–11, 38–48.
5. Frith, *Sociology*, p. 44; also pp. 38–48, **P. Willis**, *Common Culture: Symbolic Work at Play in the Everyday Cultures of the Young*, Open University Press, 1990, pp. 86–7. For other guides to sub-cultural theory, see McGuigan, *Cultural Populism*, pp. 92–7; **J. Muncie**, 'Pop Culture, Pop Music and Post-War Youth: Subculture', in **Open University**, *Politics, Ideology and Popular Culture (1)*, Open University Press, 1982, pp. 33–43.
6. **S. Hall** and **T. Jefferson** (eds), *Resistance through Rituals: Youth Subcultures in Post-War Britain*, Hutchinson, 1976. Cf. **J. Springhall**, 'Rotton to the Very Core: Leisure and Youth 1830–1914', *Youth and Policy*, **14**, 1985, and **15**, 1985/86.
7. **A. H. Halsey** (ed.), *Trends in British Society since 1900: A Guide to the Changing Social Structure of Britain*, Macmillan, 1972, p. 206; **E. Royle**, *Modern Britain: A Social History 1750–1985*, Arnold, 1987, p. 384; **Central Statistical Office**, *Key Data 1986*, HMSO, 1986. The figure of 13.3 per cent for 1980/81 refers to those aged 15–19.
8. **R. Hattersley**, in *Guardian*, Spring 1992. Also **M. Beloff**, *The Plateglass Universities*, Secker & Warburg, 1968; information from David Sanderson.
9. **C. Webster**, 'Communes: A Thematic Typology', in Hall and Jefferson (eds), *Resistance*, p. 127.
10. **M. Brake**, *The Sociology of Youth Culture and Youth Subcultures: Sex and Drugs and Rock 'n' Roll*, Routledge & Kegan Paul, 1980, p. 16.

11. Brake, *Sociology*, p. 98.
12. **P. Thompson**, *The Edwardians: The Remaking of British Society*, Paladin, 1977, p. 71. Also **S. Humphries**, *Hooligans or Rebels? An Oral History of Working-class Childhood and Youth 1889–1939*, Blackwell, 1981; **G. Pearson**, *Hooligan: A History of Respectable Fears*, Macmillan, 1983.
13. Pearson, *Hooligan*, pp. 93–4. Also **R. Roberts**, *The Classic Slum: Salford Life in the First Quarter of the Century*, Penguin, 1973, p. 155; **J. R. Gillis**, 'The Evolution of Juvenile Delinquency in England 1890–1914', *Past and Present*, **67**, 1975, p. 122; **C. E. B. Russell**, *Manchester Boys: Sketches of Manchester Lads at Work and Play*, Manchester University Press, 1913, pp. 48–51; **T. Golding**, *The Brum We Knew*, p. 13.
14. Brake, *Sociology*, p. 72. See also **S. Chibnall**, 'Whistle and Zoot: The Changing Meaning of a Suit of Clothes', *History Workshop*, **20**, 1985.
15. **T. Jefferson**, 'Cultural Responses of the Teds: The Defence of Space and Status', in Hall and Jefferson (eds), *Resistance*, p. 81. Also **F. Hartley**, *Where Sparrows Coughed*, Sheaf Publishing, 1989, pp. 48, 83–5. Cf. Lancaster, Mr R1P, p. 46.
16. Brake, *Sociology*, pp. 75–8; Muncie, 'Pop Culture', pp. 45–50.
17. **M. Brake**, *Comparative Youth Culture: The Sociology of Youth Cultures and Youth Subcultures in America, Britain and Canada*, Routledge, 1985, p. 74. Also **D. Hebdige**, 'The Meaning of Mod', in Hall and Jefferson (eds), *Resistance*, pp. 87, 90.
18. Brake, *Sociology*, p. 76.
19. Hebdige, 'Mod', p. 93.
20. **P. Barker**, 'The Margate Offenders: A Survey', in **T. Raison** (ed.), *Youth in New Society*, Hart-Davis, 1966.
21. **G. Mungham** and **G. Pearson**, 'Introduction: Troubled Youth, Troubled World', in **G. Mungham** and **G. Pearson** (eds), *Working Class Youth Culture*, Routledge & Kegan Paul, 1976, p. 2.
22. Lancaster, Mrs C8P, p. 53; Mrs P5B, p. 31; **J. Guest**, *Nobody's Perfect: An Autobiography*, Trinity Arts, 1981, p. 30; McGuigan, *Cultural Populism*, pp. 107–8; **H. George**, 'The Experience of Youth in Harrow 1948–1963', MA dissertation, University of Warwick, 1992, pp. 3, 62; Osgerby, 'Saturday Night', esp. pp. 288–9.
23. Brake, *Comparative Youth Culture*, p. 23. Cf. Humphries, *Hooligans*, p. 178; George, 'Youth', pp. 3, 36–8, 62; Lancaster, Mrs P5B, pp. 31, 34; Guest, *Nobody's Perfect*, pp. 27–30.
24. Lancaster, Mrs R3B, p. 11; Mrs R4B, p. 29; information from Clare Benson and Yvonne Sanderson; Mass-Observation, 3150, 'A Report on Teen-age Girls', 1949, p. 3; **G. Raverat**, *Period Piece: A Cambridge Childhood*, Faber & Faber, *c.* 1952, p. 255.
25. Author's recollection.
26. **S. Pixner**, 'The Oyster and the Shadow', in *Truth, Dare or Promise*, p. 96.
27. **N. James**, *A Derbyshire Life*, Postmill Press, 1981, p. 37; Willmott, *Boys*, p. 15; information from Yvonne Sanderson; Bristol, E. T. Rich to S. Humphries, 30 September 1979; R04, p. 16; Lancaster, Mr R3B, p. 24; 'Men's Wear', *Retail Business*, July 1980, p. 60.

28. See, e.g., **C. MacInnes**, *Absolute Beginners*, Penguin, 1964, pp. 10–11.
29. **J. White**, *The Worst Street in North London: Campbell Bunk, Islington, Between the Wars*, Routledge & Kegan Paul, 1986, p. 202.
30. *Express and Star*, 19 May 1964.
31. Lancaster, Mr R1P, p. 57. Also Mr S9P, p. 35; Willmott, *Boys*, p. 24.
32. Lancaster, Mrs R4B, p. 46.
33. Lancaster, Mrs B2B, p. 22. Also Mrs L2L, p. 38; George, 'Harrow', p. 39.
34. *Express and Star*, 21 May 1964; 7, 9 January 1980; **E. Hopkins**, *The Rise and Decline of the English Working Classes 1918–1990*, Weidenfeld & Nicolson, 1991, pp. 182–3.
35. Lancaster, Mr R1P, p. 32; information from Yvonne Sanderson.
36. Hartley, *Sparrows*, p. 29.
37. E.g., Bristol, R04, p. 17; E. T. Rich to S. Humphries, 30 September 1979; 515276, J. Morkunas to S. Humphries, 19 September 1979; Lancaster, Mrs R3P, p. 81; *Express and Star*, 22, 28 July 1938.
38. Willmott, *Boys*, pp. 23–4, 154.
39. **C. Ward** and **D. Hardy**, *Goodnight Campers! The History of the British Holiday Camp*, Mansell, 1986, p. 101; 'Holidays Abroad', *Mintel*, December 1981, pp. 29–30.
40. **N. Fishwick**, *English Football and Society, 1910–1950*, Manchester University Press, 1989, pp. 6–7. However, working-class youths frequently clashed with the police over playing in the street. See **S. G. Jones**, *Sport, Politics and the Working Class: Organised Labour and Sport in Interwar Britain*, Manchester University Press, 1988, pp. 136–7.
41. **R. Holt**, *Sport and the British: A Modern History*, Oxford University Press, 1990, p. 139. Also **F. Zweig**, *The British Worker*, Pelican, 1952, p. 128.
42. **O. Leaman**, 'Physical Education and Sex Differentiation', *British Journal of Physical Education*, **17**, 1986, p. 123; information from Yvonne Sanderson.
43. Leaman, 'Physical Education', p. 123. Cf. Holt, *Sport*, p. 338.
44. Zweig, *Worker*, pp. 124–30; **R. Hoggart**, *The Uses of Literacy: Aspects of Working-class Life with Special Reference to Publications and Entertainments*, Penguin, 1957, pp. 328–9.
45. Holt, *Sport*, p. 334. However, trouble was not unknown. In 1921, the boys' section at Bradford Park Avenue was closed for three months after a referee had been pelted with rubbish. Pearson, *Hooligan*, p. 30.
46. **S. Redhead**, 'An Era of the End, or the End of an Era: Football and Youth Culture', in **J. Williams** and **S. Wagg** (eds), *British Football and Social Change: Getting into Europe*, Leicester University Press, 1991, pp. 146–9.
47. **J. Williams**, 'Having an Away Day: English Football Spectators and the Hooligan Debate', in Williams and Wagg (eds), *British Football*, p. 166.
48. Holt, *Sport*, p. 336; author's recollection.
49. Holt, *Sport*, p. 340.

50. Mass-Observation, 2538, 'Preliminary Synopsis of Report on Gambling', 1947, p. 7; 'Gambling', *Mintel*, November 1978, pp. 50, 52; Fowler, 'Teenage Consumers?'.

51. **R. Samuel**, *East End Underworld: Chapters in the Life of Arthur Harding*, Routledge & Kegan Paul, 1981; *RC on Betting, Lotteries and Gaming, Report*, 1951, pp. 52, 97.

52. **C. Smith**, *Adolescence: An Introduction to the Problems of Order and the Opportunities for Continuity Presented by Adolescence in Britain*, Longman, 1968, p. 91. Also White, *Worst Street*, p. 166.

53. **A. Marwick**, *British Society since 1945*, Penguin, 1990, p. 141.

54. See, e.g., **G. Mungham**, 'Youth in Pursuit of Itself', in Mungham and Pearson (eds), *Working Class Culture*; **A. Davies**, 'Leisure Patterns among Working-Class Youths', unpublished paper, University of Warwick, January 1991.

Chapter 8

THE EMANCIPATION OF WOMEN?

The relationship between consumption and women's (so-called) emancipation has received an enormous amount of attention – some of it scholarly, some of it popular, and most of it highly polemical.[1] It is argued by those on the right that consumption helped to liberate women, empowering them in unprecedented, and often unforeseen ways. Thus according to Conservative MP Teresa Gorman 'Women actually have enormous political power in this country because they're the people who do the shopping, who spend most of the household budget'.[2] Feminists and those on the left tend to disagree most profoundly. They regard consumption as a patriarchal-cum-capitalist device which, deliberately or not, tends to confine women to the home, enslave them to fashion, and keep them subservient to men. Thus, according to feminist historian Elizabeth Wilson, it is absurd to claim that the spread of Hoovers, refrigerators and other consumer durables in the years following the Second World War afforded women anything approaching equality. For, 'Quite apart from the fact that only a minority of women had access to these aids . . . even where electricity did replace muscle power, most of the burdens and responsibilities of domesticity remained untouched.'[3]

It is clear, then, that the relationship between consumption and emancipation remains complex and contentious, and raises ideological and empirical difficulties of the most intractable kind. It is not easy to agree upon a definition of women's emancipation, it is more difficult still to measure it empirically, and it seems almost impossible to determine the extent to which such emancipation as did occur was brought about by changes in consumption, as opposed to changes, say, in the economy, in technology, in contraception or in the legal and social security systems.

It is because of – and in spite of – such complexity and uncertainty, that the purpose of this chapter is to clarify the relationship, if any, that existed between consumption and women's emancipation. It will be argued that this relationship, like that between consumption and national identity, was fundamentally contradictory. It will be shown that, although changes in consumption offered women new economic power, new social possibilities, and new opportunities for improving their social status, it did so within limits that confirmed and reinforced, rather than challenged and undermined women's conventional role and status.

Consumption certainly offered women new ways of exercising economic power. However, as so often in the study of consumption, considerable caution needs to be exercised. For while it is possible to point, without undue difficulty, to ways in which women's power over consumption changed during the period covered by this book, it is also easy to exaggerate the scale, and misunderstand the meaning, of these changes. It can be tempting to overestimate both the dependence of nineteenth-century women and the independence of their twentieth-century successors.

It is essential to recognise that nineteenth-century women of all classes exercised considerable power over household and other, generally related, forms of consumption. Even aristocratic women sometimes maintained overall – though not, of course, day-to-day – responsibility for the conduct of their households.[4] Middle-class women were, of course, much more likely to exercise day-to-day – as well as overall – responsibility for household consumption. In fact, it has been pointed out most tellingly that

> The image of the perfect Victorian lady to all intents and purposes decorative and idle, has been fractured by . . . [a] consideration of the attention to household budgeting and routine demanded of the large numbers of middle class wives responsible for making ends meet on between £100 and £300 a year.[5]

It is not difficult to recognise that running a lower-middle-class household was likely to be extremely demanding. 'The problem of making both ends meet when the income is insufficient has a most pernicious effect upon women's health,' it was explained in 1888. 'The process is thoroughly disheartening and devitalizing. It gives an anxious, worn expression easy to recognize. – Those who toil so laboriously to save must of necessity, spend themselves.'[6] It is perhaps less commonly recognised that running an upper-middle-class household could also prove most difficult and time-consuming. For, although servants were there to save housewives from unladylike drudgery, they were unable to relieve them of the burden of overall responsibility.[7] Thus when Violet Markham took over the running of her family home in 1912, she discovered that her mother had kept scrupulous accounts, and imposed a detailed timetable listing the work that each of the household's nine servants was to carry out on a daily and weekly basis.[8]

Working-class women had little choice, of course, but to exercise day-to-day – not to mention hour-to-hour – responsibility for household consumption. It was seen earlier in the book that recent oral investigations have emphasised the power that late-nineteenth- and early twentieth-century working women exercised over the scale and nature of consumer demand.[9] These studies make it clear that whereas it was the husband's duty to provide his family with as high and as steady an income as he could, it was the wife's responsibility to make it stretch as far as possible.[10]

None the less, considerable caution continues to be necessary. For it would be ironic if this new, and long overdue, awareness of women's responsibilities led, in its turn, to still further misunderstanding. For while it is true that women had responsibility for – and power over – most working-class household expenditure, this was as likely to be penance as pleasure. It was the responsibility, after all, for worrying, scrimping and struggling, for making do with far too little, for far too many, for far too long.

> Whereas more financially secure wives, including those of the upper working class, were reliant generally on the wallet of the husband, it was the purse of a mother which was the common fund amongst the families of the poor. She it was who paid the rent, who bought the clothes, who purchased the food and who applied for credit at the local corner shop. It was she who conducted all financial negotiations and it was upon her generalship that the family relied to supply it with a meal.[11]

It would be ironic, too, if this new awareness of the economic power of nineteenth-century women served to conceal, rather than reveal, the changes that took place during the course of the twentieth century. For although women's control over consumption changed very markedly over the period covered by this book, it did not necessarily do so in a straightforward or beneficial fashion. There were in fact a number of contradictory, albeit closely related, developments. Women gained power over consumption in so far as they spent more money on food and household goods: they lost power in so far as such spending constituted both a declining proportion of family expenditure and a form of consumption in which other family members began to take an interest. Women increased their power over consumption in so far as they spent more money (and a growing proportion of family expenditure) on consumer durables and medical, beauty and fashion products: they gained no power at all in so far as a surprisingly large number of women were able to buy such products only with the approval and/or generosity of their husbands.

In all events, the changes taking place in women's control over the consumption of food and household goods are by no means easy to disentangle. However, it seems, on the face of it, that women as a whole maintained, and even increased, the power that they exercised over such spending. They maintained their power largely because the family division of labour remained essentially unchanged. For, as was seen earlier in the book, even when husbands took an interest in what was bought, helped carry the shopping or went to the shops on their own, food shopping remained, as it always had been, overwhelmingly and unambiguously a female responsibility. Women increased the power that they exercised over food and household consumption chiefly because family incomes grew so substantially. For, as was also seen earlier in the book, when incomes rose, so too did the amount of money that was spent – by women – on buying food and household goods for their families.

Conversely, women's control over this form of consumption did not continue unchallenged. It was weakened in part by the operation of Engels' Law which claimed, it will be recalled, that as incomes rose, so the proportion (as opposed to the amount) of family income spent on food would begin to decline. And decline it did: from 28 per cent of consumer expenditure in 1913, to 26 per cent in 1937, 22 per cent in 1965, and just 14 per cent in 1985.[12] Nor was this all. Women's control was weakened further because, as incomes rose and shopping became less burdensome, so other family members began to take more of an interest in this aspect of the family economy. This did not mean, it must be stressed, that women relinquished their responsibility for food and household consumption – only that they relinquished some of the autonomy that they had exercised when life had been harder, and time and money in shorter supply.

Hard though it is to identify the changes taking place in women's control over food and household consumption, it is more difficult still to disaggregate these developments on a class basis. Yet it is an attempt that needs to be made. Unfortunately, the experiences of upper-class women remain particularly elusive. For such is the paucity of evidence concerning the domestic arrangements of twentieth-century aristocrats that any hypothesis seems likely to advance little beyond rather clumsy conjecture. However, it does not seem implausible to suggest that, as aristocratic fortunes declined, the responsibilities of aristocratic wives and mothers probably increased.

The experiences of middle-class women are far better documented, though little easier to disentangle. It seems, however, that for many years the combination of rising real incomes, growing white-collar employment and more readily available labour-saving devices failed to compensate fully for the decline of domestic assistance. The result was that, while middle-class women maintained, and sometimes increased, their power over household consumption, this sometimes became more – rather than less – of a burden. For a very high standard of housekeeping continued to be expected. During the inter-war years, for example, housewives were advised that consumption, like housework, needed to be planned and carried out in a thoroughly efficient and professional manner.[13] It was only in the years following the Second World War that continuing prosperity, the spread of car ownership, the growth of supermarkets, the availability of refrigerators – and the assistance of husbands – began to compensate, in any real way, for the loss of paid help in the home. So it was perhaps only in the years following the Second World War that many middle-class women began, once again, to enjoy, as well as accept, the responsibility for buying the family's food and household goods.[14]

The changing power of working-class women remains nearly as opaque. It is clear, of course, that growing female employment and rising real incomes combined together to increase the purchasing power, both collectively and individually, of millions upon millions of working-class women. However, it is surprisingly difficult to move far beyond such bald and rather anodyne statements. For despite the interest that has been shown in working-class history and women's history, remarkably little attention has been paid to the history of working-class women consumers. It seems probable, however, that working-class women, like those from the middle class, began to share the burden of food and household shopping just as it was beginning to lose some of its more unappealing aspects. It seems probable, too, that the survival of the domestic division of labour meant that working-class women continued to take a different view of consumption from other members of their families. For, as Mass-Observation concluded in 1940, the fact that the London housewife bore the basic responsibility for housing and feeding her family meant that 'Her "propensity to consume" is therefore much more rigidly conservative than that of other members of the family on whom the full burden of budgeting does not fall'.[15]

These and other features of women's control over the consumption of food and household goods during the course of the twentieth century are not at all easy to identify. However, it can be seen that although women generally increased the economic power that they were able to wield, they found themselves caught in something of a double bind. For they discovered that they retained control over household consumption so long as it remained arduous and challenging, but that they began to share control when it seemed as though it was becoming more interesting and enjoyable.

Fortunately, the changes taking place in women's control over spending on so-called 'female' products appear to be less fraught with uncertainty and ambiguity, and can therefore be discussed rather more succinctly. In all events, it seems incontrovertible that during the course of the twentieth century women of all classes spent increasing amounts of money on medical, beauty, fashion and similar products. It was seen in Chapter 1 that manufacturers, retailers and advertisers came to recognise that few women, whether housewives or not, wished to be regarded exclusively as homemakers, and adjusted their advertising accordingly. Pharmaceutical companies began to offer women the possibility of 'Radiant Health in Middle Age', while food manufacturers began to stress the convenience and slimming properties, along with the high quality and excellent value of the products that they offered. It was seen in Chapter 3 that women of all ages, and all classes, reacted with apparent enthusiasm to the growing volume and variety of clothing, footwear, cosmetics, slimming aids and similar products that were displayed so invitingly before them. Indeed, it appeared to some commentators that this was one segment of the market that would never fail to continue expanding. It was claimed in 1976, for instance, that,

> The woman who buys for herself is a creature visibly swelling in
> strength and financial integrity, and represents for marketing one
> of those very few areas which can only grow more viable with the
> coming years. With increased social and political emancipation,
> better contraception and child-care facilities, more women will work,
> and work longer, expect to be paid more and tend to resist roles
> which curtail financial freedom. In evolutionary terms, this can bring
> enormous benefits to women.[16]

These changes in supply, demand and consumption did bring considerable benefits to women, but the gains that were won should not be exaggerated. For women's power as consumers remained significantly – and sometimes severely – constrained. There were two major impediments. The first was that manufacturers, retailers and advertisers all tended, whether consciously or not, to subordinate women at the same time as they liberated them.

> On the one hand, the markets for women's personal expenditure,
> that is, those which appeal to the woman as woman, can only
> grow stronger with economic liberation and the curtailment of
> traditional roles. On the other hand, marketers for decades have
> adopted as their *raison d'être* the depiction and maintenance
> of women in economically powerless and fully traditional roles,
> that is woman as dependent, as housewife, mother, wife and
> domestic.[17]

The other major constraint upon women's power as consumers was that a surprisingly large number of married women were able to purchase medical, beauty, fashion and similar products only with the approval and/or financial support of their husbands. Nor should it be imagined for one moment that such male domination was confined to traditional working-class households. Middle-class women faced their own forms of subordination. It was common for husbands to manage a single bank account for the entire family. A Lancaster woman recalls that during the 1950s her husband, who was in a well-paid job with Hoover, had his salary paid straight into his bank account. However, this arrangement did not cause any difficulties, she maintains, because 'whatever I wanted, I just asked and I got it'.[18] It became more common, of course, for husbands and wives to share a bank account, a development which is generally regarded as representing a modest step on the road towards women's equality. But the opening of a joint account could maintain, as well as undermine, existing power relationships within the family. For it is striking that in the same way that middle-class couples started to share the burden of food and household shopping just when this form of consumption began to be less onerous, so they started to share bank accounts at much the same time as women's capacity for independent earning began to improve.[19]

It is true, however, that male control over family finances continued to be found at its most inflexible and unyielding in traditional working-class households. Indeed, it may be that this control even tightened with the decline of the practice, which had been common in Lancashire and elsewhere, of husbands 'tipping up' their pay to their wives. In all events, it remained usual well into the 1950s and 1960s for working-class women to have to ask their husbands if they wanted to spend money on themselves.[20] Thus when Norman Dennis and his colleagues published *Coal is our Life* in 1956, they discovered that male control in Ashton (Featherstone) appeared to be both secure and virtually unquestioned. There is one passage from the book that is worth citing at considerable length:

> Unlike her husband the wife in Ashton does not spend any money on herself or her amusement without detailed consultation with, and approval from, her husband. Some wives will bravely buy themselves clothes or ornaments and then present them for their husband's approval, but only when they know that 'no trouble' will ensue, or where their relationship has come to the point where she goes out of her way to assert herself despite the consequences. Normally all items outside the weekly household budget are questioned by the husband and accounted for by the wife. If a wife wishes to spend money on new clothes she tries to persuade her husband to buy them, which is usually successful, or she puts smaller items on her hire-purchase account and does her best to pay them off. Perhaps at a later date she may wish to ask for an increase in her weekly housekeeping allowance. At such a time she knows her husband would be likely to delay or refuse the increase on the ground that she was frittering money away on herself.[21]

Yet even in coal-mining families the situation was by no means unchanging. For it has been seen time and time again that economic growth and rising real incomes did much to enhance the economic importance of consumption, and that consumption was one aspect of the family economy over which women of all classes were able to exercise a significant, and generally increasing, degree of control. To this extent, at least, consumption did contribute towards women's emancipation.

Nor was this all. For consumption offered women social as well as economic opportunities. Indeed, it may well be that one welcome corollary of these changes in women's economic power over consumption was a widening in the range of social activities available to women. Women's power over – and interest in – consumption encouraged them, so it seems, to try new things, visit new places and meet new people. In fact, the relationship between consumption and women's social emancipation was not quite so straightforward as such a view might suggest. For while the range of consumption-related social activities available to women did expand very considerably between the late nineteenth and late twentieth centuries, it did so along narrow, conventional and generally predictable lines.

It is not difficult to discern the basis upon which it might be suggested that consumption contributed towards women's social emancipation. For in their different ways shopping, tourism and sport each helped to widen the range of social activities available to women. Nor perhaps could it be otherwise. For shopping, tourism and sport each required women to leave the private world of house, home and family and enter the public world of shops, resorts and stadiums.

Shopping was of critical importance. For as many women recognised (and many more men believed), shopping became of considerable – and sometimes central – importance in women's social lives. However, it is no easy matter to establish precisely the relationship between shopping and women's social emancipation. For as might be expected, shopping varied greatly in the extent to which, the ways in which, and the speed at which it affected, let alone improved, the range and quality of women's social experiences.

Upper-class women were probably little affected by the developments in retailing that so affected women from other classes. Yet in so far as they were affected, they no doubt regarded the changes – the decline of personal attention, the introduction of self-service and the spread of chain stores and supermarkets – as losses rather than gains, as causes of regret rather than congratulation.

Middle-class women were affected a great deal more profoundly. Indeed, there is one aspect of women's shopping/emancipation that it is possible to discuss with a surprising degree of authority. In fact, given the lack of interest shown generally in retailing and shopping, it is little short of remarkable that so much attention has been paid to the use that late-nineteenth and twentieth-century middle-class women made of department stores. According to that doyenne of retailing historians, Alison Adburgham, the department stores, with their variety of ready-made clothes and accessories at reasonable prices, played an important part in the emancipation of women. One could go to town for a day and get everything done in one store; and more and more, the stores in London and the big cities set out to attract shoppers from a distance by offering auxiliary, non-selling services such as restaurants, banking facilities, and exhibitions – and cloakrooms.[22]

This, of course, is to put the case at its most persuasive. None the less, there is certainly considerable evidence that department stores changed the ways in which middle-class women went about their shopping.[23] Some began to travel surprisingly long distances to patronise the stores that they liked. It seems, for example, that as early as the 1870s and 1880s shoppers came to London from as far afield as cities such as Bath and Cambridge. As the *Lady's World* explained in 1886, 'Now that the train service is so perfect between London and Bath, it is quite possible to spend a day in town and return to Bath the same evening. This is no small advantage when you have a day's shopping to get through'.[24] Most shoppers stayed closer to home, of course, patronising the department stores that sprang up in the provinces. Indeed, as Adburgham suggests, middle-class women soon realised that these stores provided them not just with a new type of outlet at which to shop, but with a new, spacious and socially acceptable space in which to spend their time. So all over the country middle-class women had their hair done in the stores' hairdressing salons, took the weight off their feet in their waiting, resting and writing rooms, had morning coffee, lunch and afternoon tea in their tea rooms, snack bars and restaurants, and made use of their – often rather splendid – dressing rooms and cloakrooms.[25] In 1908 Debenhams issued a souvenir booklet for those in London for the Franco-British Exhibition:

> You may visit the various departments, then, if you wish, have lunch or tea at very moderate charges in the quiet, elegant Restaurant, to which a Smoking-room and Gentlemen's Cloakroom are attached. The Ladies' Club Room, which adjoins a luxuriously appointed suite of Dressing and Retiring Rooms, is open to lady visitors, who may there read the papers and magazines, telephone, write letters, or meet their friends. Parcels and letters may be addressed to the Cloak Room.[26]

Working-class women were affected less profoundly, and less beneficially, by these, and related, developments in retailing provision. For although this is an aspect of shopping/emancipation that has received very little scholarly attention, it seems clear that working women derived relatively few social – never mind economic – benefits from the opening of department stores, chain stores, supermarkets and hypermarkets. It was hard for them to find the time and money needed to travel to the new stores, and they were often reluctant to abandon the shops that they knew for those that they did not.

Nevertheless, working-class women did make use, in their own way, of the social opportunities afforded by the new city-centre stores. For department stores and chain stores, like public houses, were warm, bright and inviting; and department stores and chain stores, unlike public houses, made no charge at all for admission. Thus it will be recalled from Chapter 3 that by the 1930s stores like Woolworths, Marks and Spencer, and British Home Stores were providing working people with 'a form of entertainment . . . thousands of people enter the stores just for the fun of having a look round.'[27] Other stores functioned in much the same way: as the wife of a Winchester cabinet-maker told Mass-Observation in 1949, 'I just go to Timothy Whites and have a look round sometimes. It's more or less like a departmental store, you can go and have a look without being worried to buy and I think that's a very good thing.'[28] It will be recalled from the previous chapter that by the 1950s, if not before, going shopping on a Saturday had become part of many girls' regular weekly routine. Yet none of these examples reveals fully the significance that shopping came to assume in female working-class life. For it is essential to appreciate that for women of all ages certain types of shopping were as much a form of leisure as a means of consumption. Catching the bus into town, meeting a friend, having a cup of tea, looking round the shops, and buying the odd item or two was the nearest that many working women came to a regular day out.[29]

Tourism was at once less important, and more important, than shopping in widening the social opportunities available to women. It was less important in that day trips and holidays normally took place only once, or at best a few times, a year; it was more important in that day trips and holidays, by their very nature, involved the abandonment of the day-to-day routine, and the absorption of new experiences, in new places, with new people.

Middle-class women were among the first to benefit from the opportunities on offer. For although most day trips and holidays were essentially family activities, it became increasingly common for young middle-class women to travel semi-independently and independently. Teenage girls went away with their schools, church groups and Girl Guide troops. Those in their late teens and early twenties began to take the chance to escape more completely from protective parents. It was perfectly proper, they argued, to go away with a group of friends provided that they stayed at a holiday camp or went on something like a package tour. In fact, the major attraction of holiday camps, for middle-class and working-class girls alike, was that 'in their first holiday away from the family, parents would tolerate their going away with a group of other girls . . . to one of the well known camps, in a way that they would never countenance for an individual.'[30] As they grew older, middle-class women continued to travel with considerable enthusiasm, finding with each generation that passed that they and their families were able to go further, manage better, and experience more.[31]

Working-class women also took advantage of the – fewer – opportunities that they had to travel semi-independently and independently. Teenage girls went away on day trips and holidays organised by employers, publicans, friendly societies, youth groups and religious organisations. As they grew older, some took to the outdoor life, scandalising their elders who bemoaned the appearance of 'maidens' in 'hideous uniforms' of boots, Aertex shirts and ex-Army shorts.[32] In fact, according to Richard Holt, 'Hiking and biking were very important for women in providing the first opportunities for shared physical recreation with men in a working-class world where the sexes still occupied separate spheres'.[33] This, perhaps, is to exaggerate. In any case, hiking and cycling were always very much minority interests. Older women were more likely to go away on coach trips and charabanc outings: it was a pleasure, according to Richard Hoggart, 'which particularly appeals to mothers who want a short break and lots of company'.[34] But Hoggart is referring to the 1940s and 1950s. It has been seen that in the decades that followed, working-class women, like those from the middle class, found that they were increasingly able to replace their day trips and a week at Blackpool or Southend with a continental coach tour or a week or two on the Costa del Sol.

Tourism in any form had its effect. For as time went by, women of all ages and all classes travelled more often, travelled further afield, and travelled more independently. In fact, whether they were adventurous or timid, whether they travelled alone or with their families, whether they liked or loathed what they saw, few remained unaffected. So although it may not be true that travel necessarily broadens the mind, it is certainly true that it broadened – and deepened – the range of social opportunities available to British women during the late nineteenth and twentieth centuries.

The small minority of women who spent money playing and/or watching sport found that in this form too consumption contributed towards a widening of social opportunities. Indeed sport, much more than shopping or tourism, involved women in confronting and challenging powerful cultural conventions and stereotypes. 'Sport is therefore an excellent monitor of how far women have travelled along the road to equality and the distance yet to go'.[35]

Participation was both a cause and a consequence of women's 'liberation'. Upper-class women had the time, money and confidence to swim, climb, sail, hunt, shoot and fish, and play racket sports.[36] Middle-class women too had access to many of the material and ideological resources that were required. At school, college and university they played team games like hockey and lacrosse, while later in life they took up, some of them, more individual sports like golf and tennis, squash and jogging. According to feminist historians, such sporting participation proved of great importance to middle-class women.

> Sport gave women the opportunity to be physically active, to be mobile, to be vigorous and hardy, to compete, to strive for excellence, to be congratulated for success, to accept honourable defeat, to extend comradeship to other women, to aspire to increased independence and self-fulfilment, to make important choices freely, and to experience and get to know themselves – in other words to try almost anything with a reasonable hope of succeeding. It provided a unique taste of freedom, and likely whetted appetites for more and increased confidence that it could be achieved. Sport also heightened women's consciousness of and control over their own bodies, through dress reform and greater physical activity, and in turn by doing so likely produced feelings of greater self-assurance, self-identity and self-esteem.[37]

These are considerable claims, and it is not easy either to confirm or refute them. For if it is difficult to demonstrate the impact that sport had upon women's consciousness, it is more difficult still to distinguish between the impact of participation and the impact of consumption. None the less, what can be shown quite clearly is that the late nineteenth and early twentieth centuries saw the development of intriguing, and important relationships between sport, publishing and women, and between sport, fashion and women.

Magazine publishers long sought to appeal to the sporting interests of their middle-class readers. *The Girls' Realm* (founded in 1898) published features on famous schools where sport was important, and conducted regular interviews with 'Girls Who Excel at Sports'.[38] The turn of the century saw a proliferation of special interest magazines for women: the *Lady Cyclist* (1895) and its successor the *Wheelwoman* (1897), the *Hockey Field* (1910), *Ladies' Golf* (1912) and the *Golfing Gentlewoman* (1914). The two cycling magazines, for example, carried advice, news, information and interviews, all of which were intended 'to instruct the women of England in the art and pastime of cycling . . . and to be a medium of intercommunication between women who cycle.'[39]

The fashion industry also sought to adapt its products to the needs of the sporting lady. Indeed to contemporary observers like H. G. Wells, the relationship between sport, fashion and the emancipation of women seemed simple and straightforward. The 'new woman' was one who 'rode a bicycle, played tennis or golf, showed six inches of stocking beneath her skirts, and loosened her corsets'.[40] Certainly, some lady cyclists began to follow the advice they received: they loosened their corsets and so avoided inhibiting their freedom of movement by encasing themselves 'in steel armour'.[41] In the same way, lady golfers began to wear boneless corsets, looser clothing and shorter skirts. For as the magazine *Ladies' Golf* pointed out in the early years of the century, 'A short skirt – really short, not simply a couple of inches off the ground – looks infinitely nicer and more workman-like, and makes an inestimable difference in comfort.'[42]

It was by these, and similar, developments that consumption offered women opportunities for social as well as economic advance. For sport, tourism and shopping each helped to change the ways in which women (and middle-class women in particular) spent the time and money at their disposal. Moreover, sport, tourism and shopping each helped to change the ways in which women (and middle-class women in particular) regarded themselves, and were regarded by other people. These were important changes, and their significance should not be underestimated.

On the other hand, the significance of these changes can easily be misunderstood. For the widening of social opportunities brought about by changes in shopping, tourism and sport could be restricting as well as liberating, confining as well as emancipating. For example, the gains accruing from new forms of retailing were sometimes offset by losses resulting from the demise of older, more intimate types of shopping; the gains accruing from new forms of retailing and new forms of sport were both constrained, still more strongly, by the survival of deep-seated and powerful assumptions about the role and status of women.

The new forms of retailing did not necessarily compensate for the demise of the old. For in working-class communities shopping had long performed a social as well as an economic function. Women were used to strolling down the street, browsing round the local shops, talking to their neighbours, and catching up on the local gossip.[43] It is not surprising therefore that many women were reluctant, even when they could, to abandon the local shops at which they were known and often trusted, in favour of city-centre stores at which they were unknown, might feel out of place, and were often afraid of being either patronised or ignored.[44] Their fears were not without foundation. It is not always appreciated that for many years department stores made determined efforts to keep working-class customers in their place; one at least acquired separate premises for the sale of ready-to-wear clothing, and many opened bargain basements that could be reached without having to enter the main part of the store.[45] In fact, it was probably not until relatively late in the period that working women in any numbers began to benefit from the social – as well as the economic – advantages afforded by this new form of retailing.[46]

The new forms of food retailing brought even fewer social benefits. For whatever the economic advantages of supermarket shopping, one would be hard-pressed to suggest that it widened women's social horizons or enhanced their leisure-time opportunities. It is difficult, after all, to imagine any woman, whatever her class, deciding to have a day out at her local supermarket. For while it was the standardisation, impersonality and individualism of self-service retailing that gave supermarkets their economic edge, it was this same standardisation, impersonality and individualism that made them unappealing in other respects.[47] Many women, of all classes, simply did not like the anonymity that this new form of retailing entailed. The small, individually owned shop seemed to represent a disappearing, and better, world. As a Derbyshire woman explained in 1981, 'These little shops now are on the way out, but with their going a way of life goes with them. The soulless monsters of supermarkets lack the homely service, the friendly chatter and the neighbourliness of these little shops.'[48]

These new forms of retailing, like new forms of sport, remained constrained too by prevailing assumptions about the role and status of women. Retailers, advertisers and manufacturers all continued to perceive, and categorise, many of their products as either masculine or feminine. During the 1930s, for example, St Bruno was advertised as 'a man's Tobacco', and Atkinson's Ales as 'The Flavour Men Favour'.[49] Such gendered advertising survived surprisingly unscathed. When the Automobile Association advertised its breakdown service in 1950, it explained that 'As a gesture of chivalry, help will be provided for any woman motorist who requires this service whether or not she is a member and whether or not she is accompanied or unaccompanied by children.'[50] When furniture chain ELS advertised one of its draylon three-piece suites in 1980, it explained that it comprised, along with a three-seater settee, a 'master chair' and a 'lady chair'.[51] It was not just in their advertising that chain stores and department stores continued to reinforce conventional gender divisions. The very layout of department stores reflected, and reinforced, the existing social order: men's and women's products were displayed in separate windows, and sold in separate departments, that were located, for still greater security, upon separate floors.[52]

Sport remained divided still more rigidly upon gender lines. For as Kathleen McCrone has pointed out,

> Men's and women's sports, with a few exceptions, remained strictly segregated, and women's sport was severely circumscribed by the patriarchal nature of social relations and by women's willingness, as in so many other areas, to allow men's perception of what was suitable to influence the choice and nature of their activities.[53]

This means of course that the relationship between sport, women and consumption was less straightforward – and less liberating – than it might appear at first sight.

It is true that magazine publishers sought to appeal to the sporting interests of middle-class women, but they did so in ways that maintained, as much as undermined, the sexual *status quo*. *The Lady Cyclist* and *Wheelwoman* provided information – 'to an extent that now seems absurd' – on 'how to mount, dismount, sit, steer and pedal; how to ride long distances; how to dress in a functional yet stylish manner; how to care for the skin . . . and how to "ankle" gracefully.'[54]

It is true too that clothing manufacturers sought to adapt their products to the needs of the sporting lady. But they too did so in ways that maintained, rather than threatened, the existing social order. Lady cyclists were told in 1885 that they should not dress in a style likely 'to excite undue notice': 'A lady, if she dresses quietly on and off her machine, will meet with respect and attention, where a gaudily-dressed fast girl will be treated differently'.[55] Lady golfers were advised that they could, and should, combine femininity with functionalism: for example, the J & B Athletic Girl Corset was advertised early this century as encouraging the very poise and grace that golf itself was designed to develop.[56] Lady tennis players were never allowed to forget that they were ladies first, and tennis players second. Late-nineteenth-century players were exhorted to avoid white plimsolls because 'they made the feet look large', but otherwise to wear all-white outfits because they camouflaged unladylike perspiration stains.[57] Late-twentieth-century players were advised to wear short dresses and skirts – after all, they were, it will be recalled, 'pretty enough to make any girl wish to take up the game'.[58] For Nancy Theberge, writing just after the end of the period,

> The trivialization of women's sporting experience has perhaps reached its nadir in the current feminization of the fitness craze embodied in some instances of the activities labeled Dancercise and Jazzercise and in the televised 'Twenty-Minute Workout'. I would argue that in many instances these activities are concerned with developing women's potential not in sport and athletics but in the sexual marketplace. The suggestive poses assumed by activity leaders, and breathy voices exhorting participants, convey images of dominance and submission. The ideal or goal is not the development of physical strength or even fitness but the development of women's sexual attractiveness and appeal.[59]

Thus the greatest caution is obviously called for when attempting to assess the relationship between sport, consumption and women's emancipation. However, it is now possible to discern the main contours, at least, of this complicated and contradictory relationship. For it seems that, although sport was less important than tourism and much less important than shopping, sport – or rather the consumption to which sport gave rise – was also of some significance in that it offered middle-class women new, and welcome ways of spending their leisure time.

This means that it is now possible to begin to understand the full depth, and complexity, of the relationship between consumption and women's emancipation. For two major conclusions have emerged during the course of this chapter. It has been seen that in their different ways shopping, tourism and sport each offered women new ways of exercising economic power, and that in their different ways each of them offered women new ways too of spending their leisure time.

Yet even these findings do not exhaust the complexity of the relationship between consumption and women's emancipation. For consumption was affected by, and had an effect upon, women's – and of course men's – social status.[60] Consumption, it will be shown, offered women – and men – new ways of measuring, improving and comparing their social standing. Indeed, in so far as consumption became more important as a means of defining social status, it empowered women who, it has been seen, exercised particular responsibility for household expenditure. However, it will come as little surprise to learn that, once again, the relationship was less straightforward than it might appear at first sight. For although consumption became increasingly important in defining social status, it never attained the same importance as occupation or income, and although women had particular responsibility for household expenditure, male members of the family tended to take a disproportionate interest in those forms of consumption upon which status most closely depended.

Nevertheless, the focus here is upon women and consumption, and there can be no doubt that consumption offered women new ways of measuring, comparing and improving social status. For as the period progressed, the determinants of female social status began to change: women began to judge – and be judged – less by what they earned and how they coped, and more by what they owned and how they consumed.[61] Their consumption was judged, in turn, by a number of distinct, but overlapping, criteria: the kind of supplier that was patronised; the way in which payment was made; and, of course, the type of product that was purchased.

The choice of supplier and the availability of credit were crucial and closely related, albeit contradictory, indicators of social standing. For on the one hand, it was women's growing ability to pay cash when doing the shopping, organising a day trip, or choosing a holiday that helped to raise their social status. It took, for instance, a certain level and/or security of income to shop at a co-operative store, a department store or a supermarket. For as the Manchester firm of Lewis's liked to make known, theirs was a shop for people 'who pay as they go'.[62] It was, of course, the very fact that many women found it hard to 'pay as they go' that so many of them set such enormous store by trying to do so.[63]

On the other hand, there were growing social, as well as economic, benefits to being judged credit-worthy. 'With some poor folk' in early twentieth-century Salford, recalls Robert Roberts, 'to be "taken on at a tick shop" indicated a solid foot at last in the door of establishment'.

> A wife (never a husband) would apply humbly for tick on behalf
> of her family . . . . After assessment credit would be granted and a
> credit limit fixed . . . . A tick book, honoured each week, became an
> emblem of integrity and a bulwark against hard times. The family had
> arrived.[64]

Those who were better off sometimes needed to be reassured that buying on credit would not detract from their social standing. Such reassurance was seldom hard to find. During the 1920s even co-operative societies began to organise 'mutuality clubs' based upon contributors making 'regular payments over a 20–week period for the same selection of goods as those purchased by cash customers'.[65] During the 1930s women's magazines like *Good Housekeeping* began to run regular features on the possibility, and acceptability, of using credit to buy expensive household items. It told its readers in 1932 that if they had an annual income of £500, they were justified in purchasing up to £100 worth of furniture on deferred terms. Credit generally became much more acceptable: indeed by the 1970s the ownership of a credit card (or better still several) had become a new symbol of social status.[66] For as a survey of *Consumers and Credit* concluded with apparent confidence in 1980, 'Ten years ago the vast majority of consumers from all walks of life felt that using credit was wrong, now it is regarded as a "part of everyday life".'[67]

However, it was the choice of product that constituted the key guide to women's prosperity, taste and independence – and so to their social status. Middle-class women were told between the wars that the consumption of consumer durables was fundamental to the professionalisation of housework and the elevation of the housewife's standing in society. When *Woman* published its *Every Woman's Book of Homemaking* in 1938, the aim, it told its readers, was 'to help you make that household machine run more efficiently, to save you work and worry, to point out the easy ways, the short cuts, in the intricate business of running a home.'[68] In fact, whether they were housewives or not, middle-class women knew, almost without being told, that they signalled their social status in every single act of consumption: the clothes they wore, the cars they drove, the furniture they bought, the holidays they took and the sports they enjoyed.

Working-class women generally had to content themselves with more modest signifiers of social standing. For, as Gareth Stedman

Jones pointed out in a pioneering study of late-nineteenth-century London, 'What saving there was among the casual workers, the unskilled and the poorer artisans was not for the purpose of accumulating a sum of capital, but for the purchase of articles of display or for the correct observance of ritual occasions.'[69] Indeed, it would probably be possible to draw examples from every period, and every part of the country, of working-class women recognising, and using, consumption as an indicator of social status. When an anonymous Lancashire woman looks back to her early married life in the 1950s, she remembers that she and her painter-and-decorator husband made a clear and unambiguous link between consumption, self-image and status. She and her husband deferred having children so that they could obtain the consumer durables that they wanted. So while her neighbours with young children consoled themselves with the thought that they would still be young when their children were grown up, she for her part felt superior because she and her husband were able to purchase the consumer goods by which they set so much store.[70] When Carolyn Steedman looks back on her childhood in South London, she too can see a connection between consumption, self-image and status.

> Changes in the market place, the growth of real income and the proliferation of consumer goods that marked the mid-1950s, were used by my mother to measure out her discontent: there existed a newly expanding and richly endowed material world in which she was denied a place. The new consumer goods came into the house slowly, and we were taught to understand that our material deprivations were due entirely to my father's meanness.[71]

Such attitudes often had a direct and positive, albeit unquantifiable, impact upon women's social standing. For in so far as consumption became more important as a means of defining social status, it tended to empower women who, as has been seen so often, exercised particular responsibility over household consumption. As one male observer remarked, women became much more assertive from the 1940s onwards: 'We can drive a car as well as you can, so therefore we can go out and do the shopping, we are independent.'[72] Consumption generally came to be seen as more and more important. The decisions that women took when doing the shopping or choosing a holiday were central, it seemed, not just to their own self-esteem and the contentment of their immediate family but to the success of the national – and international – economy. For as Raphael Samuel points out,

> Postwar Britain has notoriously become a more home-centred society, privatising and domesticating (as in the rise of home or home-based entertainment) what were previously mass activities. Consumer credit ('plastic money') has brought new latitudes in expenditure, dissevering

it in some sort from income, encouraging enjoyment in the here and now rather than saving for the morrow, and democratising such luxuries as foreign travel. Work statuses have been devalued in favour of those derived from the expenditure of time and money, from marriage and parenthood, style and fashion. Imaginatively the ideal home – a private utopia rather than a public one – is the summit of individual ambition.

Indeed, as Samuel goes on to explain,

> It is women who are the epicentre of these changes invading, or gaining access to, what were previously male prerogatives (such as credit) . . . . Above all, in a democracy of consumers, they are the taste leaders, doing the lion's share of what, for a customer-oriented capitalism, is the quintessential national activity, shopping.[73]

The arguments appear convincing, the weight of popular and scholarly opinion almost overwhelming. Yet once again the greatest caution is necessary. For it should not be forgotten that while consumption grew increasingly important as an indicator of women's independence, self-image and social status, it rarely if ever attained the same importance as occupation or income. Indeed, it can be no coincidence that as women's earning potential increased, and earnings came to be seen as the property of the person who received them, so women's earnings began to be redefined to make them appear less central to the family economy, and thus less important in the attribution of social status.[74]

Women's work was redefined as inessential, their earnings as 'pin money'.[75] In middle-class families, women's work was often seen as a hobby. The wife of a Lancashire car salesman who ran a play group during the late 1960s remembers her husband denying that she made a useful contribution to the family income: 'it's pocket money and that's it . . . . A great interest'.[76] In working-class families, women's work was rarely seen as a hobby, but here too it often tended to become marginalised. Elizabeth Roberts explains the combination of material and ideological developments that took place in North-west England between about 1940 and 1970:

> Although women earned more in real terms, their wages were not necessarily seen to be so important in the family economy as those of their predecessors. Their wages were no longer perceived to be for the basic necessities in life, food, clothing and shelter. Rather they were described as being for 'extras' like holidays, domestic appliances, 'better' clothing or a family car. These perceptions tended to marginalise women's wages in the eyes of both the woman and their families.[77]

Caution is also needed when evaluating the relationship between consumption and status, because it is easy to overlook the fact that male members of the family tended to take a particular interest in those forms of consumption that most directly enhanced social standing. It was seen in Chapter 3 that women's influence was at its strongest when purchasing food and 'domestic' products such as carpets, vacuum cleaners and washing machines, but that men's influence was at its most powerful when purchasing 'masculine' and/or expensive products such as televisions, video recorders and, of course, motor cars.[78] For as the editor of *Motor Magazine* pointed out as long ago as 1927, 'Every time a woman learns to drive – and thousands do every year – it is a threat to yesterday's order of things'.[79] It was a threat, not least, to men's control over the purchase – and use – of one of the most status-ridden objects that members of the family were ever likely to consume.

To some extent, then, the relationship between consumption, women and status may stand as a symbol of the broader relationship between consumption, women and emancipation. For in both cases, the relationship was complex, contradictory and contentious. On the one hand, consumption offered women new economic power, new social possibilities and new opportunities for improving their social status. On the other hand, these advances were made in ways that confirmed and reinforced, rather than challenged and undermined, women's conventional role and standing in society. Advances there were; emancipation there was not.

NOTES AND REFERENCES

1. There is no general study of women and consumption, but see **R. Scott**, *The Female Consumer*, Associated Business Programmes, 1976.

2. *Guardian*, 16 December 1990. Cf. **J. Carey**, *The Intellectuals and the Masses: Pride and Prejudice among the Literary Intelligentsia 1880–1939*, Faber & Faber, 1992, p. 122.

3. **E. Wilson**, *Only Halfway to Paradise: Women in Postwar Britain 1945–1968*, Tavistock, 1980, p. 12. Of course, feminists and those on the left hoped too that consumption would politicise women and help them to understand, for example, 'that women of all lands as the housekeepers of the nation with the power of the basket can make co-operation a means to destroy the present competitive system, and open to all mankind the portals of a community of economic prosperity.' *Labour Woman*, 1 August 1925; also December 1913, 1 January 1924, 1 February 1925, April 1956, March 1966.

4. **J. Burnett**, *Plenty and Want: A Social History of Food in England from 1815 to the Present Day*, Routledge, 1985, pp. 197–202. See also **M. Girouard**, *Life in the English Country House: A Social and Architectural History*, Penguin, 1980.

5. **J. Lewis**, *Women in England 1870–1950: Sexual Divisions and Social Change*, Wheatsheaf, 1984, p. 113.
6. **P. Branca**, *Silent Sisterhood: Middle Class Women in the Victorian Home*, Croom Helm, 1975, p. 53.
7. Burnett, *Plenty*, p. 192.
8. Lewis, *Women*, p. 115.
9. **E. Roberts**, *A Woman's Place: An Oral History of Working-Class Women 1890–1940*, Blackwell, 1984, p. 124; **C. Chinn**, *They Worked All Their Lives: Women of the Urban Poor in England, 1880–1939*, Manchester University Press, 1988, p. 51.
10. **J. Benson**, *The Working Class in Britain, 1850–1939*, Longman, 1989, p. 103.
11. Chinn, *They Worked*, p. 52.
12. **C. More**, *The Industrial Age: Economy and Society in Britain 1750–1985*, Longman, 1989, p. 373.
13. **J. Greenfield**, 'From "Angels in the House" to "The Craft Worker of Today": Women's Roles and the Ideology of Domesticity in Popular Women's Magazines in the 1930s', MA dissertation, University of Warwick, 1991, pp. 1–2, 6–8, 39, 109–16; **C. Steedman**, *Landscape for a Good Woman: A Story of Two Lives*, Virago, 1986, p. 36.
14. See **S. Bowlby**, 'Women and Food Retailing', in **J. Little**, **L. Peake** and **P. Richardson** (eds), *Women in Cities: Gender and the Urban Environment*, Macmillan, 1988, pp. 76–7; Mass-Observation, 3055, 'A Report on Shopping', 1948, p. 2.
15. *Mass-Observation Intelligence Survey Weekly*, 3 May 1940.
16. Scott, *Female Consumer*, p. 204.
17. Scott, *Female Consumer*, p. 204. Also **C. Reed**, 'Driving Force', *Guardian*, 24 April 1991.
18. Lancaster, Mrs A4L, p. 54.
19. Information from Elizabeth Roberts.
20. Lancaster Mr R3B, p. 13; Mrs P5B, p. 9; **N. Dennis**, **F. Henriques** and **C. Slaughter**, *Coal is our Life: An Analysis of a Yorkshire Mining Community*, Tavistock, 1969, p. 202; **A. Bott**, '"Who Said it was Affluent?": Household Budgeting and Buying in the 1950s in Leamington Spa', MA dissertation, University of Warwick, 1992, pp. 41–5.
21. Dennis *et al.*, *Coal*, p. 201.
22. **A. Adburgham**, *Shops and Shopping 1800–1914: Where, and in What Manner the Well-Dressed Englishwoman Bought Her Clothes*, Barrie & Jenkins, 1989, p. 231; also p. 281. For the United States, see **W. R. Leach**, 'Transformation in a Culture of Consumption: Women and Department Stores, 1890–1925', *Journal of American History*, **71**, 1984; **S. P. Benson**, *Counter Cultures: Saleswomen, Managers and Customers in American Department Stores, 1890–1940*, University of Illinois Press, 1986; **E. S. Abelson**, *When Ladies Go A-thieving: Middle-class Shoplifters in the Victorian Department Store*, Oxford University Press, 1989.
23. **M. Winstanley**, *The Shopkeeper's World 1830–1914*, Manchester University Press, 1983, pp. 34–5.
24. Adburgham, *Shops*, p. 231.

25.   Adburgham, *Shops*, pp. 154, 157, 167, 171, 216–7, 232, 273.
26.   Adburgham, *Shops*, p. 272; also p. 273.
27.   **B. S. Rowntree**, *Poverty and Progress: A Second Social Survey of York*, Longman, Green & Co., 1941, pp. 218–19.
28.   Mass-Observation, 3108, 'A Report on Chemist's Shops (with special reference to Boots)', 1949, p. 19.
29.   Scott, *Female Consumer*, p. 60; **J. B. Priestley**, *English Journey*, Penguin, 1977, p. 22; **V. Walkerdine**, 'Dreams from an Ordinary Childhood', in **L. Heron** (ed.), *Truth, Dare or Promise: Girls Growing Up in the Fifties*, Virago, 1985, pp. 72–3.
30.   **C. Ward** and **D. Hardy**, *Goodnight Campers! The History of the British Holiday Camp*, Mansell, 1986, p. 101. Also Lancaster, Mrs R2P, p. 20.
31.   E.g., Lancaster, Mrs R2P, p. 20.
32.   **R. Holt**, *Sport and the British: A Modern History*, Oxford University Press, 1990, p. 200.
33.   Holt, *Sport*, p. 200.
34.   **R. Hoggart**, *The Uses of Literacy: Aspects of Working-class Life with Special Reference to Publications and Entertainments*, Penguin, 1958, pp. 147–8.
35.   **K. E. McCrone**, *Sport and the Physical Emancipation of English Women 1870–1914*, Routledge, 1988, p. 2.
36.   McCrone, *Sport*, p. 6; **N. L. Tranter**, 'Organized Sport and the Middle-class Woman in Nineteenth-century Scotland', *International Journal of Sports History*, **6**, 1989, p. 36; *Daily Mail*, 17 January 1930.
37.   McCrone, *Sport*, p. 289; also pp. 2, 13, **J. Hargreaves**, 'The Early History of Women's Sport', *Bulletin of the Society for the Study of Labour History*, **50**, 1985, pp. 5–6. Also **J. Williams** and **J. Woodhouse**, 'Can Play, Will Play? Women and Football in Britain', in **J. Williams** and **S. Wagg** (eds), *British Football and Social Change: Getting into Europe*, Leicester University Press, 1991, pp. 88–9.
38.   McCrone, *Sport*, pp. 252–3.
39.   McCrone, *Sport*, p. 254.
40.   **J. Park**, 'Sport, Dress Reform and the Emancipation of Women in Victorian England: A Reappraisal', *International Journal of Sports History*, **6**, 1989, p. 10.
41.   Park, 'Sport', p. 22.
42.   McCrone, *Sport*, p. 236. See **L. de Vries**, *Victorian Advertisements*, John Murray, 1968, pp. 36–7, 110, 118.
43.   **M. Tebbutt**, 'Women's Talk? Gossip and "Women's Worlds" in Working-class Communities, 1880–1939', in **A. Davies** and **S. Fielding** (eds), *Workers' Worlds: Cultures and Communities in Manchester and Salford, 1880–1939*, Manchester University Press, 1992, p. 61.
44.   Information from Elizabeth Roberts.
45.   Adburgham, *Shops*, pp. 206, 276.
46.   Walkerdine, 'Dreams', pp. 72–3.
47.   **G. I. V. Mair**, 'Towards a Sociology of Shopping', MSc thesis, University of Strathclyde, 1976, pp. 91–2; **J. P. Johnston**, *A Hundred Years Eating: Food, Drink and the Daily Diet in Britain since the Late Nineteenth Century*, Gill & Macmillan, 1977, p. 86.

48. **N. James**, *A Derbyshire Life*, Post Mill Press, 1981, pp. 7–8. Also **W. G. McClelland**, 'The Supermarket and Society', *Sociological Review*, **10**, 1962, pp. 139–41.
49. *Express and Star*, 16, 17 May 1935. Also *Daily Mail*, 15–17 January 1930.
50. *Express and Star*, 2 January 1950.
51. *Express and Star*, 5 January 1980.
52. Cf. **G. Reekie**, 'Sydney's Big Stores 1880–1930: Gender and Mass Marketing', PhD thesis, University of Sydney, 1987, pp. 3, 95, 224, 332.
53. McCrone, *Sport*, p. 13. Also **N. Theberge**, 'Toward a Feminist Alternative to Sport as a Male Preserve', *Quest*, **37**, 1985, p. 195; Hargreaves, 'Early History', pp. 5–6.
54. McCrone, *Sport*, p. 254.
55. McCrone, *Sport*, p. 237. Also Park, 'Sport'.
56. McCrone, *Sport*, p. 236.
57. McCrone, *Sport*, p. 232.
58. *Express and Star*, 13 June 1964. The *Daily Mail*'s report on the British women's squash championship in 1930 commented that, 'Clear yellows and greens appear to be the favourite "squash" colours, and I particularly admired the daffodil and white ensemble of Miss Rothschild, a new and very promising player.' 24 January 1930.
59. Theberge, 'Alternative', pp. 194–5.
60. **J. H. Goldthorpe**, **D. Lockwood**, **F. Bechhofer** and **J. Platt**, *The Affluent Worker in the Class Structure*, Cambridge University Press, 1969; **R. J. Morris**, *Class and Class Consciousness in the Industrial Revolution 1780–1850*, Macmillan, 1979; **A. Marwick**, *Class: Image and Reality in Britain, France and the USA since 1830*, Fontana, 1981. It has been suggested that femininity too became materially based. See **J. White**, *The Worst Street in North London: Campbell Bunk, Islington, between the Wars*, Routledge & Kegan Paul, 1986, pp. 193–4.
61. Information from Elizabeth Roberts.
62. **M. Tebbutt**, *Making Ends Meet: Pawnbroking and Working-Class Credit*, Leicester University Press, 1983, p. 169. Also Winstanley, *Shopkeeper's World*, pp. 36–9.
63. For, while the availability of credit grew and became more bureaucratised, it also became increasingly masculinised.
64. Roberts, *Classic Slum*, pp. 81–2. Also Chinn, *They Worked*, pp. 72–3. Cf. Hoggart, *Literacy*, p. 43.
65. Greenfield, 'Angels', p. 161; also pp. 45–50.
66. Tebbutt, *Making Ends Meet*, p. 200. Also Bott, 'Leamington Spa', pp. 52–3.
67. Tebbutt, *Making Ends Meet*, p. 201.
68. Greenfield, 'Angels', pp. 133–4.
69. **G. Stedman Jones**, 'Working-class Culture and Working-class Politics in London, 1870–1900: Notes on the Remaking of a Working Class', *Journal of Social History*, **7**, 1974, p. 473. See also **P. Johnson**, 'Conspicuous Consumption and Working-class Culture in Late Victorian and Edwardian Britain', *Transactions of the Royal Historical Society*, **38**, 1988.

70. Lancaster, Mrs H5L, p. 90. Also **F. Thompson**, *Lark Rise to Candleford*, Penguin, 1979, p. 125; **G. Orwell**, *The Road to Wigan Pier*, Penguin, 1937, p. 79.
71. Steedman, *Landscape*, p. 36.
72. Lancaster, Mr R3B, p. 66.
73. **R. Samuel** (ed.), *Patriotism: The Making and Unmaking of British National Identity*, Vol. 1 *History and Politics*, Routledge, 1989, p. xxxviii.
74. **E. Roberts**, 'Women, the Family Economy and Homework: Northwest England, 1900–1970', *Labour History Review*, **56**, 1991, p. 17. Cf. Bott, 'Leamington Spa', pp. 1–2, 34.
75. Roberts, 'Women', pp. 16–17.
76. Lancaster, Mr R3B, p. 60. Also Mrs L2L, p. 17.
77. Roberts, 'Women', pp. 16–17.
78. Scott, *Female Consumer*, p. 124.
79. Reed, 'Driving Force'.

Chapter 9

THE DEFUSION OF CLASS TENSION?

The relationship between consumption and class has received still more attention than that between consumption and women.[1] However, it is a relationship which, unlike that between consumption and women, has provoked surprisingly little scholarly or popular controversy. For although it is conceded that there were circumstances in which consumption might maintain, or even strengthen, class consciousness, it seems to be generally accepted that consumption tended most often to weaken class consciousness, and so to defuse class tension. According to Paul Johnson, the study of late-nineteenth- and early-twentieth-century working-class 'spending and consuming highlights not the solidarity of workers but the degree of competition within their ranks'.[2] According to Edward Royle, the prosperity of the years following the Second World War did much to diminish class divisions: 'the working class as workers were achieving levels of consumption previously regarded as attainable only by the middle class, leading to a merging of the classes through the progressive *embourgeoisement* of the workers'.[3]

In fact, the relationship between consumption and class was a good deal more complicated than such views might lead one to suppose. For it is no easy matter to agree upon definitions of class, class consciousness and class tension; it is more difficult still to identify and measure them empirically; and it is virtually impossible to determine the extent to which changes in them were brought about by changes in consumption as opposed, say, to changes in the economy and the workplace, changes in the educational system, or changing attitudes towards, for example, country, region, age and gender.[4]

Thus it is the purpose of this chapter to subject the relationship between consumption and class to more systematic scrutiny than it has sometimes received in the past. When this has been done, it will be seen that the relationship was considerably more complex and contradictory than is often assumed. On the one hand, it will be shown that there were circumstances in which consumption maintained, reinforced and expressed two distinct forms of class consciousness: class identity (the identification of oneself as upper-class, middle-class or working-class); and class opposition (the belief that those from other classes constituted enduring opponents to oneself).[5] For consumption encouraged consumers from all classes to be aware of, and enabled them to express, their satisfaction or dissatisfaction with, the class situation in which they found themselves. On the other hand, it will be shown that there were many more circumstances in which consumption undermined class identity and class opposition, and so helped to defuse class tension. For consumption encouraged consumers from all classes to be aware of, to be proud of, and to express the geographical, age and gender identities that they shared; it encouraged them to see themselves as non-class or cross-class consumers; and it served, there seems little doubt, to distract them from the many divisions and inequalities that remained embedded in modern British society.

It is still not always appreciated how commonly consumption, class identity and class opposition were mutually reinforcing. This was certainly so in the case of the aristocracy. For the members of the upper class were only too aware – and proud – of the class character of their consumption. They knew full well that their country houses, their trips to London, their holidays abroad, their sporting interests (and their gambling debts) all served as visible manifestations of their wealth, power and status – and thus of their physical, economic and social distance from the remainder of the population.[6]

The members of the middle class were just as aware and just as proud – albeit much more anxious about – of the class character of their consumption. For they too recognised that the houses in which they lived, the shops that they patronised, the products that they purchased, the holidays that they took, and the sports that they enjoyed all sent out powerful signals, not just about their taste, but about their wealth, income, status and class identity.[7]

Middle-class shoppers were well aware of the importance, in class terms, of the shops that they used, the ways in which they paid, and the products that they purchased. They took care, often quite consciously, to shop in ways befitting their class identity – or the identity to which they and their families aspired. Their concerns changed, of course, but for many years they tended to avoid mail order and to regard variety stores and chain stores with considerable suspicion. Even the latter's attempts at providing suitable standards of service met with a good deal of distrust. George Orwell's disillusioned insurance salesman, George Bowling, despised, yet understood, 'the lad' that used to serve him in a chain-store grocery just before the outbreak of the Second World War:

> A great hefty lump of twenty, with cheeks like roses and enormous
> fore-arms, ought to be working in a blacksmith's shop. And there
> he is in his white jacket, bent double across the counter, rubbing his
> hands together with his 'Yes, sir! Very true, sir! Pleasant weather for
> the time of the year, sir! What can I have the pleasure of getting you
> today, sir?' practically asking you to kick his bum.[8]

Thus it was that middle-class shoppers continued to patronise
specialist stores which, although – indeed because – they were old-
fashioned and expensive, offered an agreeable combination of long
opening hours, free home delivery, generous credit facilities, and
expert and obsequious service. It was a combination which, whatever
its other merits, helped to confirm the class identity – and class
superiority – of the stores' customers. W. MacQueen Pope looked
back nostalgically in 1948 to the days when tradesmen knew their
place, and worked tirelessly 'to please the customer'.

> A shopkeeper was selling his goods in competition with many others.
> He had to please you or you withdrew your trade. He was not your
> master, you did not cringe and beg for favours. The boot was on the
> other leg; he did the cringing. On moving to a new district, or when
> a couple of newly wedded Middle Class young people entered their
> home, there was a state of siege. Tradesmen of all kinds came to the
> door, begging their custom. They waylaid them and solicited their
> favour. They almost came to blows over a potential customer. It was
> possible to live for a week on the free samples which poured into the
> house. And civility was the rule. Let a person in a shop be rude – a
> customer was lost for ever![9]

In fact, such standards of service and servility survived a good deal
longer than some people imagine. For example, a Brighton man
recalls starting work at his parents' butcher's shop in 1938.

> I was trained. Go to the side entrance [of the customer's house]
> and sometimes the servants wore white hats, collars, and aprons,
> and black stockings and shoes. I had to go to the door, knock
> and shout 'Butcher' – as they opened the door, always touch my
> forehead with no hat on or touch the peak of my cap. And this is
> how to address them: 'Good morning, madam, is there anything
> you'd like this morning, would you like any steak, any chops, any
> part of meat, anything for the animals, and when would you like
> me to bring it back? She'd tell me and I'd write it in my book or if
> she gave me a note I'd put it in my book, and say 'Good morning
> Madam'.[10]

This is not to suggest, of course, that middle-class shoppers were
blind to the advantages offered by the new forms of retailing that
developed during the late nineteenth and twentieth centuries.[11]
Women, it has been seen, turned with particular enthusiasm to the
department stores that opened in London and most major provincial

cities. For whatever the price, product and other benefits afforded by these stores, they too helped to confirm the class identity and superiority of their customers. Eileen Elias's shopping expeditions early this century to the Jones and Higgins department store in Peckham might have been designed almost specifically to provide her with lessons in class identity, class opposition – and class anxiety.

> Jonesandhiggins (sic) was nearly two miles away, and we had to set out early after Saturday dinner to walk there and back.
>
> The walk was a depressing one, through little back streets where children played in the gutters and women stared from open doors, their hair scraped back in topknots, leaning on their brooms with vacant eyes . . . .
>
> Jonesandhiggins was a reasonable store, everybody said; you didn't get overcharged, and you always got value for money . . . .
>
> You got a lot more than value for money, too, when you shopped at Jonesandhiggins, I used to think. You got novelty and excitement; you got friendliness from the shop assistants; you got a glimpse into a dream-world where a suburban house could be furnished from top to bottom with Turkey carpets and aspidistra-pots and kitchen labour-saving devices; you got a picture of yourself as you would like to be when you were really grown-up and a lady – with dresses like Mother's and Aunt Jane's, and any hat you liked to choose.[12]

Indeed, there is considerable evidence to suggest that department stores continued for many years to reflect the identities and aspirations – as well as the anxieties – of their customers. It has been argued, for instance, that 'During the inter war years the new provincial stores catered for the burgeoning and increasingly prosperous lower middle class. Here an element of snobbish gentility combined with theatre and stunts to attract the customers and confirm their own class perceptions.'[13] Certainly, the writer of this book can see now that during the late 1950s and early 1960s his mother believed very firmly that shopping in stores like Stones of Romford and Roomes of Upminster helped to confirm the family's much prized lower-middle-class identity.

Tourism was less important than shopping in confirming – never mind conferring – middle-class identity. For tourism, unlike shopping, normally took place only a few times a year, and then well out of sight of friends and neighbours. So tourism, unlike shopping, provided at best an intermittent and rather unreliable guide to class identity. None the less, it would be a mistake to dismiss out of hand the value of examining the relationship between tourism and middle-class identity. For middle-class tourists knew full well that their holidays (their postcards home, their photographs and slides, and their carefully cultivated sun tans) revealed – and were intended to reveal – a good deal about their prosperity, confidence and good taste, and thus about the class to which they belonged, or sought to belong.

In fact, it is possible to offer two useful, albeit fairly unexceptional, generalisations about the relationship between tourism and class identity: that day trips counted for less than holidays involving a stay away from home; and that holidays in Britain counted for less than those involving travel overseas. However, even generalisations as simple as these need to be applied with a certain amount of caution. For some day trips were regarded more highly than others. A day spent walking in the countryside or going to an industrial museum was more acceptable than one spent strolling along the sea front or enjoying the rides in a theme park or fun-fair. In the same way, some holidays were regarded more highly than others. For the means by which holiday-makers travelled, the destinations that they selected, the accommodation in which they stayed, and the activities in which they engaged all sent out powerful signals about their class identity. Molly Hughes recalls the disdain with which her family regarded the excursion trains of the 1870s:

> There were certainly 'excursion trains', but they meant all that was horrible: long and unearthly hours, packed carriages, queer company, continual shuntings aside and waiting for regular trains to go by, and worst of all the contempt of decent travellers.[14]

Such distinctions persisted. A middle-class family planning its summer holiday towards the end of the period would be equally, if perhaps less openly, aware of the importance of making choices that were consistent with its class identity and aspirations. For it was widely recognised that there were differences, in class terms, between travelling independently and going on a package tour, between flying to one's destination and travelling there by coach, between staying in a hotel and putting up in a boarding house, between visiting the Italian Lakes and staying on the Costa Brava.[15] Sometimes, indeed, the relationship between tourism, class identity and class opposition manifested itself in unforeseen and contradictory ways. For example, one summer during the 1950s a Bristol University student worked in a laundry for six weeks in order to pay for a holiday in Majorca. It was, she recalls, 'six weeks of absolute misery really, it made me a life long socialist, it made me have an enormous respect for working class people, that I had sort of always had this ambivalence about previously'.[16]

Such a transformation was most unusual, of course. For it has been seen that tourism generally was less important than shopping – and less important than might be expected – in fostering middle-class identity and opposition. However, it has been seen too that the relationship between tourism and middle-class consciousness should not be discounted altogether. In fact, in so far as tourism and middle-class identity were linked, it seems that the former tended to express, maintain and strengthen the latter.

On the other hand, sport, and the consumption to which it gave rise, was more important than tourism – and more important than might be expected – in fostering middle-class identity and opposition. Middle-class sportsmen (and women) were well aware of the class nature of their activities. Indeed, it has been claimed by some commentators that during the late nineteenth century, 'English middle-class gentlemen promoted athleticism in order to support their various efforts to distinguish their own class from the aristocracy and gentry'.[17] It is accepted much more widely that members of the middle class used sport as a means of distinguishing themselves from the working class: 'It is clear that sports in modern Britain, despite the transformation that has taken place since the Second World War, continue to mark off and unify dominant groups and the middle classes *vis-à-vis* the working class and other subordinate groups.'[18]

It was seen in Chapter 5 how close could be the connections between sport, consumption, middle-class identity and middle-class opposition. However, it is a point that bears repeating, for as has been pointed out recently, 'So much attention has been paid to the structure and dissolution of working-class communities that the careful building of networks of neighbours, friends, and acquaintances within the supposedly private and individualistic world of the middle class has been overlooked.'[19]

Some middle-class enthusiasts turned, it is true, to sports like cricket that were, or were to become, popular with all classes in society. Yet even then, they often managed to maintain their physical and social distance, forming their own clubs, captaining the teams in which they played, specialising in batting rather than bowling, and, when they watched the professional game, doing so from exclusive, segregated parts of the ground.[20] Those interested in sport turned most often, however, to activities such as Rugby, squash, tennis and golf that were too expensive, too time-consuming and too socially exclusive to be popular with the working class. Richard Holt captures beautifully the relationship between sport, consumption and the middle class:

> Tennis and golf clubs were worlds within worlds, business contacts and mutual reassurance for the reasonably well off, islands of sociability within the unfathomable seas of domestic privacy. Comfortably ensconced behind a gin and tonic at the 'nineteenth hole' or lining up a vital putt in the monthly medal, the golfer could forget the troublesome outside world and settle down to enjoy his or her modest affluence. The Depression, the poor, wars and rumours of wars, the dispiriting progress of socialism were temporarily forgotten. And if one

felt the urge to set the world to rights, there was never a shortage of orthodox political economists whose opinions on trade unionism or rising taxation were happily similar to one's own 'common-sense' view of things.[21]

However, there was more to it than this: for such complacency did not exclude, but existed alongside, a growing – and sports-driven – dissatisfaction with the rigidities of the British class system. It was these rigidities, some of the middle class came to think, that might account for the failings of British competitors in socially exclusive sports such as golf and tennis. The best evidence comes from Mass-Observation's interviews with its national panel of observers in the wake of the London Olympics of 1948. According to a female civil servant, 'Every encouragement should be given to young people. Try to give slum dwellers the facilities that Eton and Harrow take as a matter of course.' According to a factory manager, 'The majority of our Olympics Games stars came from Universities, etc. and sports clubs with special coaching facilities. The boy in the street rarely gets the opportunity to reach the top flight'. A young railway clerk believed that he had the answer:

> I think our prestige in international sport could be increased if there was less snobbery in such sports as tennis, cricket, golf, etc. The Americans coach *any* park player who shows promise of developing, but over here it is practically impossible to get to the top of any sport (except soccer) unless one wears the old school tie.[22]

So it was that sport, and the consumption associated with it, encouraged many middle-class consumers to identify themselves as middle-class; so it was that sport, and the consumption associated with it, encouraged at least some middle-class consumers to believe that those from the upper and working classes were not so much their class opponents as common captives of the British class system.

Naturally, the working class too knew that consumption sent out powerful signals about their wealth, income, taste, status and class identity. Indeed, there is reason to suppose that working people were just as aware as the middle class, nearly as proud, and a good deal more unhappy, about the class character of their consumption.

Working-class shoppers became increasingly aware of the importance, in class terms, of the shops that they used, the ways in which they paid, and (although there is no space to consider them here) the products that they purchased. They took care, like those from the middle class, to shop at stores in which they felt comfortable; they took care, in other words, to shop in ways befitting their class identity and aspirations. Thus they avoided specialist stores, and for many years tended to regard department stores and even supermarkets with a certain amount of suspicion.[23] They preferred, a surprising number of them, to use co-ops, corner shops and chain stores, all of which catered, in their different ways, for the working-class shopper. Co-ops were established by, and for, working people, and retained their popularity longer than many people imagine: it was found, for example, that even after the Second World War some 60 per cent of skilled workers in London still used the stores on a regular basis.[24] Corner shops were often run, and known to be run, by families with backgrounds similar to those of their customers. Indeed, as Peter Mathias has pointed out, 'a working-class background and consciousness could be a precious asset. Such men knew their future markets instinctively and innately.'[25] Chain stores too were aimed, and known to be aimed, at the working-class shopper. For as a respondent explained to Mass-Observation in the early 1940s, 'They are a good system for the working class pocket. Their stuff is not for rich people's standards, but for the working man's family they make the money go further.'[26]

Working-class shoppers understood, too, the differences, in class terms, between the various forms, and sources, of credit that were available to them. They knew that while they could probably obtain credit at their local corner shop, they would certainly be refused it at a city-centre specialist store. The tick book was one thing, the credit account quite another.[27] Working-class shoppers knew too that they would have credit pressed upon them by the travelling salesmen (known as 'talleymen' or 'Scotch drapers') who for many years came round door-to-door selling clothing and similar items.[28] They knew too that if they were in reasonably steady employment they would have little difficulty in buying goods on hire purchase. For working-class shoppers recognised, along with most other people, that during most of the period covered by this book hire purchase was regarded as essentially a working-class form of credit. As a Mass-Observation respondent from Chester explained in 1947, 'I think it's a very good thing for the working people. Working people haven't the money to put down'.[29]

So once again there seems to have been a clear correlation between shopping and class. For the ways in which working people paid for their shopping, the outlets at which they shopped (and the products which they purchased) reflected, and helped to shape, a sense of working-class identity – though not, so far as can be ascertained, any sense of working-class opposition. 'You know it's hard to say,' mused a Preston man, 'but you have everything that the middle class had before you. Television, fridges, cars, holidays you know. Paid holidays of course, which you didn't used to get at one time . . . we are still working class but we are certainly better off working class.'[30]

Tourism was less important than shopping in shaping working-class identity – but more important than might be expected in shaping working-class opposition. Indeed, given the economic constraints under which many of the working class continued to live, it is surprising perhaps that it played the part that it did. In fact, tourism acquired a considerable significance: for working people came to recognise that, with incomes growing and expectations rising, what they and their families did for their holidays became increasingly important in class terms.

Tourism tended in many respects to confirm working people in their working-class identity. It will be recalled from Chapter 4 that the day trip has been associated commonly – if not altogether accurately – with working-class tourism. Nor is it difficult to see why. Working people went away on excursions organised for them by employers, clergymen, publicans and other members of the middle class, excursions that sometimes culminated in expressions not just of thanks but of inter-class loyalty – and thus of working-class identity.[31] It will be recalled too that working people went away more and more in small groups of friends and relatives. But these groups too were working-class, and these groups too continued to make for recognisably working-class destinations, most often at the seaside.[32] Thus, whoever the organiser and whatever the size of the group, the association between the day trip and working-class identity remained largely unimpaired. For working people recognised only too well that day trips were regarded much less highly than holidays taken away from home: day trips, as working-class respondents are not slow to point out, were all that many of the poor were able to afford.[33]

Even when working people were able to afford holidays away from home, they did not necessarily lose sight of the relationship between tourism and working-class identity. Indeed, they could scarcely fail to appreciate that the holidays which they took were cheaper, less comfortable, and regarded as less desirable than those enjoyed by the middle and upper classes. The differences were obvious. Working-class children sometimes went away on holidays subsidised by local industrial and philanthropic organisations.[34] However they, like their parents, very often had to make do with staying with (working-class) friends and relatives. The son of a Lancaster railwayman remembers that the only holidays he ever had when growing up during the 1940s and 1950s were those spent with his family's relatives in Leigh and Glasgow: 'it was always staying with relations we never stayed in a Boarding House or a Hotel or anything.' Overcrowded and inconvenient, these were the only holidays, he maintains, that 'most people could get.'[35] Of course, working people did begin to go on other sorts of holiday; they stayed in boarding houses and hotels, they visited new places in Britain, and they travelled to resorts overseas. Yet even the most satisfied of working-class holiday-makers knew that their type of tourism was different: 'I have read, and I have heard of conducted tours being condemned by superior persons', remarked an Irish steelworker after his first trip abroad, 'but it would have been wasted time trying to convince me.'[36]

There is some suggestion here of the way in which class identity could develop into class opposition. For although working people went on day trips and holidays only a few times a year, tourism brought them into contact with middle-class life in ways that simply did not occur during the course of the normal daily round. Even day trips could have an effect. For example, a Bristol woman remembers going on a chapel excursion to Weston-super-Mare just after the turn of the century: 'A donkey ride for one penny, for two pence we could ride like a better class child in a dainty pony and cart.'[37] Holidays too sometimes encouraged working people to see the middle class as their class opponents. For as working people began to patronise boarding houses, holiday camps and package tours, so they (like the lower middle class before them) came in for a good deal of contempt and criticism.[38] Some working-class holiday-makers responded in kind. A Lancashire woman remembers vividly the way in which, even at the very end of the period, tourism brought her and her family face to face with the inequalities of the British class system:

> we used to have a caravan, a touring caravan. We had gone with mum and dad looking for a site. And then dad said, Oh this one looks nice. And I said, It's a golf club this. And we said, Oh well it doesn't matter . . . . And the bloke that came to speak to us, I was seething . . . .
> Toffee nosed and that, as to say like, You can't come on the golf club![39]

Thus the relationship between tourism, working-class identity and working-class opposition was rather closer than might be supposed. Nevertheless, the relationship between sport and class was closer still. In fact, it appears that sport, and the consumption to which it gave rise, was probably as important in shaping working-class identity and opposition as it was middle-class identity and opposition.

It would be difficult to overlook the relationship between sport and working-class identity.[40] For although it was seen in Chapter 5 that only a minority of the working population played or watched sport, it was seen too that sports such as angling, boxing, Rugby league and football became associated closely with male, working-class culture.[41] Angling clubs and associations proved, as John Lowerson points out, oddly potent vehicles for the expression of working-class identity. 'When extended fishing weekends in South Lincolnshire became possible by the early 1900s, the [Sheffield] associations were effectively operating the first major working-class package holidays.' When large firms looked for ways of providing their workers with fringe benefits during the 1920s and 1930s, some turned to sponsoring their own angling clubs.

Garswood Hall Collieries, outside Wigan, whose directors included Lord Colwyn MP, provided local waters for their workers to cut down travelling costs, offering copper kettles as match prizes: for many such works, including the car firms of the midlands, the fishing club became as solid a symbol for worker pride as the brass band.[42]

Boxing provided a more obvious expression of working-class identity. For as Stan Shipley has shown, during the half century or so between the 1890s and the 1950s it was working-class communities – and working-class communities alone – that produced 'boxer-heroes'.

Proletarian boys were attracted to professional boxing . . . not to get out of the ghetto, but to shine within it. Admiration from other social classes was valued for its ricochet effect on the local community because, on the whole, boxing's boys do marry brushmakers' daughters. They stayed put, it would seem, within loud hail of their boxing nursery, and brought up children who express pleasure in working class values. Many working men in late-Victorian England [and later] enjoyed boxing, countless more took pleasure from watching professional boxing. Boxing, as opposed to prizefighting was provided for working men. The boxer-hero was one of them. He was different only in degree.[43]

However, as might be expected, it was football that manifested most clearly the relationship between sport and working-class identity. This is an aspect of the social history of sport which, like so many others, is best approached through the work of Tony Mason and Richard Holt. It was during the late nineteenth and early twentieth centuries, Mason suggests, that football and class began to converge. For football played some part, however limited, in encouraging

the idea among working men that they were part of a group with similar experiences and interests which were not shared by the bulk of another group, the middle classes. As the numbers both playing and watching association football grew, the great majority came to be working people . . . .

The widespread experience which working men had of playing and watching association football probably aided the formation of a more general consciousness of class.[44]

It was during the 1960s, Holt points out, that football hooliganism began to hit the headlines. He concedes that the relationship between hooliganism and class was by no means clear-cut: 'Interpretations which see hooliganism as a conscious protest against poor urban conditions and employment prospects, though often finding favour with politicians, are facile.' He concludes, none the less, that there was a relationship between hooliganism and class, that hooliganism drew upon, and developed, working-class identity.

Hooliganism is partly an assertion of 'hardness' and an attachment to local territory, which the boys see as the traditional characteristics of their class. This is what seems to have been behind the 'skinhead' or 'boot-boy' phenomenon that has been a part of football hooliganism. Shaving their heads unlike long-haired middle-class students or pop singers of the period and wearing heavy workmen's boots and braces, they seemed like a caricature of the world that their parents had left.[45]

The discussion of football hooliganism serves as a reminder that sport, like tourism, sometimes contributed to the process whereby class identity developed into class opposition. Moreover, the process is less elusive than might be supposed. In fact, when pointing to the relationship between sport, consumption and working-class opposition, it is necessary to rely neither upon the supposed psychological drives of football hooligans nor upon the overtly political aspirations of those few workers who during the 1920s and 1930s joined organisations such as the British Workers' Sports Association and the National Workers' Sports Association.[46]

It is possible to rely rather upon more broadly based oral, newspaper and social survey evidence. Thus oral evidence suggests that working-class children sometimes learned while still quite young to resent the resources that middle-class families were able to devote to sport. It was when she went to grammar school in the 1960s that a working-class girl from Barrow-in-Furness first realised that other people were better off than she was: her classmates 'had their own tennis racquets and their own brand new leather satchels and all the hockey gear with them, and mine was all from my cousin'.[47]

Newspaper and social survey evidence confirms that adults too realised that sporting success did not depend solely upon ability, character and commitment. For example, in 1919 the billiards correspondent of the *Daily Herald* published 'A Message to Working Men Players'. 'With the game becoming more democratic every day, I am hoping to see in the very near future representatives from working-men's clubs throw down the gage to the best players in the amateur world for title honours.' For, as the writer concluded, 'We want no narrow class prejudices in amateur billiards.'[48] Nor were such concerns confined to journalists, activists and others with a public platform from which to air their views. Many working people seemed to resent the inferior facilities available to their children, and the snobbery that appeared to be endemic in sports such as cricket.[49] So when England lost a test match to the Australians in 1921, the Merthyr *Pioneer* reported that 'Jeremiads in profusion are being expressed at our failure, and the decadence of the race inferred from the inability of one 11 to defeat another at a game'. However, the paper drew a different conclusion: 'The welfare of the race does not depend upon the training of a few supermen, but

215

on the facilities provided for the youth of the country for healthy recreation.'[50] Twenty-five years later, Mass-Observation reported upon working-class concern that class barriers continued to inhibit British sporting success in international competition. 'There is plenty of talent', claimed an Edinburgh paper worker, 'but working children don't get the opportunity – it's not tapped.'[51] The main reason that British teams do badly, explained a painter and decorator from Exeter, is that 'the teams are picked from the few. There's too much of the old school tie.'[52]

It is clear, then, that it is possible to discern, and document, one of the two key elements in the relationship between consumption and class. For it has been shown that there were a whole number of circumstances in which shopping, tourism and sport encouraged consumers from the middle and working classes to be aware of, and dissatisfied with, the class situation in which they found themselves. Thus consumption, class identity and class opposition could be mutually reinforcing. Consumption could exacerbate class tension.

However, consumption also defused class tension. Indeed, this element of the relationship between consumption and class was the more powerful of the two. For although contentment generally left less evidence than resentment, it can be shown that shopping, tourism and sport tended most often to undermine class identity and class opposition – and so, of course, to defuse class tension. Consumption encouraged consumers from all classes to look to the geographical, age and gender identities that they shared; it encouraged them to think of themselves as consumers as well as, or instead of, members of the upper, middle or working classes; and it encouraged them to be unaware of, or satisfied with, the class situation in which they found themselves.

It has been argued in the previous three chapters that consumption tended to encourage an awareness of, and some pride in, national, regional, age and gender identities, and it is unnecessary to rehearse these arguments again at any length. It was argued in Chapter 6 that consumption played a part in fostering both British and other forms of consciousness: it encouraged consumer identification with Britain, with the white Dominions, with England, Wales and Scotland, and with particular regions and localities within the British Isles. It was argued in Chapter 7 that by the end of the period consumption had become an integral part of a new teenage culture which appeared, to some commentators at least, almost to transcend region, gender and class. It was argued in Chapter 8 that consumption did something to emancipate women: for although consumption tended to reinforce women's conventional role and standing, it also offered them new economic power, new social possibilities and new opportunities for the improvement of their social status.

These arguments are of direct relevance to the study of the

relationship between consumption and class. For whatever the theoretical and empirical limitations of the previous chapters, and whatever the inconsistencies within and between them, they all tend to point in the same direction. They all suggest that consumption defused class tension; that consumption encouraged consumers to identify themselves in ways that cut across, and undermined, conventional notions of class identity and class opposition.

Nor were these the only ways in which consumption tended to undermine class identity and class opposition. For consumption, not surprisingly, also encouraged consumers to think of themselves as consumers; to think of themselves, that is, as consumers as well as, or instead of, members of the class to which they belonged. This undermining of class identity occurred in two ways, the first much less important than the second. On the one hand, consumption helped to conceal the differences that existed between the classes; on the other hand, it helped to reveal, and perhaps exaggerate, the differences that existed within the classes.

There is certainly some evidence that consumption helped to conceal inter-class differences. It has been suggested, for example, that the middle class accepted many of the cultural values of the upper class – an acceptance that led, so it is said, to 'the decline of the industrial spirit'.[53] It has been suggested that the working class too came to accept the aristocracy as arbiters of taste: 'Many of these attitudes reached the workers through the large servant class, recruited from their number, and often returning to it with grand tales of the magnificoes of the great houses.'[54]

It has been suggested much more often – and much more plausibly – that working-class consumers began to dress in ways that made them difficult to distinguish from the middle class. Thus according to J. B. Priestley, one of the most striking features of inter-war England was to see 'factory girls looking like actresses'.[55] According to George Orwell, 'The youth who leaves school at fourteen and gets a blind-alley job is out of work at twenty, probably for life; but for two pounds ten on the hire-purchase he can buy himself a suit which, for a little while and at a little distance, looks as though it had been tailored in Savile Row.'[56] A Sheffield engineering worker put it rather more prosaically:

> The multiple shop was an innovation of the days of my youth,
> whereas previously the rich man had a tailor and the poor man bought
> his clothes off the peg, it became possible for Jack to be as well
> dressed as his Master, or very nearly.[57]

If such claims can be made for the 1920s and 1930s, it is scarcely surprising that still bolder assertions are made about the 1950s and 1960s. Indeed, it has been suggested by supporters of the so-called *embourgeoisement* thesis that the prosperity of post-war Britain did a great deal to narrow the differences between the classes. It has been argued, it will be recalled, that 'the working class as workers were achieving levels of consumption previously regarded as attainable only by the middle class, leading to a merging of the classes through the progressive *embourgeoisement* of the workers'.[58]

It was in these, and similar, ways that consumption helped to conceal the existence of inter-class differences. For if the sources of middle-class and working-class purchasing power were seen by those above them as somehow tainted, the ways in which that power was used offered those seeking to better themselves some hope at least of social acceptance.

There is a great deal more evidence to suggest that consumption helped to reveal, and perhaps exaggerate, intra-class differences. For consumption provided a means by which it was possible for members of all classes to distinguish, and discriminate, between those who stood in the same relationship as themselves to the means of production and/or appeared to enjoy broadly similar life chances.

The middle class were experts in such intra-class assessment. They knew how to distinguish between different types of shop, different types of holiday and, no doubt, different types of sporting interest. Indeed, throughout the whole of the period covered by this book the activities and aspirations of lower-middle-class consumers provoked the irritation, anger and amusement of those who prided themselves upon their social and economic superiority.

They knew that not all shops were the same. The late-nineteenth- and early twentieth-century middle class understood, for example, that London department stores varied widely in the styles they adopted, the products they sold, the customers they attracted, and thus the status that they signalled. Harrods, Whiteleys and Debenham & Freebody stood towards the top of the hierarchy, Selfridge's towards the bottom. Thus Thomas Selfridge did not expect the fashionable to patronise his store – and Eric Gill hoped that a bomb would drop on it.[59] The late-twentieth-century middle class understood that supermarkets too differed in the status that they signalled. Safeways was superior to Tesco, and Tesco more acceptable than Asda. Sainsburys, of course, stood supreme. Indeed, the ritual of the Friday-night visit to Sainsburys came to symbolise several aspects of modern middle-class life: the spread of car owner- ship, the extension of female employment, the domestication of men, and the confirmation, in a curious way, of middle-class identity itself.[60]

Nor, as the middle class knew well, were all holidays the same. For as the better-off and better-educated took pains to make clear time and time again, geographical mobility provided no guarantee at all of social mobility or social acceptance. Indeed, as the *Pall Mall Gazette* pointed out in 1865, Thomas Cook was to the traveller,

what the ingenious deceptions of the cheap haberdasher and tailor are
to the gent, who wants to make himself look like a gentleman at the
lowest possible figure. By availing himself of the facilities offered by
Mr Cook he can get up a kind of continental experience which is to
that obtained in the regular way precisely what a 'dicky' is to a shirt.[61]

Firms catering for the lower-middle-class market continued to come
in for considerable condescension and criticism. For, as the *Observer*
remarked in the mid-1920s, Thomas Cook had moved still further
down market, bringing to the French Riviera, for example, visitors
'to whom it would never have occurred before the war to go further
than Margate'.[62] It remained difficult for even the most sensitive of
tourists to get it absolutely right.

> You have to think twice about holidays. The snob thing operates. Are
> we naff in Bournemouth, vulgarian in Fiji,, loud in the Bahamas, twee
> in Cornwall, or a bit obvious, darling, in Provence?
> Go to lovely Tuscany and people will snigger about Chiantishire,
> or roguishly ask after the Shadow Cabinet, to Ireland and they will
> lower about the rain, to Majorca and you will spend time explaining
> that *of course* you are not going to Magaluf but to a little place about
> 30 kilometres North West of Palma.[63]

The working class were little less expert in intra-class assessment.
For although they had less money to spend than most of the middle
class, and less time in which to spend it, they too looked to shopping
and tourism – though not apparently to sport – as ways of ranking
their friends, relatives, neighbours and workmates. In fact, thanks
to the pioneering work of scholars such as Gareth Stedman Jones
and Paul Johnson, a good deal is now becoming known about this
aspect of the relationship between consumption and class.

It has been shown that even the poorest of the late-nineteenth-
century working class used consumption as a means of keeping up
appearances – of defining their own, and other people's, social
position. Thus Gareth Stedman Jones suggests from his examination
of the spending patterns of the London poor, that 'a concern to
demonstrate self-respect was infinitely more important that any
forms of saving based upon calculations of utility. When money
was available which did not have to be spend (*sic*) on necessities,
it was used to purchase articles for display rather than articles of
use.'[64] Paul Johnson suggests, it will be recalled, that his more
broadly based examination of working-class spending points to a
similar conclusion: it 'highlights not the solidarity of workers but
the degree of competition within their ranks'.

> It suggests a working class decomposed into many strata with
> slightly different value systems, aspirations, interests and incomes.
> It suggests a world of competition and struggle centred around the
> everyday act of spending, but of competition and struggle *within* the

working class, rather than *between* workers and owners of capital or managers. Workers and their dependants in late-nineteenth century Britain . . . defined their social position by the way they spent their money.[65]

It can be shown, too, that working people continued to use consumption as a means of evaluating their own, and other people's, position within the working class.[66] It will be recalled from the previous chapter that working-class women came more and more to believe that there existed a direct relationship between consumption, self-image, and social and class status. In this passage, a Lancashire factory worker looks back to the decade between her marriage and the birth of her first child, a period that coincided more or less with the 1950s.

> Well I skipped over twin tubs and got an automatic. And people were just . . . they were great if they had a twin tub, but I had an automatic.
> I had a split level cooker when nobody else ever had one .[67]

However, it was not just women who became caught up in intra-class competition. The son of a Barrow-in-Furness fitter remembers that towards the end of the 1950s his father bought an old car for about £10, a little less than a week's wages. 'And we got into a fight at school over it, because we had a car and somebody else didn't and they were a bit jealous.'[68] A few years later, recalls a council tenant from Preston, the key factor was whether or not one owned a television set. 'Them days it was television, if you'd got a television, if an aerial went up, Ooh they've got a television. This is how it was, wasn't it'.[69] It was the same in the west of Scotland. 'For a while television was a rare and special thing; not many people [had them] and they were well off. Then not having it rapidly became a sign of poverty.'[70] Holidays, of course, were less visible than cars and television sets, but they too could be used to confirm and bolster intra-class status. For example, an Essex factory worker knew perfectly well how to exploit the trip abroad that he and his wife took during the early 1950s: 'On receiving or visiting friends, might not our conversation boastingly begin, "When we were abroad, you know . . .?"'[71]

Thus it was that whether consumption concealed the differences between the classes, or exposed the differences within them, the consequences were much the same. For in both cases, consumption encouraged consumers to think of themselves as consumers as well as, and sometimes instead of, members of the class to which historians and social scientists would ascribe them. In both cases, consumption cut across class.

It is here that sport, and the consumption associated with it, needs to be brought into the analysis. For sport became associated with, and was used to encourage, the diversion of attention from more fundamental, class-based concerns. For just as sport could bridge geographical and age (though rarely gender) divisions, so too it could distract attention from the differences that existed between the classes.

It was not unknown for the middle class and upper class to be brought together, and distracted by, their interest in sport. Thus some middle-class sportsmen no doubt managed to persuade themselves that taking an interest in hunting, shooting, fishing and other aristocratic pastimes made them difficult to distinguish from members of the upper class. In the 1870s, claimed J. A. Hobson, the grammar school in Derby encouraged sport 'as a means of bringing us into the company of more reputable public schools on the basis of equality.'[72] Even in the 1950s and 1960s, recalls the writer of this book, grammar school sport in Romford seemed to serve something of the same purpose.[73]

> 'Sport', which came increasingly to mean organized team-games rather than hunting or shooting, was something that the squire and stockbroker could share, firing off a cricketing letter to *The Times* or enjoying the Boat Race, the Varsity rugger match, Henley or Wimbledon.[74]

It was a good deal more common for the middle class and working class to be brought together, and distracted by, their interest in sport. For as Christiane Eisenberg has argued, 'Although the idea of sport was in England originally tailored to serve the actual needs of middle-class formation, it functioned from the very beginning as a universal as well.'[75] This 'universality' came to acquire a considerable significance. For example, it is striking that both proponents and opponents of the use of the concept of social control recognise that sport was central to a number of the attempts that were made by the middle class to inculcate the working class with acceptable values and attitudes.[76]

Many in the late-nineteenth- and early twentieth-century middle class saw sport as a means of distracting the working class. They saw it as a way, along with many others, of diverting attention from the divisions and inequalities that remained embedded in British society. Thus it was hoped that even if it did not encourage those interested in sport to think of themselves as consumers, it might at least discourage them from thinking of themselves as victims. Sport, it was hoped, would defuse class tension.

Some employers were quite explicit about their motives. For as the Sheffield steel magnate Sir Robert Hadfield explained when opening his company's new playing fields in 1923, 'no one had ever heard of a good sportsman rising among the Socialists or the Bolshevists. Sport in itself was the best antidote to revolution and revolutionary ideas.'[77] Nor was this just unrepresentative rhetoric, for many large-scale firms set about supporting sport at the workplace. It was seen earlier in the chapter that during the 1920s and 1930s certain colliery companies and motor-car manufacturers sponsored angling clubs for their employees. However, the provision of sporting facilities was both more common and more varied than that brief reference might lead one to suppose: railway and gas companies, and later breweries, chemical makers and steel companies all provided their workers with the facilities to enable, and encourage, them to pursue an interest in sport.[78]

Other members of the middle class seemed to agree about the diversionary power of sport. Indeed some believed that even spectatorship did more good than harm. In 1911 F. E. Smith wondered, 'What would the devotees of athletics do if their present amusements were abolished?' He knew the answer, of course.

> Is it to be supposed, for instance, that the seething mass of humanity which streams every Saturday at mid-day out of the factories and workshops of our great towns would ever saunter in peace and contentment through museums and picture galleries, or sit listening enraptured to classical concerts . . . [or] spend his leisure studying botany or horticulture[?]

If football and cricket were abolished, he predicted, it would bring 'upon the masses nothing but misery, depression, sloth, indiscipline, and disorder'.[79] Accordingly, both participation and spectatorship were to be encouraged, for as the Mayor of Chesterfield explained to a local football club in 1922,

> One of the reasons why this country would never witness a political or social revolution or upheaval was because the average Englishman is immersed in sport . . . this was far better than hanging and slouching round street corners arguing about Socialism and Bolshevism.[80]

There can be no doubt, then, that sport (and the consumption associated with it) was seen, and sometimes sponsored, by the late-nineteenth- and early-twentieth-century middle class as a means of distracting the working class from more unsettling concerns. Yet this is not the end of the matter. For it is also necessary to determine the extent to which such middle-class faith in the ameliorative power of sport (and consumption) was realised in practice. In order for this to be done, three conditions need to be met. It has to be shown that working people were consumers of sporting goods and services; it has to be shown that they displayed little interest in the inequalities of British society; and it has to be shown that it was the former which was the cause of the latter.

It can certainly be shown that working people were consumers of sporting goods and services. After all, one of the major purposes of Chapter 5 was to demonstrate that as players, as spectators, and not least as gamblers, working men were active, and often enthusiastic, consumers of a wide, and growing, variety of sports and sports-related products. There is much other evidence besides. For instance, in 1904 a writer in the *Labour Leader* bemoaned the popularity of the 'people's game'.

> You may think that the football craze is a foolish infatuation, a form of madness, a sign of national intellectual decadence; you may think these things, but, if you value the goodwill of your fellow workmen do not so much as whisper them above your breath . . . . For the football enthusiast – and he is the mass of the male population – brooks no depreciation of his recreative hobby.[81]

Fifty years later, the Polish scholar Ferdynand Zweig described British working-class attitudes to sport in terms that would have been just as applicable at the beginning of the century.

> Sport has an indescribable fascination for the British worker. It captivates his imagination, refreshes and comforts him; it gives him courage and amusement, excitement and beauty. It may sound absurd, but one could say that sport has bewitched the British worker.[82]

It can be shown, too, that many working people displayed surprisingly little interest in the inequalities of British society. This, of course, is a much more contentious claim, for the assessment of working-class attitudes and beliefs is one of the most intractable and controversial issues confronting the historian of modern British society. However, it is a case that I have argued elsewhere, and at considerable length. I (and of course many others) have suggested that because of the attention that has been lavished upon the efforts of working-class activists in trade unions and left-wing political parties, it is not always recognised that these activists, no matter how talented and dedicated, were unable to secure the support of anything but a small minority of their fellow workers. Most working people, it must be accepted, failed to fulfil their 'historic destiny'; most working people failed conspicuously to display anything remotely resembling a revolutionary class consciousness.[83] Nor is this by any means an eccentric position to adopt. For instance, Charles More concludes his well-balanced and well-informed discussion of class consciousness in post-war Britain by drawing upon the work of scholars such as Michael Mann and W. G. Runciman.

> Attitude surveys . . . reveal that while many French manual workers perceive society as unequal and want to do something about it, British workers have a less strong perception of inequality and, even more important, see inequality between classes as more or less irrelevant to themselves.[84]

It is immensely more difficult to show that working people's lack of interest in the inequalities of British society was brought about by their consumption of sporting goods and services. Indeed, when it is put in such stark terms, the correlation appears almost impossible to substantiate. None the less, there is more evidence than might be expected to suggest that sport, and the consumption to which it gave rise, played some part at least in diverting working-class attention from the unequal distribution of power and resources that was to be found in late-nineteenth- and twentieth-century Britain.

There is certainly some evidence that workers in large-scale industry were distracted from more fundamental, class-based concerns. 'I know of nothing that is used more against our Movement', declared Ernest Bevin in 1928, 'than the many sports organisations run by employers in the way of welfare clubs.'[85] Indeed, not even trade-union activists were totally immune: in 1934 an attempt to extend an important debate at a conference of the South Wales Miners' Federation was defeated by the 'scores of delegates who wanted to go to International Rugby Match between England and Wales and who shouted Vote, Vote, Vote'.[86] Thus it is scarcely surprising to find that non-activists, especially those employed by firms providing them with sporting facilities, proved more susceptible still to the lure of sport. For as Zweig reported in 1952:

> The heads of departments play cricket with their manual workers. They 'talk cricket' and go to the local together. 'I don't know what we would do without our sports club. Our team is playing a team from another firm, and that fosters loyalty to our firm,' managers have told me.[87]

There is some evidence too that workers in other sectors of the economy were similarly diverted. Those active in the labour movement were only too well aware of the dangers. The *Labour Leader* writer who bemoaned the popularity of football in 1904 went on to explain why he was so concerned. 'We are in danger', he believed, 'of producing a race of workers who can only obey their masters and think football. This is the material out of which slaves are made; the material which gives us shouting Jingoes, ignorant electors, and craven blacklegs.'[88] Of course, this smacks strongly of special pleading, of attempting to explain – and excuse – the failure of the early socialist movement to attract wider working-class support. None the less, Tony Mason believes that the argument had some basis in fact. For, although he accepts that 'The widespread experience which working men had of playing and watching association football probably aided the formation of a more general consciousness of class', he is aware too that football could act as a palliative, undermining class identity, and defusing class tension: 'in so far as support for a team emphasised community, it probably encouraged the fragmentation of class feeling though it can hardly be considered as important in this respect as jobs, wages, housing and general expectations of life'.[89]

Football, it seemed to many observers, continued for most of the period to encourage – and even epitomise – such fragmentation and distraction. It was football, after all, that the police and strikers played together during the General Strike.[90] It was football, complained the chairman of the North East Federation of the Independent Labour Party, that distracted working people from socialist ideas.

> I do not suggest there is anything wrong with football, but there does seem something wrong with the majority of people who habitually attend football matches and fill their minds with things that don't matter . . . . Difficult though the task may be to push football out of heads and push Socialism in, the task must be undertaken, for just as surely as football doesn't matter, Socialism matters a great deal.[91]

It was football, complained a young librarian in 1949, that diverted public attention from more important issues. 'The BBC combines subtly with the Press to put over the notion that although millions are suffering intense misery in Europe, China, Malaya, it doesn't really matter as long as the Arsenal beats Chelsea.'[92] Football retained its power to distract. Indeed, on the very day early in 1993 that I wrote this passage, the *Guardian* published an extended piece on the revival of Blackburn Rovers. The writer is in no doubt at all about the game's continuing capacity for diversion: 'Brian Clarke, a bachelor in his twenties who inspects factory meters for the gas board, regards the revival as a sublime distraction from the otherwise prosaic nature of Blackburn life.'[93]

It is a great deal more difficult to decide whether, and to what extent, other sports, and sport in general, distracted working people from the inequalities of contemporary society. None the less, the weight of political, popular and scholarly opinion seems to suggest that playing sport, watching it, and betting on it all served, in their different ways, to divert working-class (and other) attention away from more fundamental concerns. According to the German Marxist Karl Kautsky, sport helped to deflect the late-nineteenth-century British working class from its historic mission: 'the emancipation of their class appears to them a foolish dream . . . it is football, boxing, horse-racing which move them the deepest and to which their entire leisure time, their individual powers, and their material means are devoted'.[94] According to sports historian Richard Holt, sport helped to bind together the classes of inter-war Britain in less obvious, but no less effective, ways:

> The fact that the English nation at least shared certain simple ethics, embodied in their admiration for men like Hobbs, may in a loose but

important sense have helped to maintain a climate of public trust. We are *not* talking here of bread and circuses. Sport, especially cricket, was never a vehicle for crude social control; rather it provided a shared vocabulary of 'fairness' and embodied a set of principles for the decent organization of public life.[95]

Moreover, virtually all those who have considered working-class gambling, agree that it was this, rather than playing or watching, which was the most potent of all sporting distractions. For gambling offered interest, hope, suspense, diversion – and of course the possibility of a win. The gambling of poor Middlesbrough housewives was, for Lady Bell, 'horribly undesirable' yet easy to understand: for in their 'sordid' daily lives, gambling contributed 'constant moments of alternating hope, fear and wonder'.[96] 'There is no doubt that hope is valuable to everyone,' explained Ferdynand Zweig, 'and the more so to people in an unsatisfactory environment.'

> 'I have nothing against the church leaders who fulminate against the pools,' a foreman with much experience of life told me, 'provided that they can sell the same commodity – hope – either cheaper or better. But it seems to me they can't. If a pool punter can buy hope, even in such a diluted and trivial form, for a shilling a week, it seems to me that it isn't a bad bargain'.[97]

The Gallup organisation summarised succinctly the relationship between gambling and class in its study, *Gambling in Britain*, which appeared in 1972.

> Men gamble to keep a dream alive that some day they will outdo their betters. Thus, gambling is what one might call a 'safety valve institution'. Without gambling the frustrations of a class society might be channelled into more destructive pursuits – or for that matter more radical political action.[98]

Thus it was that middle-class hopes – and socialist fears – continued to be realised. For sport, and the consumption to which it gave rise, was, is, and no doubt will continue to be, a telling distraction from more fundamental, class-based concerns.

It is only too clear, then, that the relationship between consumption and class was close, complicated and more contradictory than is often supposed. However, it must be conceded that the analysis undertaken in this chapter may itself be somewhat misleading. It may be misleading in so far as either the balance of the evidence or the balance of the chapter make it appear that consumption was as likely to exacerbate as to defuse class tension. For this was not the case. Consumption tended most often to undermine class identity and class opposition, and so to defuse class tension. Indeed, what dissatisfaction there was seemed to be channelled towards distinctly non-threatening ends: harder work, more careful budgeting and piecemeal political reform.[99]

Consumption, it seems, encouraged a culture of consolation, not revolution.[100]

NOTES AND REFERENCES

1 . There is no general study of consumption and class, but see **G. Cross**, *Time and Money: The Making of Consumer Culture*, Routledge, 1993.

2. **P. Johnson**, 'Conspicuous Consumption and Working-Class Culture in Late Victorian and Edwardian Britain', *Transactions of the Royal Historical Society*, **38**, 1988, p. 41. Also **G. S. Jones**, 'Working-class Culture and Working-class Politics in London, 1870–1900: Notes on the Remaking of a Working Class', *Journal of Social History*, **7**, 1974.

3. **E. Royle**, *Modern Britain: A Social History 1750–1985*, Arnold, 1987, pp. 147–8. Also pp. 151–5; **J. Benson**, *The Working Class in Britain, 1850–1939*, Longman, 1989, p. 157.

4. Benson, *Working Class*, pp. 151–5, 163–6. **J. K. Walton**, *The English Seaside Resort: A Social History 1750–1914*, Leicester University Press, p. 225.

5. See **M. Mann**, *Consciousness and Action among the Western Working Class*, Macmillan, 1973, p. 13; Benson, *Working Class*, pp. 151-5. However, there is no evidence that consumption encouraged the other two forms of class consciousness (class totality and class alternative).

6. **J. Beckett**, *The Aristocracy in England 1660–1914*, Blackwell, 1986, pp. 337–8, 366–7; **M. Blume**, *Côte d'Azur: Inventing the French Riviera*, Thames & Hudson, 1992; **S. Checkland**, *The Rise of Industrial Society in England 1815–1885*, Longman, 1964, pp. 285, 314. Cf. **R. Perrott**, *The Aristocrats: A Portrait of Britain's Nobility and Their Way of Life Today*, Weidenfeld & Nicolson, 1968, pp. 255–72 for 'inconspicuous consumption'.

7. Checkland, *Industrial Society*, p. 314. See also **T. Richards**, *The Commodity Culture of Victorian England: Advertising and Spectacle, 1851–1914*, Verso, 1991, p. 7. **G. Crossick**, 'The Emergence of the Lower Middle Class in Britain: A Discussion', in **G. Crossick** (ed.), *The Lower Middle Class in Britain 1870–1914*, Croom Helm, 1977, pp. 30–31; *NOP Political Bulletin*, June 1972, p. 19.

8. **G. Orwell**, *Coming Up for Air*, Penguin, 1962, pp. 18–19. Also Mass-Observation, 3055, 'A Report on Shopping', 1948, pp. 1, 9.

9. Cited **M. J. Winstanley**, *The Shopkeeper's World 1830–1914*, Manchester University Press, 1983, p. 54. Also **M. J. Winstanley** (ed.), *A Traditional Grocer: T. D. Smith's of Lancaster 1858–1981*, University of Lancaster, 1991, pp. 23–31; **J. Carey**, *The Intellectuals and the Masses: Pride and Prejudice among the Literary Intelligentsia, 1880–1939*, Faber & Faber, 1992, p. 167.

10. **N. Griffiths**, *Shops Book: Brighton 1900–1930*, Queenspark Books, p. 14. Also Mass-Observation, 1533, 'Supplementary Shopping Material', 1942, p. 12; Lancaster, Mrs C8P, p. 4; Mrs R4B, p. 14. **R. Cobb**, *Still Life: Sketches from a Tunbridge Wells Childhood*, Chatto & Windus, 1983, pp. 140–43.
11. Mass-Observation, 1533, pp. 5, 11-12; 1112, 'Report on Attitudes to Closing of Small Shops', 1942, p. 1.
12. **E. Elias**, *On Sundays We Wore White*, W. H. Allen, 1978, pp. 63–4, 72. I owe this reference to Diane Collins.
13. **W. Lancaster**, 'British Department Stores and Society since 1850', unpublished paper, University of Warwick, November 1989.
14. **M. Hughes**, *A London Child of the 1870s*, Oxford University Press, 1977, p. 23. See also **I. Brown**, *The Heart of England*, Batsford, 1935, pp. 14–15.
15. *Daily Mail*, 18 January 1930; **H. George**, 'The Experience of Youth in Harrow 1948–1963', MA dissertation, University of Warwick, 1992, p. 55; **D. Anderson**, 'One Man and his Yob', *Evening Standard*, 19 May 1993.
16. Lancaster, Mrs R4B, p. 62.
17. **C. Eisenberg**, 'The Middle Class and Competition: Some Considerations of the Beginnings of Modern Sport in England and Germany', *International Journal of Sports History*, 7, 1990, p. 273. Also **R. Holt**, *Sport and the British: A Modern History*, Oxford University Press, 1990, pp. 95–6, 112–15, 291–2.
18. **J. Hargreaves**, *Sport, Power and Culture: A Social and Historical Analysis of Popular Sports in Britain*, Polity, 1986, p. 109.
19. Holt, *Sport*, p. 133.
20. Holt, *Sport*, pp. 291–2. See too **M. A. Speak**, 'Social Stratification and Participation in Sport in Mid-Victorian England with Particular Reference to Lancaster, 1840–70', in **J. A. Mangan** (ed.), *Pleasure, Profit, Proselytism: British Culture and Sport at Home and Abroad 1700–1914*, Cass, 1988.
21. Holt, *Sport*, p. 133. Also **K. McCrone**, *Sport and the Physical Emancipation of English Women 1870–1914*, Routledge, 1988, pp. 133–4; **G. Pearson**, *Hooligan: A History of Respectable Fears*, Macmillan, 1983, pp. 64–9; Brown, *Heart of England*, pp. 70–71.
22. Mass-Observation, 3141, 'Report on Sport', 1949, pp. 16–17.
23. **M. Tebbutt**, *Making Ends Meet: Pawnbroking and Working-Class Credit*, Leicester University Press, 1983, p. 194.
24. Mass-Observation, 2460, 'A Report on People and the Co-op', 1947, pp. 3, 5, 40. Also Lancaster, Mrs P3L, p. 10.
25. **P. Mathias**, *Retailing Revolution: A History of Multiple Retailing in the Food Trades Based upon the Allied Suppliers Group of Companies*, Longmans, Green & Co., 1967, p. 106. Also *Small Trader*, 15 April 1915; *Sunday Worker*, 22 March 1925; *RC on Consumer Credit*, *Report*, 1971, pp. 137–8; Lancaster, Mrs C5P, p. 48; Mrs G5P, p. 9. **J. Benson**, *The Penny Capitalists: A Study of Nineteenth-Century Working-class Entrepreneurs*, Gill & Macmillan, 1984.
26. Mass-Observation, 1532, 'Report on Shopping Habits (Part III), 1942,

p. 20. Also p. 18; 1533, p. 12; Lancaster, Mrs H5L, pp. 21–2. But cf. Lancaster, Mrs P1P, pp. 53, 67.

27. **R. Roberts**, *The Classic Slum: Salford Life in the First Quarter of the Century*, Pelican, 1973, pp. 81–3; **E. Roberts**, *A Woman's Place: An Oral History of Working-class Women 1890–1940*, Blackwell, 1984, pp. 148–9.

28. **N. Dennis, F. Henriques** and **C. Slaughter**, *Coal is our Life: An Analysis of a Yorkshire Mining Community*, Tavistock, 1969, pp. 200–201; Roberts, *Woman's Place*, p. 148; Tebbutt, *Pawnbroking*, pp. 176–86.

29. Mass-Observation, 2089, 'Report on Hire-Purchase', 1944, p. 1. See also 2090, 'Report on Furnishings', 1947, p. 3.

30. Lancaster, Mr R1P, p. 72.

31. E.g., **P. Joyce**, *Work, Society and Politics: The Culture of the Factory in Later Victorian England*, Methuen, 1982, p. 186.

32. Lancaster, Mr R3B, p. 5. Also Mrs A1P, p. 28; Mr C1P, p. 70.

33. **S. R. Davey**, *Recollections*, Sheffield Women's Printing Co-op, p. 45. Also Bristol, 515276, J. Morkuras to S. Humphries, 19 September 1979; *Labour Woman*, August 1913; Lancaster, Mrs P1P, p. 53.

34. The Workers' Travel Association was founded in 1922. See *Labour Woman*, July 1934; *Express and Star*, 22 July 1938.

35. Lancaster, Mr R3B, p. 5. Also Mrs H5L, pp. 3, 39; Mrs A1P, p. 30.

36. **P. McGeown**, *Heat the Furnace Seven Times More*, Hutchinson, 1968, p. 178.

37. Bristol, E. T. Rich to S. Humphries, 30 September 1979.

38. **P. Brendon**, *Thomas Cook: 150 Years of Popular Tourism*, Secker & Warburg, 1992, p. 291; **J. Field**, 'The View from Folkestone', in **R. Samuel** (ed.), *Patriotism: The Making and Unmaking of British National Identity*, II, Routledge, 1989, pp. 4–5.

39. Lancaster, Mrs R3P, pp. 66–7.

40. **S. G. Jones**, *Sport, Politics and the Working Class: Organised Labour and Sport in Interwar Britain*, Manchester University Press, 1988, pp. 24–6.

41. Hargreaves, *Sport*, p. 109. Middle-class attempts to control working-class gambling tended, not unnaturally, to stimulate both working-class identity and opposition. See, e.g., **R. McKibbin**, 'Working-Class Gambling in Britain 1880–1939', *Past and Present*, **82**, 1979, pp. 175–7; **D. Woods**, 'Community Violence', in **J. Benson** (ed.), *The Working Class in England 1875–1914*, Croom Helm, 1984, pp. 180, 184.

42. **J. Lowerson**, 'Angling', in **T. Mason** (ed.), *Sport in Britain: A Social History*, Cambridge University Press, 1989, pp. 20, 22–3. Also **J. Lowerson**, 'Brothers of the Angle: Coarse Fishing and English Working-class Culture, 1850–1914', in Mangan (ed.), *Pleasure*.

43. **S. Shipley**, 'Tom Causer of Bermondsey: A Boxer Hero of the 1890s', *History Workshop*, Spring 1983, p. 53; also pp. 33–4, 44–5.

44. **T. Mason**, *Association Football and English Society 1863–1915*, Harvester, 1981, pp. 242, 256. See also **R. J. Holt**, 'Football and the Urban Way of Life in Nineteenth-century Britain', in Mangan (ed.), *Pleasure*.

45. Holt, *Sport*, pp. 336–7.

46. See Jones, *Sport*, esp. chs. 4 and 5; Merthyr, *Pioneer*, 28 May, 4 June 1921. **T. Mason**, *Sport in Britain*, Faber & Faber, 1988, p. 171.
47. Lancaster, Mrs P5B, p. 32. See too **A. Fell**, 'Rebel with a Cause', in **L. Heron** (ed.), *Truth, Dare or Promise: Girls Growing up in the Fifties*, Virago, 1985, p. 20.
48. *Daily Herald*, 2 April 1919. Also 5, 7, 9 April 1919.
49. E.g., *Daily Herald*, 5 November 1919; Merthyr, *Pioneer*, 21, 28 May 1921.
50. Merthyr, *Pioneer*, 4 June 1921.
51. Mass-Observation, 3045, 'A Report on British Sport', 1948, p. 18.
52. Mass-Observation, 3045, p. 15. Also *Labour*, December 1937; *Daily Worker*, 5 July 1954.
53. Beckett, *Aristocracy*, p. 5; **M. J. Wiener**, *English Culture and the Decline of the Industrial Spirit, 1850–1980*, Penguin, 1981. Cf. **W. D. Rubinstein**, *Capitalism, Culture and Decline in Britain 1750–1990*, Routledge, 1993.
54. Checkland, *Industrial Society*, p. 285. Also **W. Minchinton**, 'Patterns of Demand 1750–1914', in **C. M. Cipolla** (ed.), *The Fontana Economic History of Europe, The Industrial Revolution*, Fontana, 1973, p. 98.
55. Benson, *Working Class*, p. 146. Also **J. White**, *The Worst Street in North London: Campbell Bunk, Islington, Between the Wars*, Routledge & Kegan Paul, 1986, p. 193.
56. **G. Orwell**, *The Road to Wigan Pier*, Penguin, 1937, p. 79. See too Cross, *Time and Money*, p. 65.
57. Davey, *Recollections*, p. 25.
58. Royle, *Modern Britain*, pp. 147–8. Also **A. Marwick**, *British Society since 1945*, Penguin, 1982, p. 157; **J. H. Goldthorpe**, **D. Lockwood**, **F. Bechhofer** and **J. Platt**, *The Affluent Worker in the Class Structure*, Cambridge University Press, 1969; **F. Devine**, *Affluent Workers Revisited: Privatism and the Working Class*, Edinburgh University Press, 1992.
59. Carey, *Intellectuals*, p. 36; also p. 56; **A. Adburgham**, *Shops and Shopping 1800–1914: Where, and in What Manner the Well-dressed Englishwoman Bought her Clothes*, Barrie & Jenkins, 1989, p. 276.
60. Personal recollection.
61. Brendon, *Thomas Cook*, p. 90. See also Carey, *Intellectuals*, pp. 31–2, 74, 115, 120, 191.
62. Brendon, *Thomas Cook*, p. 260.
63. **E. Pearce**, 'Sorry You Weren't Here', *Guardian*, 9 September 1992.
64. Jones, 'Working-Class Culture', p. 474.
65. Johnson, 'Conspicuous Consumption', p. 41.
66. White, *Worst Street*, pp. 192–3; Goldthorpe, et. al., *Affluent Worker*; **D. Glover** and **M. Pickering**, 'Youth in Postwar British Fiction: The Fifties and Sixties', *Youth and Policy*, **23**, 1988, p. 26.
67. Lancaster, Mrs H5L, pp. 89–90. Cf. Mrs. P5B, p. 46.
68. Lancaster, Mr P5B, p. 3.
69. Lancaster, Mr S9P, p. 66.
70. **L. Heron**, 'Dear Green Place', in Heron (ed.), *Truth*, p. 162.
71. **J. Halliday**, *Just Ordinary, But . . . An Autobiography*, The Author, 1959, p. 230. Cf. Johnson, 'Conspicuous Consumption', p. 38.

72. **P. Bailey**, *Leisure and Class in Victorian England: Rational Recreation and the Contest for Control, 1830–1885*, Methuen, 1987, p. 86.
73. Personal recollection.
74. Holt, *Sport*, p. 96.
75. Eisenberg, 'Middle Class', p. 274. Also **G. Williams**, 'From Popular Culture to Popular Cliché: Image and Identity in Wales, 1890–1914', in Mangan (ed.), *Pleasure*.
76. See, e.g., **F. M. L. Thompson**, 'Social Control in Victorian Britain', *Economic History Review*, xxxiv, 1981; **E. Cashmore**, *Making Sense of Sport*, Routledge, 1990, pp. 69–73.
77. Mason, *Sport*, p. 97. Also **R. Fitzgerald**, *British Labour Management and Industrial Welfare 1846–1939*, Croom Helm, 1988, p. 123; **N. Fishwick**, *English Football and Society, 1910–1950*, Manchester University Press, 1989, pp. 145–6.
78. Fitzgerald, *Labour Management*, pp. 94–5, 122–3, 139–40, 179; Jones, *Sport*, pp. 62–3, 84–5.
79. Mason, *Football*, pp. 226–7.
80. **R. J. Waller**, *The Dukeries Transformed: The Social and Political Development of a Twentieth-Century Coalfield*, Oxford University Press, 1983, p. 195.
81. Mason, *Football*, pp. 236–7.
82. **F. Zweig**, *The British Worker*, Pelican, 1952, p. 124. Also Fishwick, *English Football*, pp. 142–3.
83. Benson, *Working Class*, especially introduction and chapters 6 and 7.
84. **C. More**, *The Industrial Age: Economy and Society in Britain 1750–1985*, Longman, 1989, p. 405.
85. Jones, *Sport*, p. 119. Also *Sunday Worker*, 10 May 1925; 27 January, 3, 10 February 1929.
86. Cited **H. Francis** and **D. Smith**, *The Fed: A History of the South Wales Miners in the Twentieth Century*, Lawrence & Wishart, 1980, pp. 209–10. Cf. editorial in Merthyr, *Pioneer*, 18 June 1921.
87. Zweig, *British Worker*, p. 128.
88. Mason, *Football*, p. 237.
89. Mason, *Football*, p. 242. Also **S. Tischler**, *Footballers and Businessmen: The Origins of Professional Soccer in England*, Holmes & Meier, 1981, p. 137.
90. **A. J. P. Taylor**, *English History 1914–1945*, Penguin, 1975, p. 313. Cf. Merthyr, *Pioneer*, 28 May 1921; Jones, *Sport*, pp. 58–60.
91. Jones, *Sport*, p. 28.
92. Mass-Observation, 3141, 'Report on Sport', p. 12. Cf. *Express and Star*, 10 January 1950.
93. **D. Hill**, 'Rovers' Return', *Guardian*, 6 March 1993.
94. Holt, *Sport*, pp. 146–7.
95. Holt, *Sport*, pp. 267–8. Also Mass-Observation, 6, 'Sport in War-Time', p. 1; Jones, *Sport*, pp. 7, 66, 86, 91, 117.
96. **M. Clapson**, *A Bit of a Flutter: Popular Gambling and English Society, c. 1823–1961*, Manchester University Press, 1992, p. 61; also pp. 62, 174–17. **J. B. Priestley**, *English Journey*, Penguin, 1977, p. 312.
97. Zweig, *British Worker*, pp. 142–3. Also **R. Roberts**, *The Classic Slum:*

Salford Life in the First Quarter of the Century, Pelican, 1973, pp. 162–4; **Lady Bell**, *At the Works: A Study of a Manufacturing Town*, Virago, 1985, pp. 254–70; Hoggart, *Uses of Literacy*, pp. 137–40; **R. McKibbin**, 'Working-Class Gambling'; Fishwick, *English Football*, pp. 125–6.
98. **Gallup**, *Gambling in Britain*, Gallup, 1972, p. 8
99. E.g., *Labour Woman*, 1 July 1924; April 1956.
100. For the 'culture of consolation', see Jones, 'Working-class Culture'.

CONCLUSION

The historiography of consumption offers a curious paradox, for on the one hand, the study of consumption, the consumer revolution, and the rise of the so-called consumer society has been curiously neglected. On the other hand, these same issues – consumption, the consumer revolution and the rise of consumer society – are now being proposed as a way not only of describing, but also of explaining, the nature of modern British society. It is to the unravelling of this paradox that this book has been addressed. Its aim, more specifically, has been to examine the causes, course and consequences of the changes that took place in consumption (or at least in shopping, tourism and sport) in the hundred years or so between 1880 and 1980, and to decide whether, and when, Britain underwent a consumer revolution, and became a consumer society.

It has been possible to begin to clarify the causes, course and consequences of changes in consumption. It has been shown, beyond reasonable doubt, that there were major changes both in demand and supply, and in consumers' experience of shopping, tourism and sport, and that these changes can contribute significantly to our understanding of some of the most interesting and contentious issues under discussion in modern British economic, social, cultural and political history: the consolidation of national identity, the creation of youth culture, the emancipation of women, and the defusion of class tension. 'Beyond the workplace', concludes Paul Johnson, 'individuals define themselves primarily by the way they spend their money.'[1] There can be no doubt, then, that the study of consumption must find its place in any serious, sustained and balanced examination of the development and nature of modern British society.

This does not mean, however, that modern Britain can be described as a consumer society. Indeed, abstractions of this type should always be approached with very considerable caution. It must be doubtful, after all, if it is ever possible to encapsulate the complexities and ambiguities of any society in a single epithet, however telling or memorable.[2] It is doubtful, in particular, whether the use of a geographical, age, gender and class-neutral term such as 'consumer' can possibly encapsulate the geographical, age, gender, class (ethnic, religious and other) divisions that remain embedded deep in modern British society.[3] Moreover, those tempted to describe modern Britain as a consumer society should remember that it has been described too as an affluent society, a corporate society, a leisure society and a professional society.[4] Certainly, those tempted to describe Britain as a consumer society would do well to remember that the degree to which consumption is afforded primacy will depend, in part at least, upon one's chronological and geographical perspective. So whereas Britain in the 1950s and 1960s might look like a consumer society when viewed from the vantage point of the 1880s, Eastern Europe or the developing world, it might seem much less like one when viewed from the vantage point of the 1980s, Western Europe or the United States of America.[5]

In fact, there is a great deal that needs to be done before it will be possible to comment with any confidence upon the role that consumption played in the development of modern British society. It would be useful to know more, for example, about the changing attitudes of the major political parties, the trade unions and employers' organisations towards what they came to recognise eventually as the consumer interest: it would be helpful to know more about the genesis and consequences of the consumer protection legislation of the 1960s and 1970s; and it would be more helpful still to have a greater understanding of the organisation, policies and achievements of consumer organisations, be they formal or informal, permanent or temporary, successful or unsuccessful. Who was it that organised the rent strikes and boycotts of Jewish shops during the First World War? How successful were the boycotts of Chilean, Israeli and South African products that flourished during the 1960s and 1970s? How effective was the 'I'm Backing Britain' campaign that leapt to prominence during the 1960s? Why did it collapse so ignominiously, while the Consumers' Association managed to survive, creating for itself a secure and established place in British middle-class life?[6]

What is needed above all else is an attempt to escape conventional categorisations, to move beyond a concentration either upon production or upon consumption. For neither production nor consumption can be considered properly in isolation from each other. The solution, anodyne and unexciting though it might seem, is that production and consumption, supply and demand, must each find a place in the serious study of the past.[7] The challenge now confronting the student of consumption, consumers and consumer society is to help to provide this balance, and so sharpen the descriptive-cum-explanatory tools available to historians of nineteenth- and twentieth-century Britain.

NOTES AND REFERENCES

1. **P. Johnson**, 'Conspicuous Consumption and Working-class Culture in Late Victorian and Edwardian Britain', *Transactions of the Royal Historical Society*, **38**, 1988, p. 29.
2. **A. Marwick**, *The Nature of History*, Macmillan, 1970, p. 171.
3. Cf. **G. Reekie**, 'Knowing the Female Consumer: Market Research and the Post-war Housewife', unpublished paper, Griffith University, 1990, p. 12.
4. See, e.g., **J. K. Galbraith**, *The Affluent Society*, Pelican, 1962; **L. Hannah**, *The Rise of the Corporate Economy*, Methuen, 1976; **K. Middlemas**, *Politics in Industrial Society: The Experience of the British System since 1911*, André Deutsch, 1979; **H. Perkin**, *The Rise of Professional Society: England since 1880*, Routledge, 1989.
5. **K. Thomas**, review of **J. Brewer** and **R. Porter** (eds), *Consumption and the World of Goods*, Routledge, 1993, in *Observer*, 7 March 1993.
6. For First World War rent strikes, see **D. Englander**, *Landlord and Tenant in Urban Britain 1838–1918*, Clarendon Press, 1983; for the attitudes of the Labour party towards affluence and consumption, see **C. A. R. Crosland**, *The Future of Socialism*, Cape, 1956, esp. pp. 278–94; **N. Tiratsoo**, 'Popular Politics, Affluence and the Labour Party in the 1950s', in **A. Gorst, L. Johnman** and **W. Scott Lucas** (eds), *Contemporary British History 1931–1961: Politics and the Limits of Policy*, Pinter, 1991.
7. **T. H. Breen**, 'The Meanings of Things: Interpreting the Consumer Economy in the Eighteenth Century', in Brewer and Porter (eds), *Consumption*, p. 250.

GUIDE TO FURTHER READING

INTRODUCTION

Cross, G. *Time and Money: The Making of Consumer Culture*, Routledge, 1993.

Fraser, W. H., *The Coming of the Mass Market, 1850–1914*, Macmillan, 1981.

Lunt, P. K. and **Livingstone, S. M.**, *Mass Consumption and Personal Identity*, Open University Press, 1992.

McKendrick, N., **Brewer, J.** and **Plumb, J. H.**, *The Birth of a Consumer Society: The Commercialization of Eighteenth-century England*, Hutchinson, 1982.

CHAPTER 1   CHANGES IN DEMAND

Benson, J., *The Working Class in Britain, 1850–1939*, Longman, 1989.

Deane, P. and **Cole, W. A.**, *British Economic Growth 1688–1959: Trends and Structure*, Cambridge University Press, 1969.

Fraser, W. H., *The Coming of the Mass Market, 1850–1914*, Macmillan, 1981.

Hannah, L., *Inventing Retirement: The Development of Occupational Pensions in Britain*, Cambridge University Press, 1986.

Roberts, E., *A Woman's Place: An Oral History of Working-Class Women 1890–1940*, Blackwell, 1984.

Rubinstein, W. D., *Man of Property: The Very Wealthy in Britain since the Industrial Revolution*, Croom Helm, 1981.

Thompson, F. M. L., *English Landed Society in the Nineteenth Century*, Routledge & Kegan Paul, 1963.

Veblen, T., *The Theory of the Leisure Class*, Unwin Books, 1970.

CHAPTER 2   CHANGES IN SUPPLY

Benson, J. and **Shaw, G.** (eds), *The Evolution of Retail Systems, c. 1800–1914*, Leicester University Press, 1992.

Brendon, P., *Thomas Cook: 150 Years of Popular Tourism*, Secker & Warburg, 1991.

Burnett, J., *Plenty and Want: A Social History of Food in England from 1815 to the Present Day*, Routledge, 1989.

Fraser, W. H., *The Coming of the Mass Market, 1850–1914*, Macmillan, 1981.

Richards, T., *The Commodity Culture of Victorian England: Advertising and Spectacle, 1851–1914*, Verso, 1990.

Vamplew, W., 'The Economics of a Sports Industry: Scottish Gate-money Football, 1890–1914', *Economic History Review*, **xxxv**, 1982.

Winstanley, M., *The Shopkeeper's World 1830–1914*, Manchester University Press, 1983.

CHAPTER 3   SHOPPING

Adburgham, A., *Shops and Shopping 1800–1914: Where, and in What Manner the Well-dressed Englishwoman Bought her Clothes*, Barrie & Jenkins, 1989.

Benson, J. and **Shaw, G.** (eds), *The Evolution of Retail Systems, c. 1800–1914*, Leicester University Press, 1992.

Burnett, J., *Plenty and Want: A Social History of Food in England from 1815 to the Present Day*, Routledge, 1989.

Guy, C., 'The Food and Grocery Shopping Behaviour of Disadvantaged Consumers: Some Results from the Cardiff Consumer Panel', *Transactions of the Institute of British Geographers*, **10**, 1985.

Jefferys, J. B., *The Distribution of Consumer Goods: A Factual Study of Methods and Costs in the United Kingdom in 1938*, Cambridge University Press, 1950.

McClelland, W. G., 'The Supermarket and Society', *Sociological Review*, **10**, 1962.

Scott, R., *The Female Consumer*, Associated Business Programmes, 1976.

Winstanley, M., *The Shopkeeper's World 1830–1914*, Manchester University Press, 1983.

CHAPTER 4   TOURISM

Brendon, P., *Thomas Cook: 150 Years of Popular Tourism*, Secker & Warburg, 1991.

Holloway, J. C., *The Business of Tourism*, Pitman, 1989.

Pimlott, J. A. R., *The Englishman's Holiday: A Social History*, Harvester, 1977.

Walton, J. K., *The Blackpool Landlady: A Social History*, Manchester University Press, 1978.

Walton, J. K., 'The Demand for Working-class Seaside Holidays in Victorian England', *Economic History Review*, **xxxiv**, 1981.

Walton, J. K., *The English Seaside Resort: A Social History 1750–1914*, Leicester University Press, 1983.

Ward, C. and **Hardy, D.**, *Goodnight Campers! The History of the British Holiday Camp*, Mansell, 1986.

CHAPTER 5   SPORT

Bale, J., *Sport and Place: A Geography of Sport in England, Scotland and Wales*, Hurst, 1992.

Clapson, M., *A Bit of a Flutter: Popular Gambling and English Society c. 1823–1961*, Manchester University Press, 1992.

Hargreaves, J., *Sport, Power and Culture: A Social and Historical Analysis of Popular Sports in Britain*, Polity, 1986.

Holt, R., *Sport and the British: A Modern History*, Oxford University Press, 1989.

McKibbin, R., 'Working-class Gambling in Britain 1880–1939', *Past and Present*, **82**, 1979.

Mason, T., *Sport in Britain*, Faber & Faber, 1988.

Mason, T. (ed.), *Sport in Britain: A Social History*, Cambridge University Press, 1989.

Smith, M. A., **Parker, S.** and **Smith, C. S.** (eds), *Leisure and Society in Britain*, Allen Lane, 1973.

CHAPTER 6   THE CONSOLIDATION OF NATIONAL IDENTITY?

Hargreaves, J., *Sport, Power and Culture: A Social and Historical Analysis of Popular Sports in Britain*, Polity, 1986.

Mangan, J. A. (ed.), *Pleasure, Profit, Proselytism: British Culture and Sport at Home and Abroad 1700–1914*, Cass, 1988.

Richards, T., *The Commodity Culture of Victorian England: Advertising and Spectacle, 1851–1914*, Verso, 1990.

Samuel, R. (ed.), *Patriotism: The Making and Unmaking of British National Identity*, 3 volumes, Routledge, 1989.

Williams, J. and **Wagg, S.** (eds), *British Football and Social Change: Getting into Europe*, Leicester University Press, 1991.

CHAPTER 7   THE CREATION OF YOUTH CULTURE?

Abrams, M., *Teenage Consumer Spending in 1959 (Part II): Middle Class and Working Class Boys and Girls*, London Press Exchange, 1961.

Brake, M., *The Sociology of Youth Culture and Youth Subcultures: Sex and Drugs and Rock 'n' Roll*, Routledge & Kegan Paul, 1980.

Hall, S. and **Jefferson, T.** (eds), *Resistance through Rituals: Youth Subcultures in Post-War Britain*, Hutchinson, 1976.

Mungham, G. and **Pearson, G.** (eds), *Working Class Youth Culture*, Routledge & Kegan Paul, 1976.

Pearson, G., *Hooligan: A History of Respectable Fears*, Macmillan, 1983.

CHAPTER 8   THE EMANCIPATION OF WOMEN?

McClelland, W. G., 'The Supermarket and Society', *Sociological Review*, **10**, 1962.

McCrone, K. E., *Sport and the Physical Emancipation of English Women 1870–1914*, Routledge, 1988.

Roberts, E., *A Woman's Place: An Oral History of Working-Class Women 1890–1940*, Blackwell, 1984.

Scott, R., *The Female Consumer*, Associated Business Programmes, 1976.

Tebbutt, M., *Making Ends Meet: Pawnbroking and Working-Class Credit*, Leicester University Press, 1983.

Ward, C. and **Hardy, D.**, *Goodnight Campers! The History of the British Holiday Camp*, Mansell, 1986.

CHAPTER 9   THE DEFUSION OF CLASS TENSION?

Beckett, J., *The Aristocracy in England 1660–1914*, Blackwell, 1986.

Benson, J., *The Working Class in Britain, 1850–1939*, Longman, 1989.

Brendon, P., *Thomas Cook: 150 Years of Popular Tourism*, Secker & Warburg, 1991.

Carey, J., *The Intellectuals and the Masses: Pride and Prejudice among the Literary Intelligentsia, 1880–1939*, Faber & Faber, 1992.

Cross, G., *Time and Money: The Making of Consumer Culture*, Routledge, 1993.

Johnson, P., 'Conspicuous Consumption and Working-class Culture in Late Victorian and Edwardian Britain', *Transactions of the Royal Historical Society*, **38**, 1988.

Jones, S. G., *Sport, Politics and the Working Class: Organised Labour and Sport in Interwar Britain*, Manchester University Press, 1988.

INDEX